CIRCA 1957

also by Chuck Klein

INSTINCT COMBAT SHOOTING, Defensive
Handgunning for Police

CIRCA 1957

A NOVEL BY

Chuck Klein

PATRIOT PRESS • PATRIOT, INDIANA

LIBRARY OF CONGRESS CATALOG CARD NUMBER 90-90221

ISBN 0-9627184-0-8

FOR PATTY

To Warren,
Best wishes,
Leland Sein
10-1-98

PROLOGUE

We are the children of the survivors of the Great Depression and the Second World War. Our parents' collective and silent promises had been realized. They were able to give what they had never had—to live their dreams: Free from fear, want, hunger. They had the job security from the post war boom and didn't even want us to have to worry about anything, including our future. It was a peaceful and carefree time, with only rock & roll and hot rodding to bind us together.

But kids, especially American teenagers, have never been content to rest on the laurels of others. Without the pressures of the previous generation, we created our own anxieties. Trivial as they may seem in retrospect—the worry of who had the fastest car, the most dates, the least pimples, and knew the latest songs—were real enough then. With parents who couldn't conceive of how we could have any problems and no such thing as government sponsored family counseling, we circled our own wagons...and sedans and convertibles...and learned from each other.

CHAPTER 1

Pinned back against the plastic seat covers, I could just barely see the speedometer from behind the huge tach that was clamped to the steering column; ninety, ninety-five, wham! He slammed the shift lever into third and still the force of the acceleration kept me prisoner of the seat back. I peeked again, holy cow, we were going over a hundred and then, just as suddenly as it had begun, we were back to sixty.

"Jimanetly, man, whattya have in this thing? Is this thing souped up or something? Holy cow," I stammered.

"Now don't tell your old man what we did, ya dig or I might not get any supper," my cool cousin said with a grin.

"Hey, no sweat, man, you think I'm crazy or somthin'? But tell me what made this thing so fast? It must have at least a four barrel on it? Doesn't it, Al?"

"Yeah, it's got at least that," he said out of the corner of his mouth as he matter-of-factly dusted off two little old ladies in a '51 DeSoto. "In fact it has three two barrels, a three-quarter cam, Mallory dual point distributor and a set of headers. I'd really let it all out for ya, but this things got to get me to California in the next week or so, ya dig?"

I glanced at the driver, my cousin Alfred, whom I had just met for the first, and most likely last time. He was pretty cool looking. But his car. the 1955 Chevy we were in, was the most!

My dad and I had driven to Lebanon, Ohio that morning to look at some machinery. He was always looking at machinery and stuff. In response to a call from Alfred, we had agreed to meet him there. Al was en route to California from his home in Cleveland to, as he put it, "find his niche". The plan was for him to meet us in Lebanon, and I would ride with him to our house to show him the way. After dinner, and a night's sleep in the guest room, he would again be on his way west.

Unfortunately, it all went as planned. It sure would have been neat if he had stayed for a few more high speed runs or taken me with him to the coast. But I was only fourteen then, in early 1957.

That event was the true beginning of life.

MEANWHILE BACK AT THE RANCH

CIRCA 1957

CHAPTER 2

It was in this early portion of '57 that I truly awoke. Rock & roll music was in full control, girls were suddenly of interest, and for my fifteenth birthday, my father bought me a car!

The car, a 1952 Crosley two door sedan with its tiny four cylinder engine that barely ran was a real dream to me. The dream being to convert this slow, top heavy, unattractive little old lady's car into a screaming, low slung sports car. To accomplish this would require replacing the metal body with a new, racing style fiberglass shell and hopping up the engine or maybe stuffing a V8 between the rails.

The advertisements for the plastic body in the magazine declared that the average installation time was fourteen hours. They lied. My father must have known that because what could a fifteen-year-old, sans license, do with a real sports car? Of course, not having a license didn't stop me from putting a few test miles on the stocker during post midnight joy rides when all were asleep. Once actual construction began, the car would be totally undriveable except in the various stages when tests were "required".

My only real regret was that my brother was not there to help me. I often day dreamed about taking him under my wing as we learned together. It seemed like such a long time ago... he was only ten, but I could conjure up in my mind just how he would have looked at twelve and even what he would be like as an adult. He just got sick one day.

Mom said he had a bad headache, and the next day, they took him to the hospital. I never got to say so-long or anything. Mom and Dad didn't come home for the whole day and my sister and I learned of his death when we woke a day later. They said it was a tumor in his brain or something like that.

I was the man of the house, when Dad wasn't home, and it took me a long time to really break down and cry. Then I felt guilty about it, or maybe I felt I wasn't a man. Back then men weren't supposed to cry. .

It was different when he died, different from when Granny passed away, I mean. She was old and she didn't live with us; I didn't know her as well. Maybe I was just selfish, he was my only brother. We had such good times together building jitneys and tree houses and things. I just knew that we would go on building and making stuff forever.

CIRCA 1957

Now that I had this car and the tremendous task of having to convert it to a sports car alone, it didn't seem right. Willie, that's my brother...was my brother, had a way with people even for his young age. He could con anyone. He had sorta red hair, though Mom always said it would be just plain brown when he grew up, hazel eyes like mine and a constant smile on his lightly freckled face. He would have been invaluable in talking cops out of tickets.

Whenever I would screw up and know that a verbal bashing was coming from one or both parents, I would always try to involve Willie somehow. He would smile, laugh, and con the basher into believing I wasn't such a bad kid after all. It really did work, seemed to work ... sometimes. Being such a nice guy he was just as trusting and I know he relied on me, his older brother, to protect him. Like the time the entire neighborhood gang was inspecting a house under construction, just up the street. One kid had an umbrella and some of the others were trying to talk Willie, the youngest there, into using the umbrella as a parachute to jump from the roof. I could tell Willie was excited about the idea, but when he looked to me, I just shook my head, and he turned his excitement into conning another boy into performing the jump. The other boy broke his leg and missed two weeks of school.

Our house, on four acres of land, was at the tip of a low and steeply sided ridge. Just across the narrow paved village street and in the front yard of our neighbor, old lady Palmer, was a brook with well-manicured banks and a dam at one end to act as a water fall and create a small, shallow pond. Further up, the street dead-ended into woods that had a path to the streets of the next little village where bus service was available. This path, about a hundred yards long, was made from years of bicycle and foot traffic and was well worn from the daily use of maids and laundresses that came to work in the neighborhood after riding the bus from the inner city. The land between these two villages where this path wandered was sort of a no man's land. We didn't know very many of the kids from the other village, and if we were caught alone in this area by kids from the other town, they might beat us up. Of course, if we made an expedition in this area with the full force of the gang , well we would beat up or shoot with BB guns anyone found there not from our turf.

I won my first fight in this no man's land. Actually, it wasn't much of a fight, I just plain beat this kid up. He had drifted to the brook and was playing in the fast waters just after a rain, when I saw him from my bedroom window. It was just before dark on a warm spring day and I opened my window and yelled for him to go home and get away from our waterfall. He yelled something back and gave me the finger. I guessed him to be about my size and age (I think I was about twelve or thirteen then) so I tore out of the house and started for the path I knew he had to take to get back to his own domain. Only this was my bailiwick, and I knew how to slip through the woods so as not to alert. I didn't want to let him know that I was after him so just in case he was bigger or tougher than he looked, I would be able to avoid a confrontation.

I caught him just where I planned, which boosted my confidence, and once confronted, he started to shake and ball. I was scared too, but I just punched him in the stomach and hit him with a left cross, and he went down. I didn't stick around to see if he was alright because maybe some of his friends were near. It all evened out though, I had been shot with BB's and terrorized by some of 'them' in the past as had Willie and most of the rest of our gang.

Amberley Village, where all this took place, was, in the Fifties, made up of a few dairy farms and maybe a few hundred homes inside its five-square mile borders. Most of the homes were on at least one-acre plats and were built during the thirties and forties. It wasn't until the 1960s that the village became a suburb with the building boom and flight from the inner city. Amberley was ten miles from downtown Cincinnati where all the movie theaters and department stores were. West of our street, Fair Oaks Drive, was a dairy farm which ran all the way to the factory buildings that lined the railroad tracks, marking the border between the Village and the City limits.

As kids we chased cows over the hills and went with our parents to buy milk there. East of our home was the Benedict estate where large work horses with enormous hoofs plowed the rich earth that always smelled so good. We used to hide in our tree house, enveloped in the limbs of the giant Maple and throw small sticks at the horses trying to spook them. The old man holding the plows would shake his fist at us calling us "whippersnappers", but the huge horses would never miss a step.

Horses and wildlife were common everyday occurrences for all —but of special significance or interest to Willie. He was always pointing out a Red Tail Hawk, Fox, or the sound of the

CIRCA 1957

Bobwhite Quail. He didn't always know the names of what he saw or heard, but he usually was aware of wildlife before anyone else. He seemed to sense living things, and dogs and cats always came to him first. He was just an "I Like Ike" kinda guy; always going along with the group—people and animals just naturally liked him.

Growing up there was fun and tension free, as discrimination was totally unknown, even though the neighborhood was comprised of Catholics, Jews and Protestants. Our only contact with the colored was with domestic servants of the families in the area. It never seemed to make any difference to us whom we hiked in the woods with or played ball with, well, so long as they weren't girls.

GOT IT MADE IN THE SHADE WITH COOL LEMONADE.

CHAPTER 3

Playing ball and stuff was for kids, I was fifteen now and had an automobile, <u>a race car </u>to build. Only I wasn't so sure, as I was experiencing pressures and anxieties for the first time. What if I couldn't do it, or it turned out to be a real mess? At least, if Willie were here, I could blame some of it on him. Building a car was different from school sports. In fact, it was different from anything and everything I had ever attempted.

In sports I was pretty good at swimming, but if I were going to build a real car and pass in school, I just wouldn't have time for the swimming team. The thought of getting fat and out of shape from not playing sports was depressing. It was a tough decision to make; maybe fifteen wasn't so old and wise after all. At least on the team everything was planned for me—the practices, where and when the meets were and what stroke to work on. To build a car required a lot of decisions. I would be working on this project alone most of the time, whereas on the swimming team, someone was always around to practice with and critique my progress. The team was familiar ground, and I knew my place and everybody else knew me in that place. But, changing my image from a "Harry-High- Schooler" to that of a hot rodder was exciting for sure; it was still a little scary. Then there was the fact that I didn't even know any real hot rodders much less any that were of the same back ground and religion as me, except maybe cousin Alfred, but he was gone. Most of these guys were real old, like 21 or even older. How was I, a kid with a rich daddy, going to fit in with a bunch of guys who had to work for a living?

I guess my confidence was finally cemented in place one Saturday afternoon when I caught my dad in one of his better moods. He was snacking on Melba toast and Philadelphia Cream Cheese and listening to the Redlegs game on the radio. I joined him because I just loved the white creamy cheese. The subject sorta came up by accident, when Waite Hoyte mentioned how scared the new ball players were their first time up to bat in the major leagues.

"That's how I feel sometimes, Dad, when I think about building that car. Like I'm going to bat for the first time in the league of grown-ups. Do you know what I'm trying to say?"

"So what is it you're telling me now? That you want to back out of making something out of the Crosley after I spend

7

all that money on the fiberglass body and all? Oy Vey!"

"No sir. It's just that I'm worried and afraid that I won't be able to do it and everybody will laugh at me when it turns out to be a mess."

"So what do you want, a guarantee? Son, you don't know the meaning of the words fear or worry. Even if you fail, you'll still be one up on everyone else who never even tried to build a car. So listen to your old man, you're not going to fail as long as you believe that you won't. Hush up now, Wally Post is in the hole with two strikes on him!"

I listened and waited. Post struck out. "Have you ever been scared? Like in the war or something?"

"Damn right I've been scared, but there are different kinds of fear: There's the kind when you're facing the enemy on a battle field and then there's the kind that, well it's a fear you have for someone else. It's hard to explain. When you're in the shooting war there's nothing you can do about it. If a bullet has your name on it then that's it. You're still scared, but resigned to the fact that you can't alter it. The other kind of fear, the kind that eats at you, is the kind when you worry about somebody else, like when I left your mother and my children to go to war. I was thirty-five when I was called up. I was not like most of the draftees because I had a family and a business I was just starting. I was scared of going to such a far off place and having to leave my family at home. Most of the younger soldiers were looking forward to this, their biggest experience in life, but not me. Am I making any sense?"

"Yes. I think I know what you mean. It's like when I've been about to begin a swimming team race. I'm scared, but there's nothing I can do about it and it's only me that is affected. I guess the other kind of fear is what it was like when Willie got sick. I was scared for him. When the ambulance guys took him to the hospital, I was scared that he might be in pain and, well, I was just scared <u>for him</u>. It was a worse kind of pain than the fear of losing a swimming race."

"Your grammar's not exactly right, but I think you've got the idea. I don't think I ever told anybody this, but fear really hit home when I had to show your mother how to use that old .380 Colt. It was just before I left to go overseas. She hated guns, but I felt—and she did too—that she should know how to use it. I didn't know when I would be coming back or even if I were coming back, and if I did come back I didn't know what I'd be coming back to. I mean it was totally unknown. I might come back to a country that was controlled by the Germans or the Japs. Maybe I would be gone for so many years that the spring in the clip would loose all its tension and the gun would fail just when your mother needed it. Those were my biggest fears. I wasn't worried about my hide, I always figured I could take care of myself. It was my fear of what might happen to you, your sister and my wife that really weighed heavy on my mind. But since a man has to do what a man has to do, he might as well make all the preparations as best he can."

"What was the war really like, Dad? I've never heard you talk about it. Did you shoot anybody? What did—"

"Son, I don't talk about it because I don't want to relive things that are best forgotten. I'll tell you this though. It's not what you see in the movies. The mind is a funny thing. It can suppress some things and enhance others. Some people only remember the good or funny events that occurred, while others, like myself, can only remember the hunger, the mud, the cold, seemingly never ending rain, short supplies, sore feet, constant fatigue, fear of going on patrol, fear of not going on patrol, getting a "Dear John letter", a buddy—his guts hanging out and wanting to know if everything's going to be okay—or the—"

"It's going, going...gone! That's Johnny Temple's first home run of the season and the Redlegs lead—" Waite Hoyte had recaptured the conversation.

It was from this discussion, and others, that I made up my mind that I was going to put everything I had into the building of this vehicle, but at the same time, I was going to do my best to at least maintain the friends I had made on the team and in other fields. I had seen others change their focus and lose touch with those with whom they had gone through the earlier years. I didn't want to become a one interest person. With the diversity of students at Woodward High, this was an opportunity and a challenge. Besides, who could tell, I might be back on the swimming team next year.

Before going to this public school, I had attended a private school through grade seven. My seventh year, at an all boys academy, was not to my liking at all. At the private school, everyone was upper middle class or higher and we had little contact with those of other races or religions. Woodward was a real awakening. There was a large contingent of Jews, some Blacks, a few Orientals and all mixes of wealth. Discrimination

9

and prejudice were almost non-existent. Oh sure, there were words such as Kike or Nigger used in close circles at times, but they weren't used with intent to hurt. They were just labels or ways to identify, and some kids were just emulating their parents. Besides, if you called someone a racial slur to his face, there was the real possibility that the biggest and baddest of his kind would beat you up when word got around.

Coming from a well-to-do family in a neighborhood of similar households, I never thought about living without TV, telephone, automobiles, or just not having enough money for a school lunch. My introduction to life at Woodward quickly taught me that I was no different than those of lesser means. We all had the same fears, wants, dreams and smarts as well as a common denominator of love of rock & roll music and fast cars. Maybe the reason I could relate to those of modest circumstance was that my parents saw to it that I never had more money than I needed. I got by on an allowance during the school year that was just enough to provide lunch, with a few bucks left over each week for entertainment, Some kids worked after school jobs; others put their free time into sports. We were all still teenagers, in love with rock & roll and struggling to pass each class.

WHAT'S YA GOT IN THE BOWL, BITCH?

CHAPTER 4

The start of construction of the Crosley sports car began with the separation of the body from the chassis. To do this required the removal of steering, seats, linkage, wiring and all the bolts, screws and pins. Not an easy task for a novice! Oh, I had worked on cars before, but I had never completely dismantled one. Aside from tearing down and rebuilding lawn mower engines and making minor adjustments to my sister's car, my hands-on experience was limited to watching or helping others.

The proficiency I gained from this allowed me to be able to combine lawn mower engines with homemade jitneys and thus provide a set of wheels for Willie and me—on the rare days that the thing worked. Motorbikes were a different thing all together. Too dangerous, Mom had always said. Maybe it was the accident Willie had when he broke his arm, the time the steering rope broke on the jitney. Willie and I had been racing against the stop watch—the one I got for Christmas for timing my swimming—and the rope that was attached to the front axle snapped and Willie slammed into the side of the garage, breaking his arm. Willie could always beat me in these little races around the circular part of the driveway because he was lighter, but I don't think he could have beaten me if it wasn't for that fact. Now I'll never know for sure. I guess Mom figured one banged up child at a time was enough. With a motorbike we could ride double and thus might both get hurt at the same time should we crash. Accidents were inevitable because just riding these motorized junk piles was never enough; we just always had to see how fast we could go.

I did get a few rides on a motorbike though. A neighbor boy had a Whizzer with a very temperamental carburetor and whenever he couldn't get it running he would bring it to me. Most of the time I could make it operational in short order but would tell him that it would take a few days to make the necessary repairs. After he was gone and the adjustments made, I would tell Mom that I was going to push the bike back to the kids house. Once out of her sight, I would hide the motorbike in the bushes. Later, after dinner I would just say I was going to hitch-hike down to Roselawn to see some of the guys. Only, this time I would retrieve the Whizzer and off I'd be.

This is how I usually got to see Karen. She was thirteen-years-old and lived in one of those old Victorian houses in the

CIRCA 1957

Avondale section of the city, with parents who looked more like grand parents. A twenty minute motorbike ride away made the trip almost as much fun as the visit. Of course, if I thumbed, it took over a half hour to get there in the early evening, when there were lots of cars, but it could take as long as an hour or more to get home in the late night when the traffic was light.

Karen was the first girl who let me play with her tits, and I don't just mean a little feel through her clothes. She had small but nice firm ones that she liked to have me rub, and on occasion, suck. The problem was that she had gotten into a fast crowd before she met me and had gotten into some trouble. She wouldn't talk about it, and I guess that's why she wasn't allowed to go out on dates. So whenever I could I went to visit her and we'd sit in her parlor in this giant old stately house and make out while her parents sat in the kitchen. With her parents so close, she couldn't take her clothes off so she would usually just wear a sweater and no bra. The floors creaked so bad in that old house we could hear if her mother was coming, and we would straighten out our clothes in a hurry and sit erect at the sound of footsteps. The problem was that sometimes the floor creaked when no was coming and we'd have to start all over again after catching our breath. I didn't care if we got caught, which was my first revelation of the old saying that a stiff cock has no conscience. I'm sure her mother thought me ill-mannered because I didn't get up whenever she entered the room. I didn't get up because I had a hard-on from the minute we sat down in that parlor until I was half way home. When it was finally time for me to leave, Karen would stand in her bedroom window over looking the driveway and let me watch her take off all her clothes. It was sure tough to walk away from there with a big stiff one, much less ride a motorbike.

She was my first real "hands on" experience with a member of the opposite sex. From her I learned that girls nipples got hard just like a man's cock. I had often wondered why some of the pictures of nude women in the girly magazines had nipples that stood up and others didn't. I'd play with those titties and they'd get nice and hard, and then we'd hear her mother walking around and we'd have to straighten up. By the time I got back to playing they would be soft again. Neat!

As I got deeper into building the sports car I would have less time for girls. All my spare time, after school, all day Saturday and Sundays, would be spent building and daydreaming about the car.

By early summer, 1957 I had the body off, the floor boards separated from it and faced the grinding task of cleaning the remains. The drudgery of this work was mind numbing and the dirt and filth was so heavy that I had to spend a good portion of each day just cleaning the garage. At least if Willie were here I could get him to help. Then again maybe not. By now he'd have had his own friends to play with. This garage where I was allowed to house my soon to be race car was a two-car attached and was given to me because my father had a new three car garage built at a right angle to it. This was not totally out of consideration to me. He needed the space for two reasons: One, my sister had gotten her licence and was given a car to drive, a 1956 Ford; and two, the Cadillacs my mother and father drove were getting too big to fit side by side in the old garage. The garage was surrounded by shade trees and the area remained quite cool in the summer as the house was not air-conditioned. On one outside wall, under the wood double hung windows, was the heart of the workshop; a large work bench, some eight feet long. We made this bench from wood Willie and I had swiped from some of the new houses they were building up the street a few years ago. This creation was made of plywood and two-by-fours and held together with nails, since by that stage of life we hadn't discovered threaded fasteners. It was sturdy enough with a full length shelf under and eye-ball level to a floor that sloped to the center drain.

Before school was out for summer vacation, my favorite teacher, Mr. Herne, the metal shop instructor, told me about a hot rod club some of his former pupils belonged to and how to get in touch with them. I went to my first meeting in the back alley club garage in the Bond Hill area of the city the next night. Wow, real hot rodders, just like in the car magazines! After introducing myself and explaining how I came to learn of them and that I was in the process of building a car, a guy wearing an Iskenderian Cam T-shirt volunteered to sponsor me at the next meeting. This was really cool. Isky, so called because he always wore those T-shirts, was 22 years old, worked for the phone company as an engineer, and drove a 1953 Studebaker coupe with a Cadillac engine under the hood—a Stude-lac. After the meeting, he offered to take me home in this hot machine. Man, I was really livin' now! As if that wasn't enough, Isky also had a 1932 Ford roadster that he was putting a Cadillac engine in.

CIRCA 1957

The Stude-lac, he explained, was his street machine and the roadster was going to be just for the drag strip.

This club, The Knights of the Twentieth Century, boasted some of the finest rods in the city. In various stages of completion there was Stan's Merc-o-lac, Bobby's '40 Ford that had been chopped and channeled, Bart's '49 Ford with a full flathead, and Harry Stone's '56 Chev custom to mention a few. I learned right off that these fellows were serious about racing and that they were intent on forming an association to build and operate a real drag strip. Club members could be fined for racing on the street or even thrown out of the club if the violations were harmful to the image of the Knights. But, because there was no drag strip, some could be goaded into a street race on occasion.

Informal street races could be run from a stop light, while more formal illegal drags were held on the Lockland Highway. The Lockland Timing Association (LTA), as we jokingly referred to this section of road, was from the divided highway signs just east of the Paddock Road entrance, eastbound to the foot bridge, which marked the end of the quarter mile. Spectators could, of course, watch the races from this viaduct. Some of the races were just between dogs, while others paired very hot machines that could reach over 100 MPH in the quarter mile.

To stage a race on the LTA, it took four cars: Two to race; one to block traffic from the rear so the cops couldn't chase the racers; and one car to wait at the turnaround past the foot bridge to signal with headlights when it was clear. Most times that the police could get close enough to give chase they were outrun by the faster hot rods. The city's answer to this was the introduction of the police interceptor, a 1957 Chevrolet two door unmarked sedan with three on the tree and a V8 engine including power pack under the hood. Oh, I guess they could go fast enough, but there weren't very many of them. Besides, times were different. There wasn't much traffic and not nearly so many cops. What cops there were seemed to be relaxed about drag racing and wouldn't hassle hot rodders if they appeared to be serious about the sport. It was the politicians who made the most noise about catching speeders.

I spent many nights helping fellow club member Bart put the finishing touches on his full race '49 Ford. Big Bart had spent most of his earnings as an apprentice machinist for Lodge & Shipley, on adding everything he could to that old flathead to make it go faster. On the first night he got the bomb running I was lucky enough to be there. After a short drive around his neighborhood to make sure there were no major leaks or other problems, we headed for Carters' Drive-in restaurant to show off. After one pass through the lot, we pulled out onto Reading Road where he laid down a strip of rubber all the way to the Valley Theater where a cop was parked in full view. Well, he pulled BB (for Big Bart or Broads & Booze) over, but he didn't need his red light or siren 'cuz BB stopped just as soon as he saw him.

"Yeah, I know, it was an accident, your foot slipped off the clutch and you just happened to lay a patch all the way down the street. Let me see your licence, son," the cop said, spitting the words out sarcastically.

"No sir, it wasn't an accident. I did it on purpose 'cuz this is the first time I've had it running and, well, I just wanted to see what it would do. I'm sorry and I won't do it again, honest, sir," BB whined as he fumbled for his licence.

"I don't care if you kids all kill yourself just as long as you don't do it when I'm working. I saw a plaque hanging from your rear bumper. Are you one of those hot rod clubbers?" The cop asked, examining Bart's licence.

"Yes sir. I, ah, we...belong to the Knights."

"Yeah, I've heard of your club. My brother's kid belongs to one called the Hell Cats. What've you got in this thing to make it lay that much rubber? Let me see under the hood."

Breathing a sigh of relief, Bart slid out from behind the wheel and opened the hood. The cop was obviously impressed upon seeing the six Stromberg 97s nestled between two polished Offenhauser aluminum high compression heads. After a brief description of how BB had bored and stroked, ported and polished the block and added a full Clay Smith cam the cop let us go with the promise that it was the only time he would.

The rest of the summer of '57 was like a merry-go-round with only stops for food and sleep. Every day there were new rock & roll songs on the air and lots of time to spend working on my car and other club members' hot rods. The nights were taken up by much of the same, plus an almost nightly ritual of hanging out at Carters' with an occasional jam session thrown in. Part of the summer was expended in actual labor—building the drag strip. This work was alright because it was still related to cars and the sooner we got it finished the sooner we could race on it. The strip was the result of a lot of hard work and public relations on the part of the various hot rod clubs in the Cincinnati area. The clubs had printed up small cards that said: **"YOU HAVE BEEN ASSISTED BY A MEMBER OF THE _____ HOT ROD CLUB WHICH IS DEDICATED TO SAFETY."** The idea was to pass out the cards whenever a member helped a stranded motorist. At least that's what I was told when handed my supply of cards. I wasn't quite sure what good they would do since I was not yet a licenced motorist. I did give one out to a neighbor lady when her clutch return spring came off and I was able to replace it.

THE Drag Strip, more formally known as The Southern Ohio Timing Association (SOTA), was built by hand complete with rest rooms, timing stands and fencing. The financing was done with the sale of bonds. Only enough money was raised to pave the quarter mile so we had to stop on dirt and gravel. The spectator and pit areas were grass beaten into dirt which yielded great clouds of dust when ever the wind blew. But nobody really cared—we saw our hard work rewarded when we finally raced. Those who weren't racing, either because they didn't have their rod ready or, because like me, they didn't have a licence, were expected to work at the various jobs. Not having a licence didn't prevent my driving on the strip, because when an errand needed to be run from one end of the strip to the other I was usually the first to volunteer to drive SOTA's '52 Ford pickup. I couldn't go over 10 MPH on the return lane for safety reasons and also because the dust was so bad when it was dry, but on the strip I floored the old truck to reach the wild speed of at least 50 MPH!

My stature among schoolmates was greatly enhanced as I was acknowledged by some of the upper classmen, who had come to race their daddy's car. They's just say, "Like how's it goin' Paul?" as I painted their number and class on their window with Bon-ami. It was really neat. Here I was, a fifteen-year-old with an official SOTA arm band, a Knights T-shirt and rubbing shoulders with the gods of the local car world. It never occurred to me that perhaps it was these older classmates' stature that was increased; to them, maybe I was one of the gods. This lofty position was responsible for an introduction to Kathy, my first real true love.

She was in the spectator section with a friend of a friend who introduced us. Actually, he was in last year's English class. He called to me as I was performing the task of walking the fence, at the time decked out in Jeans, Knights T-shirt and SOTA armband. I stopped and went over to where he and two girls were standing. I don't remember much of what was said after hearing the name Kathy. She was beautiful. I'm not sure what I said other than I had to finish walking the fence to keep spectators from climbing on it, but she asked if she could walk with me. The race day was almost over, so we didn't get much of a chance to talk while I completed my task. Mostly, we talked about what music we liked; yes, I liked Elvis, but thought Little Richard was the most. Kathy loved Elvis and Buddy Holly. We both agreed that Buddy Knox's rendition of "Party Doll" was better than Steve Lawrence's and anybody who didn't like Fats Domino was gone. Man, the merry-go-round was spinning faster. I was cool enough to get her phone number, which she had to write on a dollar bill because neither one of us had any paper. She used a lipstick and wrote her name on one side and her number on the other. Ah, Willie, I wish you could see me now. Life couldn't get any better.

I caught a ride home with Benny in his '57 Chevy fuel injected convertible because BB's '49 had broken an axle on its maiden run down the strip. Bart had picked me up early that morning in his flathead that made so much noise, with its straight pipes, we must have awakened half the neighborhood. It was a neat trip down, never getting out of second gear because the mill wouldn't run under 1500 RPM, due to the advanced ignition and full cam. Now the broken bomb was silently being towed behind the '57 with a length of chain, Big Bart sitting hunched up behind the wheel, not looking very happy. The once deafeningly loud beast at least still looked cool with it's hub caps gone, class number still painted on the rear side windows, and splotches of red primer contrasting the dull green paint where Big Bart had started a nose and deck job.

I told Benny about the neat chick I'd met and how a girl who liked drag racing and rock & roll music was the one for me. His only comment was "The higher you go the harder you fall," while Sonny James', "Young Love" blared over the speakers in the dash. I wondered what he meant.

When I got home that night Mom was worried because I had missed dinner. In fact, I had missed breakfast and lunch and had eaten only a couple of hot dogs at the strip. I was starved. I sat down in the big kitchen at the counter and without sounding too demanding asked my sister, Bobbi, if she would fix me something. Bobbi said, "Mother, look at him! He's a walking pig pen. I don't even want to be in the same room with him."

"Paul go up and take a shower and put on some clean clothes, and we'll fix you something to eat," Mom sighed.

"I could really dig a big juicy steak and some fries," I said.

"You'll get the leftovers from the dinner that you missed. Now get up and get going and don't forget to throw your dirty clothes down the chute—all of them!" Mom asserted.

"So you dig it, man," Bobbi said, sarcastically.

"Hey, I'm cool," I retorted, as I got up to go upstairs.

Once upstairs I studied myself in the mirror as I undressed. Except for the pimple that was sprouting next to my nose, and aside from a little dirt and the fact that my flat top was ruffled by the dirt and wind, I didn't look too bad. I showered and shampooed, watching the white bath tub turn brown with dirt. Only on my face did I take care to clean with a face brush and Acne Dome soap which a dermatologist had recommended last year. It didn't seem to work as I was still plagued with a few pimples in various stages. The one next to my nose was going to be a humdinger if I didn't get a hot compress on it tonight. If I could only wash my face and use the compress every hour, I'm sure my face would be clear and smooth. It wasn't as bad as some guys, who have had their faces sandpapered by a doctor. I was sure it would go away by next week.

Dinner was warmed over pot roast and noodles which was very good; anything would have been good, as hungry as I was. While I ate I tried to tell Mom and Bobbi about my day. They listened without comment, doing the dishes, while I told about how Big Bart had twisted off an axle and that the top eliminator of the day, a guy from Dayton, had turned over 130! There was no comment until I mentioned that I had met a good looking chick.

"What's her name," asked Bobbi.

"I'm not tellin', so don't bug me," I said, stonewalling.

"She must be some hot rod girl who wears short-shorts. Are you ashamed of her? Why won't you tell us her name?"

"I'll bet you'd wear short-shorts too if you didn't have such a big rear end," I shot back.

"Mother, tell him not to talk to me like that."

"Paul!" Mom said.

"Well then tell her not to bug me about my friends," I

replied."Next thing you know you'll be growing duck tails and become a bigger hood than you already are," Bobbi said, not missing a chance to slip one in on me.

"I doubt that, man, but at least I don't bleach my hair."

"That's enough children," was Mom's final word.

Barbara Ann, Bobbi, was alright for a sister even though she did needle me about some of my friends. She was nineteen and had just completed her first year at Miami University in Oxford and was really hot stuff, if you can dig what I mean. I couldn't really talk to her because she seemed like an adult already. She didn't dig rock & roll music and certainly not fast cars. The guy she dated, "old four eyes," I called him, was a big man on campus. He drove a stock '54 chev, with an automatic transmission yet. He wasn't cool like in real cool but he was alright though, for a square. Last year he let me go with him and some of his fraternity brothers to see the "500" time trials in Indianapolis. On the way back he actually floored the old Chevy and we hit 95 on an open stretch of two lane highway just outside of Greensburg. Somebody yelled, "Streamline the car," and we closed the windows, which allowed the little six banger to push the car to a hundred miles per hour! We all cheered. John had a little cool. I wondered if they ever did it. Naw, not with my sister. She probably didn't know what it meant, even though she had a blonde streak bleached in her hair and drank wine at college frat parties. Naw.

I was beat, but I just had to call the number on the dollar bill before going to bed. I dialed, trying to imagine what kind of house she lived in, what she was doing now and if she would even remember me. What if she didn't?

"Is Kathy there?"

"Just a moment please."

"Hello." I recognized the voice; it was musical.

"Kathy? Hi, it's Paul, Paul Auer; you know, we met at the strip today."

"Oh, hi Paul." Then a little softer, "I was hoping you'd call."

"Yeah, I thought I'd call before I hit the hay. I'm really beat. It was a long day. I got to the strip about 7:30 this morning and just got home a little while ago."

"How come you got home so late? I thought the races were over when we left, which must have been about five," Kathy said.

"Well, BB, that's the guy I was with, his '49 dropped an axle and we had to rig a tow chain and tow him home. Then we pulled the rear end out to see how much damage was done. Man, you should have seen the axle. This section of solid steel, that must be at least an inch and a half in diameter, was just twisted in two like...like a piece of licorice." I explained.

"You must be awful tired."

"I am. Do you go to the strip often or was this your first time?"

"It was my first time. I only went because my girl friend, Donna, that's the girl I was with, dragged me along because she had a date with Joey and she didn't want to be alone with him,"

"Joey, you mean the cat I saw you with?" I asked.

"Yes, he said he knows you from school."

"I think he was in a class with me last year."

"At Woodward?"

"Yeah, where do you go to school?"

"I go to Walnut Hills."

"That's where my sister went, I know a few cats that go there. Do you know Mike Kahn or Ed Goldman?"

"I know who they are," Kathy replied.

"Why didn't your friend want to be alone with Joey?" I asked.

"She only went out with him as a friend. She's trying to break up with him. What's your sister's name? Was she in a sorority?"

"Yeah, she was in STP, but she graduated a year ago. Her name's Bobbi."

"Did you hear the song "Whole Lotta Shakin' Goin' On", by Jerry Lee Lewis?" Kathy asked.

"Cool man, you can really dance to that one. Do you collect records?"

"No. Do you?"

"No. I've got to put money into my car."

"I have to go now I hear my mom calling to get off the phone. It was nice talking to you, Paul."

"Yeah, I've got to get to bed. If you're not doing anything next Saturday night, I'd like to see you. Maybe we could double with somebody to the drive-in or something," I suggested, holding my breath for the answer to whether I lived or died.

"That might be okay. Will you call me during the week?" She said, in an up-beat tone.

We said our good-byes, but I could have talked forever. I felt I had known her a long time with what I had already learned. She was about five-feet-three, just a little shorted than me, had light brown hair, much lighter than my dark brown hair, that she wore in a pony tail. I wasn't sure about the color of her eyes. I'd better check that next time, first thing, in case she asks if I know. She told me at the strip that she lived on Grand Vista, in Pleasant Ridge, which was only a couple of miles from me, but impossible to thumb to. Besides I don't think I want her to know that I hitch- hiked. It just doesn't sound cool. It was time to shag ass and get some z's.

I talked to Kathy every night the next week while the days were spent mostly working on the Crosley, which had been progressing slowly. Everything had been stripped and cleaned, including the engine and was now ready for reassembly, which would be the fun part. The garage had chassis parts hanging from every inch of wall and window space while the engine was spread out on an old sheet in one corner of the smooth cement floor. Before putting it all back together, I decided to paint everything that would take paint and chrome the overhead valve cover and a few other parts on the engine. It would cost me time and money but the end result would be a cool looking mill. Maybe I was just putting off the inevitable job of fitting the body to the frame.

The fiberglass body had arrived the week before from Almquist and a quick check of the dimensions showed that there was no way it would fit and look right. There were no instructions, just a shell, two curved pieces that had to be fitted and a made into doors, and a copy of the invoice showing that the amount of $295.00 had been paid. For the finished car to look right and handle correctly, the frame would have to be "Z'd" and "C'd" and the engine would have to be moved back and down, stuff I had only read about in Hot Rod magazine. If I mounted the body on the stock frame as indicated by the sales literature, the engine would not be in the center of the hood opening and the car would have a very high center of gravity. Definitely not the "low slung sports car" I imagined it should resemble. I figured that it had to be all back together in stock condition before I could begin to take accurate measurements about where to cut the frame. I needed help, not just to lift the engine and body, but to double check dimensions and someone to bounce ideas off. I still had a few weeks of work before I would be ready to start the modifications, and by then I would be back in school where maybe I could find someone.

Willie would have been almost thirteen by now and no doubt big enough to help with the physical part. He was big boned; I remember Mom saying that about him a long time ago. She said he was built like her father, whom I remember as being big and barrel chested, not like me. Mom thought I was built like my great Uncle Will whom Willie was named after. Old Uncle Will was average height and build and was pretty hep for an old man of seventy-eight. Most all of my relatives had died before I was twelve, there was only Uncle Will and a few cousins and uncles, most of whom lived on the West Coast.

Anyway, Saturday night was set. We were going to the passion pit. I had thumbed to Carters' Thursday night to look for a double, somebody with wheels, and found Big Bart sipping coffee alone inside at the counter. Bart was Big Bart because he was, well, big. He was at least six-two and must have tipped the scales at something around 195; not fat, all muscle with biceps that were prominently displayed when he rolled his ever present pack of Lucky's in his T-shirt sleeve. His hair was light blond, and he usually had a two-day growth of beard, which wasn't noticeable due to the light color. His finger nails, like all hot rodders, were embedded with dirt and grease from working on cars. He had on the standard attire of the day: T-shirt, Levi's and black leather engineer boots.

I sat down next to him, ordered a small lemonade from the hovering waitress who was obviously smitten with Big Bart, and asked, "Hey, punk did you get a new axle in the coupe?"

"Punk? I'll kick your ass you little squirrel."

"Squirrel? It wasn't me that pealed out of here and got stopped by the cops, man!"

"I'm hep man, crazy man, crazy."

"Say Bart, I was wondering—"

"No, you can't borrow my car. You don't even have a licence."

"Naw, man I don't want to borrow your junker, unless you're drivin' it, dig."

"What's this shit gonna cost me?"

"As I was sayin'," I started again. "I was thinkin' that maybe if you had a date this Saturday night we could double."

"Where'd you wanna go? Janice and I were talking about going to the drive-in. Who do you have a date with? Not some

22

whore, I hope." "Hey, man, I got a date with a real nice chick I met at the strip. She lives in Pee Ridge and goes to Walnut Hills," I said, trying to defend Kathy's honor. "Like man you didn't tell me," I continued, "if you got the axle fixed, and then I got another question for ya."

"Yeah, but I had to get one at the junk yard. I was hoping to just weld the old one back together at work but there wasn't enough spline left to weld onto. Now what else are going to bug me about?"

"Well, I need to know what will happen if I bore the venturi out in the carb on my Crosley and increase the size of the jet at the same time. Will it work? I mean will it increase the power?" I asked.

"Paul," Bart said, getting serious. "The venturi is built into the Carburetor for the purpose of increasing the speed in which the air flows through the fuel nozzle, which creates the partial vacuum that draws the fuel into the venturi to mix with the air. The size of the butterfly valve and the air horn is directly related to the size of the venturi. I think if you increase one without proportionally increasing the others then all you'll get is poor gas mileage and very flat acceleration, if it runs at all."

"Yeah, I dig what you're saying but I think the main purpose of the venturi is to increase the air speed only at low engine speed, so the engine will idle. At higher engine speed, and I'm talking about 4000 RPM and up, the restriction of the venturi is a hinderance. In other words, if I'm correct the top end should improve while the low speed response drops way off. That's okay with me. I'm willing to sacrifice the bottom end for more power on the top end. Ya dig?"

"I still say it won't work because you have to keep the ratio the same between the venturi and the butterfly. If what you're saying was true we'd have read about some guy on the West Coast doin' it a long time ago."

"Maybe so," I persisted. "But those guys on the coast don't know all the tricks. I've got a spare carb base, so I think I'll try it if you'll lend me some number drills so I can drill out the jets in succession."

"Sure you can borrow the bits just let me know which ones and when. I gotta shag ass outta here. Come on I'll give you a lift home if you want," Bart offered.

We went out and climbed into his old '35 Ford four door

sedan, which was BB's main mode of transportation since the '49 had become a "Sunday" car only. The '35 was completely stock; well, except maybe for the chrome racing air cleaner under the hood. BB, a true hot rodder couldn't stand to drive a factory stock car. I surveyed the back seat where I would be spending Saturday night and hoped that it would be a cool evening. Those old wool seats get awful hot.

"How long have you and Janice been going together?" I asked.

"About a year now,I guess."

"'Bout time for you to be getting married and settle down and quit this racing stuff isn't it?" I joked.

"You sound like my mother. She's always bugging me to get married, I'm not tying the knot until I finish night school."

"Night school? I didn't know you were in school."

As we drove home Bart explained how he had failed to keep his grades up in high school and now he would have to wait until he had earned enough money from his work as a machinist's apprentice to pay his way through night school at the University of Cincinnati. The earliest he could start, if he saved money every week, would be the second semester which began in January of 1958.

Once home I asked him if he would take a look at my car. We went into the garage, where I told him of the problem facing me in fitting the glass body to the Crosley frame. After looking over the various parts, spread around the area, Bart said, "Looks simple enough to me. All we have to do is decide where we have to cut, get a few pieces of channel iron and weld in the new parts."

"Well, if it looks so easy how 'bout giving me a hand with the major task of measuring and cutting since I can't lift the body myself?" I asked.

"Sure, but you'll have to put it all back together first. Think you can have it done by next Saturday? It shouldn't take us more than a few days at most to do the whole job."

Bart was a true optimist. Who else would try to force a 200- plus horsepower engine into a vehicle designed for less than 100 horses and wonder why the axle broke?

After we agreed that he meant Saturday-a-week and not the day after tomorrow we would begin the work that appeared so easy to Bart. I was elated. I had the "expert" help I needed and the car would be done within the month. Bart cut-out after confirming again that this Saturday we would double to the drive-in.

It was too late to call Kathy, so I turned on the old radio in the garage, jiggled the antenna wire that was hanging from the rafters and daydreamed about how it would be. I could just see myself, snug and secure, behind the wheel of a low slung, snazzy sports car with a good lookin' chick in the co-pilots seat; strains of Chuck Berry or Elvis coming over a radio as we cruised through Carters' or Frisch's.

Saturday dawned hot and humid and promised to be just as bad by drive-in time, or worse if it rained. I had hoped to work on the Crosley but knew, as soon as my father came down for breakfast, that most of the day would be spent cutting the grass. Cutting grass wasn't so bad because it allowed me to operate a motorized vehicle. I don't just mean the lawn mower, In order to cut, I had to bring the mower from my father's factory, about a mile down the country road, to the house with a farm tractor pulling a trailer which carried the mower. The old man gave me a ride to the plant where I rigged the tractor and mower. Driving anything, even a farm tractor and even if it was only a mile was a thrill. The cutting and trimming would take most of a day and was always done on Saturday, weather permitting. The work was never performed Sunday as it was an unwritten rule of the neighborhood that nobody cut on the day of rest which was the day most relaxed in their screened in porches. Cutting after the dinner hour was also forbidden for the same reason.

Around 7:15 that evening BB and Janice, in the '35, picked me up and we then went to pick up Kathy. She lived in a two-story brick house on a street of similar middle class homes. Her mother greeted me at the door.

"Hi, Mrs. Becker, I'm Paul Auer. Is Kathy ready?"

"Why yes Paul, please come in. She'll be down in a minute."

"Thank you," I said, as I turned to hold one finger up to signal Bart, sitting in the car at the curb, that it would be a minute. Once inside I was ushered into the kitchen, where I met Kathy's brother, after which I made the mistake of asking, "Is Mr. Becker home?"

"No. Mr. Becker died in the war. He died a month before Kathy was born," Mrs. Becker stated solemnly.

"Oh, I'm sorry. I didn't know."

25

But before an awkward silence could develope, Kathy breezed into the room. She was very pretty with a light tan skirt and white lace blouse, white bobby socks and brown and white saddles. She had a yellow ribbon tied around her pony tail all of which contrasted to my faded red T-shirt, engineer boots and faded jeans.

"Hi, Paul, I'm ready if you are. Bye Mom, bye Joe, I won't be late," Kathy said, all in one breath.

Greatly relieved, I immediately started after her down the hall toward the front door. But before we got out the door, Mrs. Becker touched my arm, saying, "Please see that she is home by midnight," and looking out the door to the old black sedan parked at the curb, its rear sagging from a broken spring. She added, "Is that car safe?"

"Yes ma'am. The show should be over by 11:30 and the car has been converted to hydraulic brakes. It stops real good," I stammered, as I stumbled out the door, trying to keep up with Kathy who was now half way to the car.

Once in the car, and after the introductions were made, Bart said that since the show wouldn't start for an hour or so, he wanted to stop by Norwood Ford to look at the new cars and pick up some literature. The girls got acquainted, I guess, while Bart and I checked out the new T-Bird parked in the show room. We could have spent all night in there looking at the new cars and discussing the changes we'd make if we could afford to buy one, but the chicks insisted on cutting-out for the pit. We went to the Montgomery Drive-in because the main feature was "The Man Who Knew Too Much" and it was only a dollar a car load, whereas other passion pits all charged per person.

Bart and Janice, secure in the knowledge that they would have the whole car to themselves later, took the front seat out and sat on it, leaning up against the front bumper. Kathy and I then had the privacy of the back seat to ourselves. The first order of business, once were alone, was to tell her how I screwed up by asking her Mom about her Father.

"Well, don't feel bad. You didn't know," she reassured me. After a moment of silence Kathy continued, "You know I never did know my father, so I don't know what I missed, and Mom never talks about him. All I've seen is a photo of him in uniform and a Purple Heart that is in my Mom's dresser. Are your parents living?"

"Yeah, but my little brother died a couple of years ago,

26

so I know how your Mom must feel when someone talks about somebody who should be there. He died of a brain tumor and I don't like to talk about it. It makes me sad. We were gonna...we had...." I looked out the window, blinking my eyes. Damn, this was not the way it was supposed to be.

"Now it's my turn to be sorry. I didn't know, but why does it make you sad to remember him?" she asked.

"I don't know, it just does. Can we talk about something else?"

She snuggled closer just as the credits were flickering on the screen for the start of the movie. Hey, this is great, get a little sympathy and the chicks just melt. I'd have to remember that. Thanks Willie! I put my arm around her in hopes that she might want to kiss, but she was intent on watching the flick. No sweat, there was plenty of time to put a move on her as I felt my pecker starting to push out against my tight jeans. It was not easy to concentrate on the movie with such a good lookin' chick pressed against my side. My mind raced to think of what to say to put her in the mood. After what seem like half the movie I asked, "Wanna get some popcorn?"

"Yes, that's a good idea, it's very hot in here."

I let her get out first because the speaker was on my side and I needed a second to make sure that the bulge in my pants was not too noticeable. We walked back to the car holding hands with a box of popcorn and one coke that we would have to share because that's all the jack I had. Once settled in the dark back seat of the old Ford we both realized that the story line of the feature had passed us by. Great, but how do I get to first base with all this food we were holding? Maybe she sensed what I wanted because she put the coke on the floor, took the box of popcorn from my hand, and then put her arms around me and we kissed. It was the best kiss I had ever experienced. Her soft lips, the smell of perfume, the pressure of her breasts against my chest was like, Wow! I couldn't think, I couldn't breathe it was not at all like when I was with Karen. With Karen I was always planning my next move, like where I was going to put my hands. When we broke I reached for more, but Kathy just straightened her skirt and picked up the coke offering me a sip. I didn't understand this chick. One minute she knocks my brain out of whack and the next, like nothing's happened, she's drinking coke. Trying to be cool, I said, with a voice that squeaked, "Put the coke down and come here."

"No not now, somebody might see us. Now pass the popcorn and tell me what you're going to do in school. Are you going to rush? Which fraternity do you like?"

"Get hep, nobody's going to see us. Don't sweat it."

In a cool and detached voice only a nun could muster she said, "Paul, NO,and please don't talk like that, at least, not when you're around me."

"Talk like what," I demanded, getting defensive. "Didn't you like the kiss," I blurted suddenly beginning to feel insecure.

"You know, all that cool cat talk. I don't like it."

"Yeah, okay, but how about the kiss." Now I was really beginning to feel dejected, as I fought to try to remember the heavenly contact we so recently held. I couldn't remember anything; whether my mouth was open or closed or if I pressed to hard. Maybe she had detected my hard-on and was alarmed. She didn't have to worry about it now. It had shriveled up to nothing. Maybe the Five-Day deodorant pad I used after my shower only a few hours ago had failed, or my breath had begun to smell. I could hear the kids all talking behind my back—Auer smells...pass it on. Discreetly I checked.

"Well?" I bravely asked fearing the worst.

"Paul, I liked it alright, maybe too much. That's why I want to stop, I hardly know you, and I'm not that kind of girl. Can't we just talk?" she said, taking hold of my hand and looking at me with eyes that said I dig you.

Whew, I think, I didn't know what to think; my brain was like crazy, man. I did know I wanted her and I would do anything to get another kiss like the last one.

"What kind of girl are you, anyhow?" I asked. "You get a guy all heated up and then shut off tight like a new engine. Are you a PT?" I felt a little more sure of myself now that I hadn't been rejected for something I had done.

"Let's not argue, I really like you, Paul it's just that I don't want to do this in the back seat of a car. It seems so, so cheap."

I felt bad. How could I hold onto this beautiful lady when we would have to rely on a back seat for over six months until I got my license. What happened? It seemed that a few minutes ago I was on top of the world and now everything was all over. The title to a recent hit by Ivory Joe Hunter came to mind: "Since I Met You Baby, I Almost Lost My Mind" kept going round and round in my head. Damn, the movie was over and Bart and

Janice were struggling with the front seat. I thought about getting out to help when Kathy put her arms around my neck and we just hugged. Everything was cool again. She was amazing! I wondered if she was making me go up and down on purpose; I didn't want to believe that. Janice saw and said, "Alright you love birds, break it up."

Kathy, whom I thought would be embarrassed, replied to Janice, "We had our heads above the seats, which is more than I can say for you two. We could feel the whole car shake whenever you were doing whatever you were doing up there on that make shift bed."

Janice, with a look of mock indignation said, "Just what do you think, in your dirty little mind, we were doing 'up there' in front of god and everybody." We all laughed.

We put the speaker back, threw out the empty popcorn box, and got in line to leave as cars with spotlights played tag on the now dark screen

It was almost midnight so we had to take Kathy right home. I walked her to the door and told her I hoped that we could do it again. She came real close, close enough that I could feel her breasts touch my chest and just when I thought she was going to lay one on me she kissed my cheek and said for me to call her tomorrow. My head was reeling again. I almost ran back to the old Ford. I felt light and loose, like, well I wasn't sure. I had never felt like this before. Janice must have known because as soon as I slid in next to her in the front seat she said, "I think Paul's in love. Do you love her?"

"Hey, don't bug me, she's alright," I said, trying to act cool.

Three in the front seat was pretty tight, especially with someone the size of BB in addition to a floor shift. So Bart put his arm around Janice and I shifted when Bart shoved in the clutch. We drove like that all the way to Carters' where they dropped me off.

The first thing I did upon entering the restaurant was to put my last quarter in the juke box to play the Fat Man's, "I'm In Love Again", followed by Frankie Lymon and the Teen-agers, "Why Do Fools Fall In Love" and Sonny James, "Young Love". As I turned to look for someone to sit with, Fats was already singing:

"Yes, it's me and I'm in love again,

29

Had no lovin' since you know when...."

It must be love because I had never felt like that before. I had a hard time going to sleep that night, fighting half-heartedly the urge to pound my puddin', which throbbed. I kept trying to tell my putz that it wasn't like that with Kathy, but my hand and cock had other ideas.

THAT'S ABOUT THE SIZE OF IT.

CHAPTER 5

Sunday, Isky picked me up for the strip at the usual hour— 7:30 A.M.—BB having pawned me off to him because he, BB, didn't have to work the strip that Sunday. Isky was going to be the announcer for the day while I was to fill in wherever they needed a shelp. BB had promised to be down later, to run the '49 again now that it had a new axle. Isky's '32 still wasn't ready to race, so we motored down through Pee Ridge, Hyde Park and Mt. Lookout in his Stude-lac, the deep twin Glas-pacs shattering the morning stillness as he backed off for hills and stop lights. Being among the first to arrive, we stopped at the check-in to register and paint "C" GAS and the number one on his rear side window before heading to the pit area. I was left with the job of readying the coupe for the race by pulling the spinner hub caps and removing the spare tire to cut weight down. Isky took off for the announcer's stand which stood a full two stories above the landscape.

I was assigned to the staging area, with a broom to sweep the burned rubber and other debris off the strip. I was thankful for the job, since it didn't require much thought. My mind was still in a daze from last night and I couldn't stop thinking about Kathy. Ah, but the strip was magic and nothing could dampen the exuberance of a hot rodder nestled among dreams on wheels. The taste of oil tainted dust, the unmistakable smells of gasoline, alcohol and other exotic fuels had a calming, yet exciting, grip on us all. Early arrivals were greeted by sounds of Bob-white Quail, crickets and other natural morning sounds only to later ride the crest of a wave of eardrum numbing roars of the fire shooting machines whose exhaust looked like giant acetylene torches.

As the pit began to fill up with hot-rodders and squirrels, I saw Joey in a '57 Chev with "B/S 22" on the window. While the practice runs were going on I walked over to his car to talk.

"Where'd you get the wheels, man?" I asked.

"I borrowed my dad's car, It's stock but at least it's a stick," he said, as he struggled to pull the air cleaner off.

"Does he know that you're going to race it?"

"Hell no, I told him I was going on a school picnic."

"Shit man, school ain't started yet."

"I'm hep, but I told him it was a pre-school meeting of the drama club, ya dig."

31

"You don't think he'll be a little suspicious when you come rollin' in with numbers painted on the window, no hub caps and covered with dust?" I asked incredulously.

"Fuck no, we'll take it to a car wash first."

"Where's that chick I saw you with last time. What's her name, Donna?"

"She didn't want to come. I heard you had a date with Kathy last night, ah, how'd you make out."

"Like what's it to ya." I said, turning to leave.

"It ain't nothing to me, man, but Donna told me she was going to Coney today."

"I don't give a shit," I threw back over my shoulder as I tried to be cool walking away. I hoped Joey got caught by his old man drag racing the family bus. I wanted to ask who she was going to Coney with, was it a guy? Why didn't she tell me. Damn. Fuckin' women.

I got back to the staging area, picked up my broom and swept up a storm while thoughts of Kathy with another guy banged around inside my head. Maybe she was just going with her brother and mother. Shit, maybe she had date with some big bruiser and they were rolling around on the sand right now. I had to find a phone. The thought of her in a bathing suit was, like crazy, and the thought of her in a bathing suit with another guy was—I didn't want to think about it. If he was a big beast, maybe I could get some of the Knights to kick his ass. The sound of a revved engine brought me back to reality. I didn't feel so good.

I don't remember too much of the rest of the day other than Isky won the "C" Gas trophy and BB blew his pressure plate, again on his maiden run. It didn't look like he was ever going to get to the end of the strip. The only highlight of the whole day, if you can call it that, was when Joey, in his daddy's car, blew the clutch. It didn't just break or quit. It came all apart and with no flywheel shield, the parts of the disk and plate came through the floor board, through the dash board and through the windshield. That nice new car was a total wreck. Somehow I didn't feel sorry for him. I mean fuck him, talking like Kathy might be out with some other guy and hinting that we made out. Yeah, fuck him. I felt better already. He was a dork.

On the way home Isky asked, "You haven't said much today. Is anything wrong?"

"Naw, I'm just hot, tired and in need of a bath...and I had a date with this chick last night—"

"Oh, you've got it bad. What did she do to you?"

"Man, I don't know. We had a date last night, went to the Montgomery with BB and Janice, and then some guy at the strip said something and—"

"Hey, man, slow down. You're not making any sense. Did she dump you, or what about this guy at the strip?"

"I don't know, man, I just don't know anything."

"Man, you ought—"

"Shhhh," I cut Isky off as I reached for the volume knob on the radio, turning it up to hear:

> "Had no lovin' since you know when
> You know I love you, yes I do...."

It was becoming our song. Maybe she felt the same, fat chance.

"I'm sorry, what were you saying?" I asked.

"Man, you really got it bad. But I will try to enlighten you with Isky's words to live by: When it comes to women just try to remember the rule of the four 'F's.

"Yeah, I know, Find 'em, feel 'em, fuck 'em, and forget 'em."

"Only make sure you put the emphasis on the 'forget 'em' part," Isky related in a fatherly tone.

I thought about that as Isky rambled on about chicks and how to handle them. I had found her, but to feel her seemed kinda dirty and to fuck her, too crude. Get in her pants? Just as bad, but I better not think about it or I'll probably come in my jeans. Forget her? I didn't want to. Too much shit to think about.

We didn't talk much on the rest of the way home and Isky left me with the request to use a small part of my garage to build his engine for the '32. I said it was okay by me.

I was beat. It was almost 6:00 P.M. and I just had to call Kathy. No answer. I showered and got to the dinner table just in time for a hot meal; some kind of fish with rice. It looked good, but I just didn't seem to be hungry. When I realized that I hadn't eaten all day I forced myself to put away two helpings. I wasn't like me not to be hungry, I wondered what was wrong. After dinner I tried to call again; still no answer. Maybe Isky was right. This chick could drive me to drink, if I drank. I decided to lie down and take a nap and then try again. I never woke up.

I woke late the next morning and right away my head

started to think about all the stuff I had to do; call Kathy, work on the car, call Kathy, get dressed, call—shit, I might as well call her and get it over with. She answered on the second ring.

"Kathy? Hi it's me."

"Hi, Paul. I was hoping you'd call. I missed not talking to you yesterday. Did you have a good time at the strip?"

Now what. She just said she missed me. Maybe I was wrong, but I better find out just in case.

"What, I'm sorry I didn't hear what you said," I pleaded.

"I said," Kathy began again, "how was your day at the strip, did Janice go with Bart?"

"No, I think she had to be with her family so BB came alone. He blew his clutch and didn't get to finish even the first practice run." I summoned up some courage and continued. "Did you have a good time at Coney?"

"How did you know I went to Coney?"

"Hey, get hep. I keep tabs on all the good lookin' chicks."

"You must have talked to my mother or brother. Did you?"

"No," I said, starting to feel very confident.

"Well then, how did you know and did you miss me?"

"Yeah, I would have liked to have seen you at the strip. If you'd been there, you could have seen Joey ruin his daddy's shiny new car when the clutch let go."

"Oh, that's who told you. It was Joey wasn't it?"

"Yeah, he just mentioned that you were going to Coney, that's all," I said, tiring of playing a game. "Who'd you go with," I asked.

"Just my brother, my mother and a neighbor boy."

"Who's the neighbor kid. How old is he?"

"His name's Billy and he's sixteen. He lives two doors up the street, if you must know," she said, testily.

"Is he a boy friend, or what?"

"No he's just a friend. I've known him since, like forever. Are you jealous?" Kathy taunted.

"Not me, we're not going steady or anything are we?"

Almost in a whisper she said, "No."

Silence....

It's wonders what a good night's sleep can do to clear one's head, I thought, as I began to enjoy the idea that she just might be worried that I might be worried. My heart still said to keep talking, talk for ever, but my now clear brain said to shag ass.

"Kathy, I've got to go now. I'm like starved and if I hurry, maybe I can get Bessie to fix me something to eat."

"Who's Bessie" If you came over here, I'd fix you something."

"If I had wheels I'd be there."

"Who's Bessie?"

"Just a chick I know," I teased.

"How old is this 'chick' and where does she live?"

"Sounds to me like you're the one who's jealous."

"We're not going steady or anything," she mimicked.

"Hey, I'm like gone, I hear Bessie in the kitchen. Just for your information though, Bessie is our laundress and besides that, she's colored."

"You have somebody to do your wash? Why doesn't your mother do it? Does she work? Kathy blurted out.

"I don't know why. She doesn't work. The old man makes enough that she doesn't have to and besides, Bessie has always done the laundry. Now I really got to go. I'll call you tonight."

I still didn't know where I stood, but I felt better. I had a lot to digest in addition to food. After a satisfying meal of three eggs fried in bacon grease, and a stack of toast, I went out to the garage and at once decided to start to put the engine together before finishing the frame. Isky arrived late in the afternoon and we unloaded his Caddy engine block from the trunk of the Stude-lac, placing it in the only free corner left in the garage. We didn't talk much, both having work to do. My task seemed insurmountable with the time I had left. I had to have the job done by Saturday, not only because BB was coming over to help fit the body, but school would start the day after Labor Day, a week from tomorrow. Sunday I would have to help my parents get ready for a big pool party they were giving that night, which meant no drag strip, and Monday, Labor Day, was reserved for cleaning up after the party.

I worked every day that week on the Crosley, and a few nights too. Kathy and I talked on the phone every night, sometimes for hours on end. Mostly she wanted to know about Willie and what I remembered of him. I didn't want to talk about him because it upset me that I had really forgotten a lot of things about him. She put me down about this, but I got her attention when I told her that someday when I owned a big company I would name it Willie Enterprises. She didn't say anything more about the boy next door and I didn't ask, but in the back of my mind I knew that trouble could come from that type of relationship. After all, didn't Mickey Rooney and Judy Garland live next door to each other in the Andy Hardy movies? Come to think of it I had a girl next door. Judy Bloom, a real looker. In fact she had just been over to swim last week, with her mother. She even stopped in the garage and watched me work, asking all kinds of questions about the job at hand. I don't think I was very nice to her because at the time I was doing the frustrating operation of setting the valves and had to devote all my attention to that. Maybe she liked me. Shit! I don't need more girl problems. However, I just might mention her to Kathy if she ever said anything about the cat who lived next to her. Why does everything have to be so damn complicated?

Saturday rolled around with a light rain falling. I called BB to see when he would be over and to my elation he said he was on his way. Now we would get down to some serious rod building. We spent over four hours measuring again, with only a short break for lunch which we had to fix ourselves because Mom was busy getting ready for the party. She had Bessie come in to help because Bobbi had gone back to college last Thursday in her '56. Around three in the afternoon, Bart said, "It looks like the cut to "Z" the frame should be for six inches, which will allow about three inches ground clearance, or about the width of a pack of cigarettes."

I agreed, adding, "Then if our calculations are correct the engine will have to move down the same and back a total of twenty- one, which will still give us three inches over the tie rod." After a few moments of silence, Bart asked in an astounding tone, "Well, what are you waiting for? Start cutting.."

"Holy shit, man, I'm afraid to take the first cut; if we're wrong...once. we make the cut on the frame it's too late to—" I cried.

"Fuck it, man, I'll do it. It ain't my car." And while I watched, with a pit growing in my stomach, Bart picked up a hack saw and cut one side of the frame in half. There was no turning back now. Within thirty minutes the frame was in three pieces.

"What the fuck did I get myself into," I wondered aloud. "If this doesn't work, I'll kill myself and come back and haunt you, you car wrecking monster!"

I seated myself on the work bench, the one that Willie and I had stolen the lumber for so many years ago, just as Shirley and Lee's "Let the Good Times Roll" came over the old clock radio. It was a good sign.

"...Come on baby let the good times roll...
Roll all night long...."

It was almost seven when we finally decided to call it a day. I was scared of all the possibilities of things that could go wrong, but Bart spoke with confidence, even though he admitted this was the first frame altering job he'd ever done. When I reminded him of the fact that it wasn't his car or reputation that was at stake, he tried to cheer me up with his Alfred E. Newman, "What me Worry," impression.

Mom fixed us both soup and a sandwich which she made us eat in the garage because the kitchen was filled with stuff for the party and we were very dirty. Still hungry, I conned Mom for a few bucks for a piece of pie at Carters' while BB washed up in the water from the spigot in the garage. I did the same, and then used a little axle grease to help my crew cut stand up.

Home from Carters', I was exhausted and drained from the days tension, I had to call Kathy and tell her about the progress. She wasn't interested so we talked about school and I had to punish myself by asking how she was going to get to school.

"Billy got a car, so he said he'll drive me every day," Kathy answered without a trace of emotion.

"Is it a car pool, or is it just you and Billy?"

"Well, let's see, It's Billy and me and my brother and maybe Barbara. Why are you worried? We're not going steady or anything."

"Would you go steady with me, if I asked?"

"Are you asking?"

"Yeah I'd like to go steady with you."

"Oh, Paul, I don't know. Are you in love with me?" She asked in a hushed tone.

"I think so. How 'bout you Kathy?"

"I know you're in love with your car. Lets not talk about this on the phone. When can I see you?"

"Maybe tomorrow night. You know that big party my parents are throwing? Well, I think I'll be the official valet. See the driveway isn't big enough to hold all the cars, so I'll take the guests' cars when they arrive and park them on the road next to the house. Then, while the party's going on, I might be able to drive one of them over for a visit," I boasted.

"Paul, I don't want you to do anything illegal. What if you get caught?"

"Don't sweat it. Will you come out if you see a strange car outside and hear a horn?"

"Oh, I don't know, I don't want you to get in trouble."

"I'll take my chances. See ya, and I can't wait for tomorrow night. Hey wait. By the way, who's the chick Barbara you said was going to ride to school with you?"

"Oh, she's just a neighbor kid—too young for you—only in the seventh grade."

The merry-go-round was starting to move again. It must have slowed there for a while when I was having delusions about the cat who lived next to Kathy. I knew she loved me, the rod was coming along alright and everything was going to be okay.

Sunday morning was dry and the sun even looked like it might make an appearance. Bill, the part time Company gardener, and I worked all day cutting the grass, trimming hedges and washing down the pool furniture. While cutting the grass between the woods and the road, as there were no sidewalks, Jimmy walked by.

"Hey daddy-o, where you been? I haven't seen you all summer," I asked once I got the big Whirlwind mower shut down.

"Shit, my old man's had me working for him since the last day of school. But he told me if I could save a hundred bucks by the start of school, he'd buy me a car. I've got a hundred and twenty now. Where the fuck have you been besides working on your car? How's it coming, anyway?" Jimmy said, in rapid fire.

"That's it, just working' on the damn car, cutting this fuckin' grass and going to strip. What kind of rod is your old man gonna get ya?"

"I think I might get lucky. He's talking about a convertible, a Chevy."

"Do you think he'll go for a two-seventy and a stick?" I asked with obvious enthusiasm.

"Not a chance. It will have to be an automatic because my Mom will want to drive it. It will still be a hell of a pussy wagon if he gets the flop top."

"Where are you going now?" I asked.

"I'm just going to get the mail that everybody forgot to get yesterday. I would have driven, but I thought I saw a cop go up the street a little while ago."

"Yeah, I saw him too. It was one of the new ones, a young guy that actually looked friendly," I told Jimmy. "Anyway, If you're not doing anything tonight, why don't you come over? Mom and Dad are having a party and I'm going to park the cars. I'm sure the old man wouldn't mind if you helped."

"Yeah, that sounds cool. Like what time?"

"About seven. I think."

"If you really want to be a good guy, you could finish cutting this grass and then I'll let you blow me," I joked.

"Fuck you, pussy."

"Speakin' of pussy. Did you get any?" I teased.

"No, but my Uncle Jim promised to take me to Flo's for my sixteenth birthday. He's a pretty cool guy, if you catch my drift."

"Neat. I wish I had an uncle like that. I got to get this grass finished, so I'll see ya about seven, okay?"

"Okay, don't get any on ya," Jimmy said, as I wrapped the starting rope around the hub.

Everything went according to plan. As the guests arrived Jimmy and I took their cars down the drive, parked them half on the grass and half on the road because the street was very narrow with no gravel shoulder, center line or curb. After we parked each car we would jog back through the woods, following the path to the top of the ridge and then to the driveway to pick up another stocker. By nine it appeared that all that were coming had arrived, so Jimmy and I surveyed the collection of cars for the one we wanted to take for a spin. We decided on a '56 Chevy stage coach with a stick shift behind a V8 power pack engine. The car belonged to Mr. Addison who had something to do with the old man's business.

We quietly slipped our selected rod from its parking place and headed for Kathy's. In front of her house I parked at the curb and hit the horn two short ones, while teasing the gas pedal to make the engine race. It wasn't long and the porch light came on. I held my breath, hoping it wouldn't be her Mom or worse, her brother. Cool, it was Kathy. She came over to the driver's side where I sat, eyes wide open with excitement and said, "Move over and let me in."

"No, get in the other side." I wasn't giving up my seat behind the wheel to anyone. She ran around to the other door and Jimmy got out to let her sit between us.

"Aren't you afraid of getting caught and aren't you going to introduce me to your friend?"

"Oh yeah, Kathy, this is Jimmy."

"Hi, it's nice to meet you Jimmy. Now, would you do me a favor and let us have a few minutes alone?" Jimmy, with a look of rejection, got out and started to walk up the street. Kathy turned around on the seat with her back to the dash and pulled her bare feet up on the seat. Her breasts were straining the buttons on her tight sleeveless blouse that was tied in a knot at the middle, exposing smooth skin just above her shorts. Jimmy had hardly walked a few steps when she threw her arms around me, catching me by surprise. I couldn't turn the engine off or even take the car out of gear, so I held the brake tight and just let the clutch out slowly to stall the engine. As we hugged and kissed, I couldn't help telling her, "I love you, Kathy, can we go steady? You're... you're the, well, the most." She just sighed and hugged me tighter. I don't know how long we were going at it, but Jimmy came back, asking through the open window, "Are you two going to do this all night? Man, we've got to get this set of wheels back, if you catch my drift dad."

I didn't care if I did thirty years to life for Grand Theft Auto. It was worth it. Kathy turned around, tugged at her blouse that had slipped around to expose the better part of a bra covered mound and said to Jimmy, "Paul and I are going steady, so please make sure he gets home safely."

I was at a loss for words as Kathy got out and ran to the house yelling over her shoulder for me to call her tomorrow. I sat there not able to move, my face burning from the rush of blood, her face having been pressed against it. After a moment Jimmy, reached over and poked my leg saying, "Come on, man, let's roll."

Gaining composure and feeling like a real cool cat, I started the engine and we made our way out of the maze of streets and back to Montgomery Road.

"She's pretty good lookin'. where'd you find her?"

Trying to regain my cool, I took my time answering, so my voice would sound normal. "I met her at the strip."

"Shit, maybe I should have been going to the strip instead of working all summer."

"Let's see what this thing will do," I muttered, As we

passed Section Road and home, continuing on out Ridge Road.

"It's okay by me, but we've been gone at least a hour already," Jimmy reminded me.

"Okay, just one run on the highway and then we'll go straight home."

We followed Ridge to Reading, turned north being careful to obey the traffic laws in Reading, made it to By-pass 50 in Evendale where we turned west. At the entrance to the Lockland highway, I came to a stop after lining up parallel with the dotted white lines separating the two southbound lanes. It was dark now with only my headlights and the traffic signal at Shepard Lane, about a mile down the road, visible. I put the car in first gear, revved the engine and let my foot slip off the clutch. The car lurched and stopped dead.

"It's a dog. I better give it more gas," I said, trying to convince Jimmy that it was the car's fault and not mine. The next time I got it right, spinning the wheels and producing a respectable fishtail which I corrected before reaching maximum RPM first gear. At what sounded like the engine's peak, I slammed the shift lever into second and got a chirp of rubber. The feel of acceleration pushing me back into the seat was exhilarating as the car reached over eighty miles per hour before I eased it into third and backed off for the light at Shepard Lane. The light was red and I was going to peal out again when the light turned, but there was another car coming down Shepard Lane and I wanted to make sure it wasn't a cop. I did a normal take off and, once secure in my mind that the other car wasn't john law, down shifted back into second and punched it. We were going over a hundred as we roared through the towering walls of the Highway where the pavement narrows to just four lanes with no median or guard rail. The walls, some twenty-feet high where they cut through the heart of the City of Lockland, produced a neat sound as the noise of the engine bounced from side to side. We took the Highway to its beginning at Paddock Road, past the foot bridge which marked the end of the quarter mile of the LTA, and headed home. Jimmy hadn't spoken other than to say, "Jesus Christ", when we finally stopped at Paddock.

Luck was still with us as we drove slowly up our street, past the cars we had so carefully parked a few hours earlier. Before reaching the driveway, I saw Mr. and Mrs. Addison staggering down the middle of the road. I stopped as Mr. Addison stumbled up to the window and said, with slurred words, "That's very nice of you, Paul, I was just looking for my car."

"I'm sorry I didn't realize sooner that you wanted to leave, or I would have had the car in the drive. If you want I'll turn it around for you, sir," I said, in the nicest tone of voice I could muster, my legs still shaking from the excitement of the high speed run.

"Why that's very nice of you. You're a good boy." He was so drunk he didn't notice the smell of burning rubber that permeated the car.

The guest were starting to leave en mass, so Jimmy an I walked down to the pool to see if we could help with the cleanup. By midnight the last of the company had staggered out. Jimmy and I found a bottle of vodka and some orange juice and toasted a very successful night.

I must have gotten a load of bad orange juice, because on Monday morning I didn't feel so good. I called Kathy around noon and we had our first fight. She said she didn't want to go steady with me if I was going to go around stealing cars. I tried to point out to her that she didn't seem to mind getting into the stolen car last night, but it only made her madder. To get out of this mess I told her that I had to help Mom clean up the mess from the party and I would call her later. I then called Jimmy and we agreed to meet at the bus stop on Losantiville in the morning to thumb to school together.

Bobbi came home in the afternoon and we all had a good family dinner together. It had been a long time since we all sat down to a meal at the same time where someone didn't have to run off afterward. Bobbi told about her class schedule and how she still needed certain credits for her English major and that John was talking marriage, but she didn't think she was ready. I saw her in a different light. Bobbi suddenly seemed older, even like more of an adult with real problems, and not so much like a sister or student. I felt more alone in the way that if I confided to Bobbi, it would be like talking to an adult, not a teenaged sister. I didn't want to think about it. I could talk to Kathy if I had any problems. Who needs a sister? Kathy and I were one. It was a natural chain of events in my mind, how going steady would lead to an engagement, followed by marriage, with a home and kids. It was all so simple. Any fool could see that. I decided that I was completely happy and content and I wouldn't even look at another girl again. I looked at Bobbi and tried to imagine if John could feel about Bobbi the way I felt about Kathy. No way. What do they know about love? Shit, I was fifteen, had been in love, fought men and had driven fast cars. What could they know that I hadn't already experienced.

Ah, the summer of '57; girls, hot rods and rock & roll music. And nothing could sum it up better that the unofficial national anthem of the time than Chuck Berry's, "Maybellene"! I mean it had everything: An untrue woman who is caught by a V8 Ford, high speed on the open road, and a beat that made you want to get up and dance. The lyrics entwined the high speed chase of an jilted lover, his overheating hot rod loosing ground until it begins to rain, in pursuit of his heart throb, Maybellene, in her Cadillac. After the rain cools his engine, the heartsick hot rodder finally catches the Caddy at the top of a hill where he wails the rhetorical questions of unfaithfulness.

The consensus was that a Cadillac, being the quality car that it was, would run a long way at a hundred miles per hour, but a Ford, even a V-8 Ford wouldn't. Hopping up a car for the quarter mile drag was one thing. But, it was entirely unrealistic to expect a hopped-up engine to stay cool at sustained high speed. The Ford had to have been a flat-head, as early overhead valve mills were dogs.

The music was so important it was inseparable from us teen- agers. That song, and others, such as "Black Denim Trousers", and "Tell Laura I love Her", were scenarios we day-dreamed about.

We literally <u>lived</u>, <u>ate</u>, <u>slept</u>, and <u>breathed</u> cars. We <u>lived</u> the lives of those depicted in the hot rod magazines and read, talked and fantasized about cars, cars and cars. We <u>ate</u> with axle grease impregnated fingers, while we sat on dirty garage floors and loved every minute of it. We <u>slept</u> and dreamed of cars and we <u>breathed</u> the fumes of gas and oil, burned or un-burned, that were as sweet a smell to us as a Bordeaux was to a Rothschild.

SHOOT THE JUICE TO ME BRUCE

CIRCA 1957

CHAPTER 6

Summer was over. Oh, there were plenty of hot days left, and the Beechmont Dragway would be there every Sunday as long as the crowds came, but the first day of school was, well, the end of summer. No more sleeping till I woke up or going to Carters' every night, or going anywhere for that matter. I would be down to only a few hours per day, if that, to work on my car. "Shit, shit, shit," I said aloud to myself as I struggled to force my feet into the more confining penny loafers I would now have to wear. My feet had been used to the loose engineer boots and gym shoes I had worn all summer. One day and everything had to change. I wished that I had a job where everything was the same every day, and I didn't have to make all these adjustments in my life; naw, long summer vacations were too good. Isky, BB, and the other guys in the Knights all had to work everyday all summer and right up through Christmas with only one day off. Maybe school wasn't so bad after all.

Mom had two eggs and toast ready for me when I came down, which I inhaled in less than five minutes.

"Slow down, Paul, you have plenty of time. Do you have your paper and pencils? I left your lunch money on the counter next to the bread box. "Mom said, with that anxious look only moms can muster.

"Yeah, I got the money, thanks."

"Do you want me to drive you to school?"

"No thanks. I'm meeting Jimmy on Losantiville. We're going to thumb together."

"I wish you wouldn't hitch hike. Why don't you take the bus?" I'll be glad to give you extra money for the fare."

"Ah, Mom, you know I hate to take the bus. Besides I can get to school faster by bumming rides."

"But, it's so dangerous," she said, with that pitiful condescending smile she was so good at.

"What's the danger? Do you think some guy is going to kidnap a couple of men while he's on his way to work?"

"You're not a man, Paul and—"

"I'm big enough to take care of myself," I said, unconsciously straightening up and tightening my muscles.

"Well, if you ever change your mind...now hurry or you'll be late."

"Okay, see ya after school," I said, as I headed out to door

45

en route to the path through the woods to meet Jimmy—the same path through no-mans-land where I had beat up that kid and been in all those BB gun fights.

Jimmy was already there dressed like me in a print short sleeve sport shirt with the sleeves rolled up and pleated slacks held up by a thin black belt. He stepped off the curb and stuck his thumb out as soon as he saw me coming. One of the very first cars stopped and I had to run to slide in next to him in the '56 Plymouth that had pulled over to the curb.

"You fellows going to New Woodward?" The middle aged driver asked.

"Yes, sir," Jimmy and I both answered. "Do you come this way every day, Sir?" Jimmy asked the driver, hoping to cultivate a steady ride.

"Most of the time," He answered.

Since the second day of eighth grade I had thumbed rides and had never been late. Many of the rides came from the same people, though friendships never developed with the drivers. In all the years of bumming rides, I had had only one bad ride. Some guy put his hand on my knee when we stopped for a light and then smiled at me. I got out at once leaving his car door open in the middle of a long line of traffic. I heard him swear at me as horns blew while he struggled to close the door. On rainy days I could get Mom to drive, but I had never ridden with my sister because she drove a car pool and left too early. Bobbi was a senior when I started the eighth grade, so there would have been only one year I could have gone with her anyway. Jimmy had only begun to hitch hike with me late last year after he moved into the old Stewart place up the street.

We rode the rest of the way to school in silence, believing it to be bad manners to speak unless spoken to while a guest in a benefactor's car. My thoughts, while we waited for traffic at Reading Road, were about Willie. This would have been his first day of school at New Woodward and it would have been Willie and I hitch-hiking together today. Willie had only thumbed with me once. It was the time we decided to go to the Valley Theater one Sunday afternoon and didn't want to ride our bikes because it was too cold. Some old guy in a beat up pick-up truck gave us a ride and Willie talked to him and asked him questions all the way to Reading Road where we got out. It was strange that I should think of that now. I sensed Jimmy sitting next to me and felt resentment, but quickly dismissed the feeling. It wasn't

Jimmy's fault. He was a pretty good guy and fast becoming a good friend.

New Woodward High School was called that because, well, it was "new". The "old Woodward", where my father graduated in 1926, was downtown and now named Abigail Cutter. New Woodward was only four years old and was just plain Woodward to the students, not ever having any firsthand knowledge of the old Woodward. This structure, at the corner of Reading Road and Seymour Avenue, was a three- story, buff colored brick with lots of windows. Actually it was a five-story building, if the basement and sub-basement were counted, and they counted if a trip from the swimming pool in the sub to the lunch room on the third floor was required. All of the floors were a terrazzo tile while the walls were half-glazed block and plaster. It was very solid and always immaculately clean which was saying a lot, considering that there were about three-thousand students in daily attendance. I felt good about being part of such a big and modern school.

Each classroom, including most of the basement rooms, had one wall of windows, to let in lots of light and a cool breeze during hot days. Quite a contrast to our arch rival, Walnut Hills, with its dark halls and stairs with wood framed windows in lieu of our bright aluminum trim. Of course, they claimed their's was more aesthetically pleasing to the eye with all that old carved woodwork, but what did they know? Besides, we won more times than they did in football, basketball and swimming. To say there was a little rivalry would be an understatement since many families had children in both schools. Walnut Hills High School was an elective school deep in the City and those living out as far as we did had to, more often than not, rely on car pooling as a means of transportation because bus service required a transfer and at least an extra half-hour of travel time. Hitch-hiking was not practical due to the distance and direction changes—or maybe it was just because most of those guys were really candy-asses at heart.

Across Reading Road from the half-circle drive in front of Woodward was the almost completed Swifton Shopping Center, one of the first of its kind in the country. Before Swifton, that corner of Reading and Seymour was just a huge lot, about a quarter-mile square, with one giant tree right in the middle. This tree had a big branch which came straight out from the trunk about fifteen or twenty feet from the ground and always

looked to me like the perfect hangman's tree. Gazing out classroom windows when an eighth grader, I often daydreamed
about bad guys being hung from that giant branch in the old
days and wondered if any of their bones would be buried there.

North of the school and across Seymour was the bowling
alley and a field with a well worn path that led to the residential
area of south Roselawn. Catty-corner from Woodward was the
Jewish country club, Crest Hills, with its manicured hedges and
fairways stretching all the way to Losantiville Road.

Jimmy and I walked up the long semi-circular sidewalk
to the groups of kids standing under the marque renewing old
acquaintances. The girls were talking about boys, clothes, boys,
who's going with whom, boys, rumors about girls, and boys. The
boy's banter was always the same. In the crudest of terms they
discussed cars and girls while always insulting each other or
trying for the perfect put down.

"Hey, here comes Auer and Cohen. What have you
pussies been doin' all summer? Fuckin' your fist?" Laughter.

"Blow me asshole."

"I'll get on my knees if you get on your back." More
laughter.

"Hey, dad, look at the tits on that cunt!" Somebody else
said to the group in general.

"Man, I'd eat a mile of her shit just to see where it came
from!" Murmurs of agreement, all within earshot.

I moved through the group to another gathering of boys.

"Hey, Auer, you schmuck, I heard you've been running
the drag strip."

"No, I'm just one of the shleps. Were you there?" I asked,
impressed that someone had acknowledged my new stature.

"Fuck no, but if my old man gets that Bonneville like he
said, I'll be there."

"Your old man catch you at the strip, he'll have your
tuchis for lunch. Did you hear what happened to Joey what's his
name, you know the DB with the '57 Chev?" I asked.

"You mean Anderson? The one on the track team? What
happened?"

"He told his old man he was going out on a picnic in his
dad's brand new '57. Only he went to the strip instead and blew
the clutch. I mean pieces of it went through the floor board, dash
and windshield!"

"Oy vey! What happened to him? Did his old man kill

him?"

"Naw, he told me if he could get you to suck his old man's cock, again, all would be forgiven," I joked. Much laughter.

"Ah, eat me, Auer."

"Hey, it is true about the car. It'll probably be covered under warranty if they just say it happened when he slapped second gear to pass somebody."

"You think the goyim are that smart?"

"Well, they're smart enough to have a new '57, what are you driving, schmuck?" I said, with a twist of contempt.

"Hey, easy, dad, I didn't mean anything by it."

The first bell rang, signaling the beginning of another school year and the official end of summer.

Both Woodward and Walnut Hills drew from Amberley, Golf Manor, Roselawn, Bond Hill, Avondale, Carthage, Hartwell, Pleasant Ridge, Kennedy Heights, Silverton, Edgemont and Deer Park. The student body for the combined schools totaled over five-thousand and was made up of approximately 60% white protestants, 35% Jews, 5% colored, and a smattering of others. We all got along very well with interfaith dating, common and religious slurs almost non- existent. The only place the line was drawn was with the fraternities and sororities. There you didn't have a choice. You were what you were: Jews in Jewish social clubs and gentiles in their own, just like the country clubs of our parents. This presented a real problem for me as I had many friends both Jewish and gentile. Not only that, my best friends were in many different clubs. The sophomore year, the class I was just entering, was the traditional time for students to pledge. When the time came for me to align myself with a group, I vacillated, finally deciding not to decide. I knew I risked being a social outcast because many— not all, but many—of my friends were either in a fraternity or rushing one. For comradeship and a feeling of belonging I would have to rely on the Knights, who didn't seem to care what my religious beliefs were, only that I believed in hot rods. I think there was one other guy in the Knights who was Jewish, but I never asked him because it just didn't seem to matter. The fact that my Daddy was very prosperous—to some I could be perceived as a "poor little rich kid"—also never presented itself among my fellow club members. Only the certainty of my belief in hot rods was required for acceptance.

As I walked to my homeroom down the now familiar

halls packed with other students, I couldn't keep my eyes off all the tits. Everywhere I looked there were big tits, little tits, sharp pointed tits and round soft tits not to mention the ass packed into tight skirts or a dress cinched up around a tiny waist. Why anybody would want to go to an all boys school was beyond me.

I caught up to Jimmy as we entered our homeroom together. After a brief comparison of our schedules, we learned that this was the only class we would have together. We took seats near the back of the room and Jimmy asked, "Tell me about this chick we almost got arrested for just so you could see her."

"We didn't almost get arrested and I didn't just see her."

"Yeah, I noticed. She was all over you. Are you gettin' any?"

"You schmuck, she's not that kind of girl, and besides, you don't think I'd tell you if I was."

"All chicks put out. It just takes the right guy at the right time and place. If not you, then some other guy."

"Fuck you," I said, under my breath, as Miss Nathan called the class to order.

"Not me, dummy, her," Jimmy slipped in.

The words of wisdom from a fellow fifteen-year-old sank in as I felt a knot in my stomach thinking about Kathy with another boy. Damn. Maybe I could transfer to Walnut Hills, so I could keep an eye on the situation.

The bell rang ending the ten minute homeroom, and everyone headed their separate ways. There were only two classes I was really interested in, Metal Shop with Mr. Herne and English. Algebra would be a snap, Biology sounded awful and Physics could be interesting, but....

First bell was English, where I learned that we would go over a lot of the same shit we had last year, in addition to having to do a book report each semester and write themes. Half-way through the class I got my first hard-on of the day. I wasn't thinking about anything except the subject at hand, and then there it was, this big protrusion trying to poke its head through my pants. Wearing pleated trousers was certainly one of the best inventions ever, because it made concealment much easier than a tight pair of jeans. I struggled to discreetly rearrange myself while sweat formed on my forehead in the anticipation of the teacher calling me to stand before the class. Every boy's greatest fear. I remember that happening to a kid in the eighth grade. All the girls giggled, but he just kept right on talking like nothing was wrong. He was either very cool or so far gone he was oblivious that they were laughing at him. I wondered if they put salt peter, as the rumor went, in the meat served in the lunch room. If they offered it in homeroom, I'd take a double dose. Well, at least I was smart enough to bring a note book with me to act as a shield in case "it" wasn't gone by the time I had to walk to second period. With all this concern, I missed whatever the teacher had said for the past few minutes. No wonder girls got better grades than boys, they didn't have to tie up their brain cells with worries about stuff like that. Well, maybe they had the anxiety of blood running down their leg or staining the back of their skirt, but shit that was only once a month. We had to worry every day, all day.

By the time fourth bell came around I was so loaded down with books that I had to stop at off at my locker and dump them. I kept the note book with me, just in case, though I wouldn't need it for the next class, Metal Shop 1.

Mr. Herne was glad to see me and shook my hand while telling me, "Paul, I think you're going to like Metal 1. It's a lot different than the classes you had in junior high. You have a good summer?"

"Yes sir, and I really want to thank you for telling me about the Knights. They let me join as a junior member."

"Oh, that's right, I did tell you about them. Are you still working on that car? what was it—"

"It's a Crosley that I'm going to put a fiberglass body on and make into a sports car."   "How's it coming?" Mr. Herne asked sincerely.

"I'm ready to start welding on the frame. Something I hope to learn here."

"Well, you're in luck because that's one of the first things we're going to take up. Now grab a seat and we'll get the class going."

After calling the class to order. Mr. Herne started right out by introducing me.

"Paul stand up. Class, this is Paul Auer and he's going to build the finest sports car this school has ever seen. And he's going to build it with the knowledge he'll gain right here in this class. Isn't that right, Paul?"

"Ah, Mr. Herne, I don't know if I'll ever be able to finish it."

"Any student of mine that fails in a project, I'll kick his

butt." Laughter. I sat down.

"Now, Paul, and the rest of you hot rodders, there is one thing I want you to remember. I want you to think of this every time you turn the key. You guys just keep this one simple fact in mind and most of your problems will be solved: Just remember...keep the rubber side down. Now let's go to work fellows." More laughter.

Mr. Herne was pretty cool, for a teacher. He knew how to talk to kids and didn't get upset if someone used a cuss word when projects weren't going right, and he certainly wasn't embarrassed if somebody cut loose with a fart or belch. He occasionally laced some of his instructions with swear words, always admonishing us not to tell anyone, like it was our little secret.

"The first thing we're going to do is review the safety rules," Mr. Herne continued. "There are no exceptions to these few simple rules and anyone not abiding by them will be removed from the class. Permanently! Rule number one is that all loose clothing must be removed. Rule number two: No jewelry of any kind can be worn when operating any machine or tool. This includes all rings. I don't care if the ring you have on is your great grandfather's family heirloom and you can't get it off. We'll cut it off for you if you want to take this class. Rule number three: No ties other than bow ties. I know most of you don't have to wear ties, but sometimes you might be required to for class pictures and such. On those days you'll have to remove the tie, and I don't give a damn if you have to go home and have your mommy retie it. That's why I wear this stupid bow tie. Due to the alleged infinite wisdom of the school board, who insist that all teachers wear ties, I find this is the only way I can conform. The last rule is: No horseplay of any kind. If you go up and goose somebody while they're running a lathe it could cause a serious accident. I don't care if you cut my class sometimes or screw up a project, you can still pass. But, if you break the rules that's it. You'll be takin' Home Ec."

It was strict, but fair, and I never saw anyone break the rules, although he had to remind many of us to remove rings and ID bracelets on occasions.

I found Jimmy in the main hall after last bell and we decided to walk to Pasquale's for a twenty-five cent pizza and a coke before thumbing home. As we walked, I asked, "Who'd you get for English?"

"Some new chick with great big tits. Who'd you get?"

"I got old lady Cantrell, but I'm not worried about English. It's Biology that's going to be the ball breaker. Man, I've got it last bell and when it's hot, like today, and the smell of that formaldehyde can really wipe you out."

"Yeah, I can dig it. Hey, did you see Stan Schwartz?" Jimmy asked.

"Which one? The Jew or the goy?"

"The Jew."

"No, what about him?"

"Man, remember how small he was. He must have grown two feet since last year," Jimmy exaggerated.

Pasquale's was too crowded to even get in the door, so we just kibitzed with the kids standing outside while trying to figure out what to do next when Lou Goldstein drove up. Jimmy called to him, "Hey Goldstein, how 'bout a ride home?"

"Yeah, sure, I've got to take her home anyway, hop in." Her was Natalie Klein, a ninth grader who looked like a senior already. We piled in the back of the old '53 Chev many door to hear Lou ask, "What are you doin' dressed as a harry-high-schooler, Auer? I heard you were a real greaser, hangin' around with all those hot rodders."

"You got it half right, Goldstein. I'm a hot rodder, but you don't see any duck tails or my collar turned up do ya'?"

Louie tried to peal out but the old six banger just lurched. Nobody laughed. Louie was one tough guy. Goldstein and I went back a long way. We first met while still in grade school. His was Bond Hill while I went to Lotspeich, but we became friends through the Bohi Rifle Club, which our fathers got us into. He and I were about the same size then. Now I was at least an inch taller and though I wasn't a weakling by any means, Louie had been lifting weights and taking boxing lessons for the past two years and was just plain tough. He always seemed ready for a fight, especially with anyone even suspected of being anti-semitic as was so admirably demonstrated by his very decisive attack on the nazi sympathizer, Terry Hall, in the boys rest room at school last year.

Jimmy and I thanked Lou for the ride when he let us out at my drive and I said to Jimmy, once the '53 was gone, "That Natalie sure turned out to be one fine lookin' chick, didn't she?"

"Yeah, but I wouldn't try taking her away from him."

"I'm hep, you think I'm meshug? Louie and I are friends,

but not that good of friends. "We both laughed, knowing it would be suicidal to attempt to even flirt with any girl that Lou Goldstein had an interest in.

"You want to come in for a snack?" I asked.

"Naw, I better get home, it being the first day of school and all," Jimmy said, as he turned to leave.

"Okay, see ya at the bus stop tomorrow. Stay cool."

I went in the house and grabbed an apple and called Kathy.

"Hi, baby. How was your first day?" I asked.

"It was great. I got all the teachers I wanted, and Donna's in two of my classes. Did you miss me?"

"Naw."

"Paul!" "I'm only kidding, of course I missed you," I said, as I thought of all the cute chicks I had seen at school.

"Don't kid about that...I missed you. I even wrote your name all over my notebook, and Danny, he's a boy in my Algebra class, saw it and said he knew you."

"Danny who? What's his last name?"

"I don't know, but he's cute."

Bad news. I suddenly wished I was like Louie and could just put the word out not to mess with my chick or I'd kick some ass.

"Paul?"

"What? Oh, I'm sorry, I was just thinking that if you would go to Woodward I wouldn't have to worry about all the cute guys and I'd get to see you everyday."

"Ah, Danny's only in the ninth grade, and besides, why would I want to go to Woodward when I'm already going to the best school in the city," she said, trying to put me down.

"Best school? Ha, just a bunch of candies."

"Well, at least they're not all hoods and greasers."

"Yeah, well anytime your cats want to have a rumble-"

"Oh Paul, that sounds so juvenile. Anyway I'm glad you called because I wanted to tell you there's going to be a sock hop at the new Pepsi plant Friday night. Where's the Pepsi plant. Do you know?"

"It's on Sunnybrook just off Reading Road and over the railroad tracks," I said, feeling the sting of her put-down.

"They're going to have a real disc-jockey from WSAI and he's going to be live on the air. Joe said he'd give Donna and me a ride. Can you come?"

"Yeah, I might stop in to check it out," I said, trying to regain my cool and knowing that I would have to be there not only to see Kathy, but also to keep other cats away.

"Well, anyway I have to go, I have a ton of homework. I love you, Paul."

"Me too, you."

"Can't you talk?"

"Right."

"Is your mom there?"

"Right again."

"I Just have to hear you tell me. Call me tonight, will ya?"

"Okay, just think of Fats Domino in the meantime."

"Why should I think of him?" Kathy asked, in a quizzical voice.

"I'll tell you tonight when I call.

Dinner was exactly at six-thirty as it always was because that's the time when my father came home from the office. He was a big man in almost every sense of the word. He was big in size, big in stature, and very big in power, but he lacked the art of conversation, at least with the family. It seemed that the only talking he did was to ask questions like what Bobbi's or my friends' fathers did for a living. He usually just collected information and then made his decisions informing the effected persons later.

The buying of the Crosley was a typical such episode. One evening he showed me an ad for a fiberglass body and asked me if I thought I could build a car like the one pictured. When I told him "No sweat" he said for me to write to the companies— there were only two—for literature. He studied the broadsides when they came and then about two weeks later, on a Saturday, informed me that he had found a 1952 Crosley at a dealer in Reading. We took the car around the block with the dealer driving while my father negotiated the price. And just like that told the guy if he'd deliver it that day they had a deal. I'm sure he put a lot of thought and work into getting me started because as I was to find out, in future dealings with him, he never did anything on the spur of the moment. Armed with this insight, Tuesday's dinner was not too early to make my next request.

"Say, Dad," I said, while Mom was serving. "I need a torch to put the frame back together on the Crosley, so can I borrow the one from the plant?"

"Torch? You mean the acetylene torch? Why does the frame have to be welded?"

"I had to cut the chassis down a little to make the new body fit and what I plan to do is tack weld it together with the torch and then later have it arc welded," I explained.

"How do you plan to get the welding outfit up here? Do you know how to use it? How long will you need it? Are the fire extinguishers in place in the garage?"

It was like the Spanish Inquisition. I answered his questions, exaggerating the part about my experience with the torch. I believed I could figure out how to braze with a little help from BB and Mr. Herne. The old man gave me his standard answer—"We'll see"—which usually meant okay as long as I did my chores and didn't step on my dick in the meantime.

I helped Mom clear the dinner dishes, took out the trash, and then went up to begin my homework. I got the Algebra done, but before I could get into the Biology assignment Isky drove up. He had just picked up the new pistons for the Cadillac engine and was going to fit them to the bored block. After about a half-hour of watching him, I returned to my room for another try at the Biology. I had visions of taking the same course again, in summer school, when the urge to call Kathy forced me to put the book down one more time.

"Yes, it's me and I'm in love again," I softly sang into the phone when she answered.

"Well, what's that supposed to mean?"

"That's the Fats Domino song I told you to think about. I don't know why, but every time I hear it, I think of you."

"I know why. It was playing on Joey's car radio when we first met at the drag strip. Don't you remember?"

"Yeah, maybe that's it. It can be our song," I said.

"It already is. From now on, whenever we hear it we'll think of each other. It's so romantic I love it."

The rest of the week was just like Chuck Berry's "School Days". Up every morning and trudge to school just to hear the teacher preach the golden rule. Now that always confused me. Mom said the golden rule was: Do unto others as you would have them do unto you. Dad said it was: Do unto others before they did it to you. By the time I got home from school on Friday, it had already started to turn cold, which was alright with me because I could now wear my Knights Jacket. I called Kathy, but she wasn't home so I asked her mom to tell her that I'd be at the sock hop around nine. I changed into my blue jeans and spent the next three hours, with a half-hour off for dinner, readying the car and garage for the torch. At dinner the night before, the old man said that I should come into the office on Saturday morning and he would check with the machinist to see if they could spare the welding outfit for a while.

Around eight-thirty I thumbed to the Pepsi plant. I could have gone with Jimmy. Some of the Phi Ep boys were picking him up to check him out and I could have gone too, but I didn't want to be obligated.

The Pepsi plant was packed and it took me quite a while to locate Kathy. She was off to one side talking with Donna. I made note of her location while working my way to the DJ. After he put the next record on I asked him if he would play "I'm in Love Again". He said he'd try, while taking Kathy's and my name for the dedication. I found Kathy, but it was almost impossible to say much with the music so loud and everybody else talking. We really didn't need to say words. We'd been doing that all week long on the phone. I know all I wanted to do was touch her and hold her. I sensed she wanted the same. If only I had wheels. We danced to "Whole Lotta Shakin' Goin' On" and "Honky Tonk, Part Two" then slow danced to "In the Still of the Night".

When the DJ went to a break, we walked to one of the far corners to get away from the crowd and noise.

"I like your Knights coat. Can I wear it," Kathy asked.

"Yeah, sure, do you want it now? Are you cold?"

"No, I mean can I take it home?"

"Hey, this is the first time I've worn it. It's used, you know. I bought it from Isky, he's the cat with the Stude-lac, it didn't fit him anymore so he let me have for a double saw buck."

"Well, you haven't given me anything like a ring or something since we've been going steady. Donna doesn't believe we're going steady," she whined.

"Okay, if it's such a big deal, I'll give you the coat, but not tonight. I need it to keep warm on the way home."

We both heard ours names over the PA followed by the Fat Man:

> "Yes it's me and I'm in love again,
> Had no lovin' since you know when,
> You know I love you, yes I do...."

CIRCA 1957

We pantomimed, holding hands, seeing only each other, hearing only the words and knowing they were meant just for us. I felt my heart racing, I saw her lips quiver...we were like two full race duce-coupes all revved up waiting for the drop of the flag.

We pressed tight to each other, kissing and hugging, standing on the outer edges of the dance floor, oblivious to anyone and anything until Donna came over to tell Kathy that the girls they had come with were ready to leave. The dance was almost over anyway, and most of the kids had already left. We parted with my promise to bring her my black wool jacket. The one with KNIGHTS embroidered on the back in three-inch-high, old English-style letters over a patch of a hoodless roaster.

I caught a ride to Carters' with a kid from my English class. It was just starting to rain. I didn't see any familiar faces so I had to decide if I should wait to see if somebody showed up to give me a ride home, or start thumbing now before the rain got worse. I decided on the latter walking the two blocks to Section Road to catch a ride. I stood out in the cold rain for ten minutes before seeing the first car. It passed me by, even though I used my most pathetic look while emphasizing my thumb in an exaggerated way. The third or forth car had a bubble gum machine on top. I tucked my thumb in my fist and turned to walk to the sidewalk. I was sure I could be arrested for soliciting a ride or something. The car stopped next to me and I walked over to the passenger door which opened.

"Where are you going fellah?" Came the question from the officer behind the wheel.

"Just up to Fair Oaks, sir."

"Do you live in the Village?"

"Yes sir."

"Come on hop in, I'll give you a lift home."

I climbed in, noticing it was a 1957 Chev V8 with standard shift. This was real cool.

"What's your name?" the cop asked.

"Paul Auer. My father is Sidney Auer. That's his plant just over the tracks."

"I don't know too many people here. I've only been on the force about a month now. By the way, my name's Tony, Tony Bloomfield."

"Nice to meet you, sir," I said, noticing that he couldn't be any older than Isky or most of the other club members.

"What does the back of your coat say?" the officer asked in a non-interrogating tone.

"Knights, Knights of the Twentieth Century. It's a hot rod club, sir."

"You' don't have to call me "sir", and I'll bet you're one of the kids Sergeant Prince told me to watch for."

"I don't doubt that. He's ah, ah, a prick. Now Cap'n McDaniel...he knows me and he's an alright guy."

"I know what you mean about Prince, but don't tell him I said so."

"Okay by me. I don't want anything to do with him."

I directed Tony to our driveway and before getting out I thanked him and invited him to stop by sometime and see the Crosley. Say, maybe cops weren't so bad after all.

THAT'S THE $64,000.00 QUESTION

CIRCA 1957

CHAPTER 7

Saturday BB and I went to Dad's plant, a medium-sized paper converting factory, to pick up the torch. Due to the lateness of the season and the recent rain, I wouldn't have to cut grass that day. This allowed me the entire day to work on the rod.

Using two pieces of channel iron BB had "requisitioned" from his place of employment, we began the tedious job of aligning the frame with its relationship to the front and rear axles. The crude instruments available to us didn't make it very easy to set an eight degree positive caster, which we could only hope would be okay. There were no instruction books available for this kind of work so it was mostly, by guess and by golly. Like hot rodders before us, if we made a mistake now we wouldn't know it until the car was almost complete. Rectifying errors then would be a major job, if it were possible at all. Around five we actually could see the frame taking shape, the "Z" section being firmly held in place by tack welds. The plan was to tack weld everything we could, make any final adjustments, then tow the bodiless chassis to Jimmy Batz's garage in Roselawn to be professionally arc welded. It would be a long time before we were ready for that.

Still to be done were many jobs that we couldn't do ourselves, such as lengthening the steering column and shortening the drive shaft. These operations required precision alignment that only a few shops had. Other procedures that we could perform, such as lengthening the pitman arm by cutting it with a hacksaw and welding in a new section with a piece of scrap steel, sounds easy. But how long should a pitman arm be? Too long and the manual steering would be too hard to turn the heavy front end; too short and desired ratio wouldn't be met. Hope and pray!

Before heading for Bart's around seven that evening, we stopped by Kathy's so I could give her my Knights jacket. She wasn't home so I had to leave it with her mom. Since BB had helped me all day, I had to help him pull the transmission out of the '49 to get at the clutch, which he hadn't replaced since the last run at the strip. By the time we got it out some of the other club members had started to filter into the basement garage, many with instruments. It was a rather odd assortment, including a guitar, stand up bass, sax, and an accordion. They didn't sound exactly like the original artists they copied, but it was music to our ears. The jam session continued until about midnight and then we all piled into hot rods for the required visit to Carters'.

The next few weeks were much of the same. School all day, work on the sports car, homework, phone calls to Kathy, Carters' on the weekend and an occasional jam session. Having Kathy was the absolute greatest. My grades were improving, the car was going to be really neat. Everything was perfect. What could go wrong? The highlight of this period was the introduction of the '58 model cars. Ford had abandoned its two seat Thunderbird for a four-place version, most likely because they couldn't keep up with the Corvette, which had been given a face lift and a few more horses.

Work had been progressing slowly on the Crosley, due to the waiting required on all the parts that had to come from outside sources. Everything was cool except that I hadn't been able to spend much time with Kathy, having seen her only twice since the sock hop. Those two times were after school when she came to Swifton with a group of her girl friends so we didn't have much privacy. At the first Knights meeting in December, the club decided to have a Christmas dance in order to raise money for the club car, a still under construction class "A" dragster. This was great. I couldn't wait to get home and call Kathy to tell her we'd be going. I was so elated with the prospect of being able to show her off to all the guys that I forgot to ask around to see if there was anyone I could double with. No sweat, I was sure somebody would take me in, especially if I had the price of admission.

Isky took me home, since he wanted to put some of the finishing touches on the Cad engine. I turned on the light in the garage and said, "I'd like to help you, but I got to call somebody."

"This somebody your chick?"

"Yeah, I've got to call before nine."

"Before nine, eh? What happens after nine, does she cut your water off?" Isky asked in jest.

"No man, it's just that her mom gets meshug if I call too late."

"Sounds to me like you're pussy whipped and what's masug mean?"

"Meshug is yiddish for crazy."

"You mean when a Jewish cat wants to say something

cool, he says, 'meshug man, meshug'?" Isky asked trying to be funny.

"Man, you're the one who is really crazy and I don't mean as in cool, ya dig! Besides, it's better to be pussy whipped than jackin' off into an exhaust header," I tossed over my shoulder as I started for the door to the house. Isky threw a greasy rag at me but missed.

"Yes, it's me," I sorta sang into the phone when she answered.

"Hi, Paul."

"What's wrong? Can't you talk?"

"Sure I can talk, what do you want to talk about?"

What's wrong here? She didn't sound like the usually cheerful, I love you Paul. I decided to press on, being in a good mood. "I just got back from the club meeting and we're going to have a dance the Saturday before Christmas."

"That's nice," Kathy, matter-of-factly said.

"We'll be together and you'll get to meet all the members," I added, pushing on.

"Well, I don't know, Paul."

Oh, shit. Now what's wrong, I thought, as anxiety began to twist my stomach. "What do you mean, you don't know?"

"Well what do you expect? You call me up when ever you feel like it and now just tell me that we're going to a dance without even asking me."

"We are going steady, aren't we? I mean who else are you going to go out with?" I stated, knowing the minute I said it, it was wrong and now I was in big trouble.

"That's what I wanted to talk to you about."

"Okay, maybe you're right, I'm sorry," I said, trying to cover my tracks. "Would you like to go to the dance with me?" I continued in a soft voice.

"That's not what I meant."

"I don't understand, what are you talking about?" The rock in my stomach starting to move again.

"Paul, I...my Mother doesn't want me to go steady."

"Your mother! What about you? Do you want to?"

"Oh Paul, I don't know. It's just that when I'm with you that's all I want, but when we're not together...I just don't know."

As she spoke I knew the world was ending. Sweat was breaking out on my forehead, I felt sick, there was a ringing in my ears. Damn cars, if I had a license, if we even went to the same school —if, if, if. Oh Kathy, baby, I had planned our marriage, in my mind, a thousand times; how am I going to face my friends. Shit, without a license I can't even get to a bridge to jump off. I wanted to speak these things, but somehow the words wouldn't come out, my throat was, I don't know, just closed.

"Paul, Paul are you there?" her sweet voice probed.

"Yeah, yeah, I'm here," I said, in an utterance that I was sure showed my hurt.

"Paul, I still love you. It's that I just don't...can't go steady anymore.

Wait, was I hearing right. Was there a light at the end of the long dark exhaust tube? I thought I heard her say she loved me. Maybe it was true, maybe her mother, the old biddy, was really trying to keep us apart. We could run away and get married, yeah that's it—. "I love you Kathy, I want to marry you," I blurted out.

"Paul, Honey, we can't do that. You don't even have a license yet, and besides, I don't want to get married, not now anyway."

Thoughts were coming through my head faster than I could sort them out. She called me honey. Maybe it will work out. I've got to get some wheels. Maybe I can steal a car and keep it hidden somewhere like I did the old Whizzer or I could—shit I didn't know what I wanted to do this. I needed time to think. "That's not exactly what I meant," I said, trying to salvage what cool I had left, if any.

"I have to go now. If you want to pick up your coat, you can."

"How 'bout Friday night? Can we, will you go out with me if I can get a double?"

"I can't. I'm going to a GK slumber party."

"Would Saturday night be okay? I think Isky said something about a date he was taking to a movie?" I said, trying not to sound like I was pleading.

"I can't go out then either, Paul. How about tomorrow?"

"Why can't you go out Saturday? Do you have a date with somebody else?"

"It's not exactly a date."

Oh shit, here we go again. There's another guy. I need time to think, I better not talk anymore or I'll really say something stupid, not that I already haven't."

"Okay. Tomorrow. When?"

"Anytime after about noon. I'm not going to school tomorrow because I have a dentist appointment in the morning. Mom is going to take me there, and then I'll get a bus home around noon. Do you want to come after school?"

Trying not to sound dejected, I said, "Okay I'll see you tomorrow." But somewhere in the back of my mind I could hear Elvis:

> "Now, since my baby left me
> I've found a new place to dwell,
> down at the end of lonely street
> At heartbreak hotel...I'm so lonely,
> I'm so lonely, that I could die....
> ...for broken hearted lovers to cry
> there in the gloom...."

I had to get my cool back. Maybe it wasn't as bad as it seemed. After all, she did say she loved me, or did she? Maybe it was me who said the word. I know she called me honey, that's got to count for something. I needed a plan. Let's see, she did say that she would be home around noon and if I got my buddy Stan Schwartz, the gentile, to write me an early excuse slip then I'll get there when she did. And since her mother worked and her brother would be in school, we'll be all alone and then—. I had reached the garage door and would have to think about this further.

"How's it goin', Isky?" I asked, not really caring, but glad to have some one to talk to.

"Crazy man, you're just in time. Help me turn this monster over."

"Okay, but I can't get any grease on these school pants or my mother will kill me. Ya dig daddy-o?" After repositioning the block and getting a little dirt on my pants Isky turned his attention to the Crosley which helped my sagging morale.

"I've been looking at the work you've been doing on the sports car, Gov'ner," Isky said, in an exaggerated English accent. It looks pretty good so far. I'm sure you're doing the right thing by "Z'ing" the frame, instead of just doing a channel job on the body. I've seen cars that were altered that way and, like man, they didn't look right. Now what you really need to do is fit an engine like this Cad in it."

CIRCA 1957

"Ah, come on man, it wouldn't fit, but I would like to put a flathead '60 in it."

"A flathead? Man, you've been hanging around Big Bart too long. Flatheads are dead," Isky joked.

"Shit. I'll bet his '49 will pull your '53."

"We'll never know until he gets to the end of the strip."

We both laughed.

Soon after, Isky left and I tried to do some homework. Impossible! My mind wouldn't stop thinking about Kathy.

I caught up with Jimmy the next morning in "no man's land", as we both headed for Losantiville Road to begin the daily thumb. I had to tell somebody about my problems, so I just came right out and told him that the chick we went to see in the '56 back in the summer was going to dump me. His first comment was a question, "Did you get in her pants?"

Embarrassed to answer such a query about a girl like Kathy, I answered, "No."   "Well, that's your problem," Jimmy continued in a fatherly tone. "Is she a virgin?"

"Yeah, I guess so, I don't think she's ever gone with anyone before."

"You get a girl's cherry and she'll love you for ever, guaranteed, no shit!"

"That's not so easy when you don't have wheels, man," I countered, getting defensive.

"Hey, dad, I didn't say it was easy. All I said was that if you're the cat to pop the hymen, then you're the cat she'll never forget. It's a known fact," Jimmy stated like a real cocksman.

A car slowed to pick us up as I asked, "How do you know? Did you ever get a cherry?"

"Please."

I looked at my friend in a slightly different light as we piled into the waiting car. Maybe he was getting a little nookie from some of those girls that always seemed to be hanging around him. He was certainly good looking enough with his blond hair constantly falling over his eye brows and those blue eyes. Chicks always dug blue eyes, not green like mine, hazel, my mother called them. I'll bet chicks really did go for him especially since he'd had a nose job as a Bar Mitzvah gift from his parents. Jimmy had an easy going way about him. He never got mad and when he said tough words like "fuck you", he really didn't mean it in a threatening way, sorta like the way Willie would have been. I might be able to learn something from him, but first things first. I had to find Schwartz, the gentile, and put my plan into action.

Late in the eighth grade I, along with others, learned that the school did compare signatures from note to note of our parents. These letters were required to excuse an absence or gain early dismissal for doctor's appointments, funerals, etc. Therefore, the first time I was legitimately absent from school, in the ninth, and had a bonafide note from my mother; I tore it up and had Stan write the note. This established his copy of my mother's handwriting as the official signature and thus he could and did sign all notes, both dubious and legit. These requests for early excuses had to be tendered to the main office where a "green slip", noting the time and date, was then issued, complete with the Vice Principal's rubber stamp signature. Of course, one could only have so many doctor's appointments or deaths with out arousing suspicion so other means of acquiring the coveted "green slips" were in order, such as having a friend steal them.

I found Stan in his homeroom. "Hey Schwartz, ole buddy, I think I need a dental appointment today. Do you think you can fit me in?"

"Sure, what time is your tooth going to start to ache?"

"How about two o'clock," I said, producing a clean sheet of paper and a pen.

I hurried to the office and secured the "green slip", knowing they never checked if the early request was for an hour or less. Once the slip was in my possession and I was out of the office, I promptly added a "one" in front of the two, thus changing it to read "12:00". Now all that remained was to show the slip to my fifth and sixth bell teachers for their signatures. This way they wouldn't report me when they didn't see my name on the absence list sent to each room everyday.

It took two rides and I had to walk the last mile. It was cold, but I didn't feel it. My spirits were high with the prospect of a clandestine meeting with my girl. I rang the bell, suddenly feeling the cold. No answer. Shit. Did I get stood up? Did I waste an early excuse, one that took me out of Biology that I was surely going to flunk now. I rang again. Maybe the bus she was riding was in a wreck and she was hurt, calling my name. Wait a minute this is crazy. I must be totally meshugge. The door opened and there she was.

"Come on in. You must be freezing. How did you get out

of school? Are you going to get into trouble," She said, in a non-stop sentence.

I stepped in, dropping my books on the floor, and grabbed her arms, pulling her to me.

"Your hands are like ice," Kathy said, pulling away from me.

"Well, come here and warm me up."

"No."

"What do you mean, no," I said. The old feeling of rejection building up inside me.

"Paul, we shouldn't be doing this. My mother will kill me if she knew we were alone in the house."

I quickly decided to cool it, walking into the living room. I sat on the big over stuffed couch. Kathy turned on a light in the already sunlight drenched room and proceeded to straighten things that appeared to be in order to me. I watched her stoop, bend, and twist, fantasizing about touching her where I really didn't want to touch. I wanted to save that kind of thing for when we were married, but Jimmy's revelation threaded its way through my mind. She had on a tight wool skirt and an angora sweater that clung to her round and larger-than-I-remembered breasts. I had warmed up, in fact I was now hot. Standing to remove my coat I said, "Kathy, come over and sit with me. Tell me what's wrong."

"Okay, but just to talk. Now tell me how you got out of school?"

I explained the notes, the "green slips" and how I had to spend an hour in the cold to get her, trying to gain a little sympathy as I slipped my arm around her.

"Paul, why didn't you pledge a fraternity?"

"I already told you that I've got friends in all the fraternities, and I couldn't just go with one group. Besides I already belong to a "social" club.

"You mean The Knights?"

"Yeah. Why is it so important that I join a fraternity?"

"Well, I don't know. I just think that it's important."

"Is that what this is all about?" I asked as the phone rang. She reached across me to the table that held the phone pressing her breasts against my pounding chest.

"Hello." I could hear a man's voice. "I'm okay, but I can't talk now." He talked. I felt sick. "Okay after school. Bye." She hung up.

"Who was that?" I asked, not really wanting to know.

"It was...it was my brother. He just wanted to see if I got home alright."

I didn't believe her. I wanted to, but I knew deep down she was not telling me the truth.

"You don't believe me, do you?"

"No, who was it?" I had to find out.

"It's just some guy that wants to go out with me."

The death knell had sounded, but I wasn't going to let her know my hurt. That would be uncool. She sensed my thoughts saying, "I really like you Paul, I don't want to hurt you. Can't we talk about something else?"

"Like me? I...I thought you said you loved me," I said. Realizing at once that I sounded like I was pleading.

"I do love you, in a very special way."

"You mean like a boy friend, someone you want to go steady with?" It was getting worse. Time for some new approach.

"Well, not exactly. I'm too young to go steady. I want to go out with other people and go to fraternity dances and things."

I took her face in my free hand, turned it toward me and we kissed. It was different. She wasn't pressing back. I let my hand drop to her breast, but before I could even begin to caress her she pulled away saying, "Don't, Paul. Let me get your Knights jacket."

She got up and walked to the other room. For an instant I wished the house would catch fire, and I could save her. Then she would have to love me. She was back in a flash, but she stood by the front door. I better pull myself together, I sure didn't want her to see me cry or anything. I got up, walked over to her, took the jacket and put it on. She didn't look at me. Her eyes were looking at the floor. I walked back to the living room, grabbed the coat I'd worn over here and walked straight toward the door. She put her hand on my arm saying, "Can't we be friends? Don't leave like this. I'm sorry about what happened on the couch. Paul talk to me."

I knew if I said anything my voice would crack. I walked out into the cold bright sunshine. Life was over. By the time I reached the street, I was mad. I wanted to scream. I wanted to hit something. I looked up the road, hoping to see her neighbor, Billy, not knowing or caring if he was the cat on the phone or not. If he came down the street right now, I thought, I'll cold-cock him, beat the shit out of him. Oh, Kathy, it hurts. I suddenly felt compassion, even for Billy. I wanted to turn and run back to her house, hold her, and hear her sweet voice tell me it was all a bad dream. I pinched myself. Shit. Fuckin' women. Fuck 'em all. From now on it was just the car, the Knights and Jimmy...well maybe other guys too, but no more cunts. Jimmy must be right. I should have tried to get her cherry, if the cunt had one, back when she really loved me. I shouldn't have been so fuckin' respectable.

It took two rides and almost an hour to get home. I went straight to my room, lay on the bed, and cried. I lay there until I heard Mom call for dinner; thinking, thinking of the hurt. So this is what they must mean by a broken heart. It was different from when Willie died. I felt sad then and hurt, but it was somehow different. I didn't want to think about it. I had other things to do.

So, if your baby leaves
and you have a tale to tell,
Just take a walk down Lonely street
...to Heartbreak Hotel....

RACE BOWL OPENS THE 27th

CHAPTER 8

Christmas was only a matter of days a way and I hadn't gotten any presents for anyone due to the usual lack of money. It was cold. I didn't have a girl, and I didn't even have a date for the big dance. Even if I could get a date, I would have to borrow the money for the ticket. I was lonely, with only my car and the radio to keep me sane. Jimmy and most of the other guys from school were involved in fraternity doings. Maybe I had made a mistake by not joining.

The work on the car had progressed to the stage where I was ready to have the frame arc welded. On Friday, I asked Jimmy if he would help me tow the Crosley to Roselawn to be welded because BB was going to have to work overtime. He'd been doing a lot of that lately and had not been available to help me. On top of that he was going to start night school next month, and then I'd be completely alone on this project, Isky having taken his now finished engine out of the garage. I called Jimmy Saturday morning asking when I could expect him.

"How long is this going to take? I have to go to a Phi Ep meeting this afternoon. I'm on the damn committee for the next dance."

"Well, if you could get here by ten, I could have the tractor from the plant here, and then all we have to do is tow it to Jimmy Batz's for him to weld. It shouldn't take over an hour, I guess."

"Okay, but I've got to be home no later than noon. That's when they're picking me up," Jimmy said.

"Crazy man. See ya around ten and dress warm. There ain't no heater. In fact there ain't no body, ya dig."

I used a piece of wood taped to the frame and the drive shaft as a seat for Jimmy. It really took some doing on Jimmy's part. Not only did he have to hold on with both hands, but he had to lift his foot higher than his belly to stab at the brake pedal to keep slack out of the tow chain. It was slow going because if we broke a weld now, it would be a lot of work to fix.

Jimmy Batz was an old colored man known among the hot rodders as the master when it came to arc welding. We left the chassis and tractor at the ramshackle shop, after being advised that it would take about an hour to do it right. Jimmy and I walked to Carters' to warm up and wait. Sipping hot chocolate, I asked my friend, "So tell me about Phi Ep. Do you like being in a fraternity?"

"Yeah, there's a real feeling of belonging. All the guys are like a team. I guess that's how it is. I've never really been on a sports team, but I'm sure that's what it must be like. Why didn't you join? I don't think I lost any of my gentile friends by joining, and I'm sure you wouldn't have either."

"Ah man, I don't know. Sometimes I think I should have, and other times I'm glad I didn't. I might still be going with old what's her name if I had. I know she wanted me to join real bad," I said.

Yeah, well, that's one of the advantages of a fraternity. The chicks seem to really dig them. Of course you've got the Knights so you must get the picture.

"Yeah, but it's not the same. A lot of nice girls won't even look at a cat with a hot rod jacket on. They think we're all hoods or greasers. They don't know the difference and what's more they don't care. Anyway, I'm through with chicks. From now on I'm just going to work on the car and then, when I get my license, I just might go the four 'F' routine."

"I can dig it. I think it was really shitty what Kathy did to you." Jimmy commiserated.

"What about you? Who are you going to take to the frat dance? Are you going to try for that chick, Gail, the one I saw you talking with in the hall yesterday?"

"Boy, I'd like to. She's easy on the eyes and she's been helping me with my English but—"

"But, shumt! Why don't you just ask her out. You're a big Phi Ep man now and women will be just begging to squeeze your cock," I ribbed.

"I don't know, I think she only wants to be friends."

"Well, if I may borrow your famous words of wisdom, `just get her cherry and she will want to be real friends forever'," I joked.

"And if I may borrow your equally good response, `easier said than done'," Jimmy said, with a laugh.

"Hey, let's make like a tree and leaf. Mr. Batz should have the welding done by now.

"Ah, shit man, it's almost noon now. I thought you said this would only take an hour."

"I lied."

Jimmy Batz had done a beautiful job of welding as expected. I paid him the agreed twenty dollars, which now left me flat broke. Jimmy drove the tractor back so I could check out how the frame handled now that it was solidly welded. Even being towed and without an engine, I could tell the work Bart and I had done appeared to be okay. The rear wheels tracked straight in line and the steering wheel snapped right back after a turn indicating the positive caster was correct.

Some of the Phi Ep boys were waiting at my house when we got back. Lou Goldstein made me promise to take him for a ride when I got the car finished. How could I refuse? I felt real good. After the fraternity boys left, I took the tractor back to the plant and then walked the short distance into Roselawn to pick up some nuts and bolts I knew I would need for such extraneous items like the gas tank and seats. The little hardware store was my only source for these parts because we had a charge there and I didn't need cash. My old man paid the bill every month without complaint or comment.

It had started to snow hard by the time I stuck my thumb out to get home. "Silver Bells" was playing over the speakers at each corner of the building that housed the hardware store, drug store and a furniture store. Now it was really starting to feel like Christmas. By the time I got a ride the streets were snow covered, and I had to give the guy, who gave me a ride, a push to get him started after he let me out.

Once home, I turned on the radio in the garage and sat on the work bench admiring my work, thinking about how it would be to be the owner and driver of a real sports car. I thought about all the work I'd done and all the work that lay ahead. I thought about all the chicks that would want to ride in the car. Then I thought about Kathy, and I thought about Willie. That's when the idea hit me. I struck the torch and as carefully as I could, using brazing rod, I welded the name Willie into the inside of one of the frame rails. I put it where no one would see it. Most guys named their cars after a chick, but chicks had a way of cutting out, leaving a broken heart. Kathy had left me and so had Willie, but it wasn't Willie's fault that he left. After I was done I realized that I could never tell anyone that I had named the car after Willie because some might think I was a sissy or worse yet, Willie was a sissy having a car named after him.

The thoughts of Kathy had stirred up a mixture of feelings that I really didn't want to experience again. I had too much to do and there was no way to change the name of the car now, even if she realized her mistake and begged me to come back. I hadn't heard from her since that day at her house except when she called to tell me I had left my books there. I had to ask her to give them to Donna to give to Joey. It took two days, but Joey finally brought them to school for me.

Christmas day was the typical midwestern weather, the snow having melted days ago. Now everything was brown and grey and wet. I got clothes and money as gifts. The clothes I didn't care about, but the money was what I needed to buy the necessary speed equipment for the engine.

I had heard about an old man in Edgemont that raced Crosley's indoors at the Gardens, and was selling some of his stuff. The next day, a Thursday, I thumbed to the old man's house.

A white-haired older gentleman answered my knock at the door.

"Mr. Crifield?" I inquired.

"Yes, sonny. What can I do for you?"

"My name's Paul Auer. I live a couple of miles up Section Road in Amberley and I heard that you might have some Crosley engine parts for sale, sir."

"That I have, son. That I have. Let me get my coat and we can go out in the shed to see what I've got." He put on an old and frayed Navy Pea coat with insignia and stripes on the sleeves and led me to the shop he had in the back of the house. Inside was a Crosley Hot Shot and parts and tools covering the entire wall space. The Hot Shot was on a trailer and had a big number fifteen painted in red on a white circle on the door. "What kind of parts are you looking for, son," he asked.

I explained how I was building a sports car and now I needed some speed equipment for the engine. When I was finished he said, "I'd like to see that car when you get it done. I think you've picked a good engine to work with, and I'm sure I can be of some help. This was my last year of racing the little cars, and now I'd be happy to sell some of these parts to a younger man. How fast do you expect to take your little engine? " And without waiting for an answer he continued. "Now this here little Hot Shot will go plumb off the scale of that there brand new twelve-thousand RPM Stewart Warner tachometer. It's got a..." He talked on and on while I threw in a couple of yes sirs and wows. It was fascinating, and he sure knew all about the little cars. Before I left he ended up selling, actually giving, me a high lift Harmon Collins cam, and other invaluable speed equipment. I thanked him over and over as I carefully carried the box of goodies out of his shop promising to visit him when the car was done. Now I was really set.

The rest of Christmas vacation was spent meticulously assembling the engine and worrying about my only homework assignment, to write an essay or poem for English. If it was to be an essay it had to be at least five hundred words, which was real work. A poem could be any length, but I had never actually been able to write poetry. The merry-go-round must have started up again because in the shower one night it came to me, just like that. I got out of the tub and without drying off, wrote down my first poem ever. I loved it. I only hoped the teacher would.

I was on my way to the hop
when I squealed to a stop
at the light, ready for a fight.
I looked to my right
and there sat Bev in his Chev
'a revvin' her up.
The light turned green
that Chev looked mean
But, I put my foot down
like it was bound.
Then as I shifted from strange range
to queer gear, I shed a little tear
for Bev and his Chev.

I titled it, <u>All Tore up by Who Ain't Stock</u>, and took it at once to my mother who laughed and then wanted to know what strange range and queer gear meant. I explained they were slang for gears in an automatic transmission.

FUCK WITH THE FALCON, YOU BETTER KNOW HOW TO FLY

CIRCA 1957

CHAPTER 9

Three days before New Years, and I didn't have a date. The more I thought about it the more I didn't care. Jimmy's call to tell me about his plans didn't help my deepening depression.

"Hey, schmuck, I just called to tell ya that I got a date with Gail for New Years. What are you gonna do?"

"If I do anything at all, it will be to go to a jam session at one of the Knights' houses. Or maybe I'll just stay home and beat off. Where are you going and who are you doubling with?"

"We're doubling with Goldstein. Do you want me to see if I can fix you up? Maybe you can triple with us," Jimmy said, trying to raise my spirits.

"Naw, I've still had it with girls. Where are you gonna to be?"

"I think there's a party at one of the member's homes. His parents are out of town and some of the seniors are getting some beer and wine. Sure you don't want me to try and get you a date?"

"Yeah, I'm sure. Is this Gail thing gonna be more than just friends? I hear she fucks like a mink," I joked with pure jealousy.

"You cocksucker," Jimmy jested and then added, "If she does it's only for Phi Ep's, so you'll never get any, putz."

I went to Ed Moser's for the scheduled jam session where everybody got plastered by midnight. The hot rod band had come a long way and were now calling themselves, "The Keynotes". They even had a few jobs for pay lined up for the spring and had written an instrumental, which they played for us. Janice took me home around one in Bart's '35, with BB passed out in the back seat.

It was 1958, the year I would get my license. Only a few more months of lost identity and bumming rides. Jimmy's dad had bought a '58 Chev rag top and even though it was an automatic, Jimmy was elated. He wouldn't get his license until May, a few months after I would get mine, but the prospect of such a cock wagon made the wait almost bearable. The permit to drive, and what we would do once we had it, was all we talked about every day going to school. Jimmy said that the first thing he wanted to do when he got his license was to drive through the front circle at Woodward with the top down, rain or shine. I said I didn't know what I wanted to do for my first official and legal act, though I had an idea.

Christmas vacation had been a welcome break, but I was having a difficult time getting my mind back in school gear. Right off in English we discovered that everybody would have to read their poem or essay aloud and then the rest of the class would be allowed to critique the work. I would be one of the first because we were going in alphabetical order. Naturally, when it was time for me to stand and read I had the beginnings of a hard-on, the 342nd of the day, or so it seemed. I got a good laugh from the class when I finished reading though, I wasn't sure if they were laughing with me or at me. Mrs. Cantrell restored order saying, "Well, Paul, that certainly was original. I don't think I have heard anything quite like it before. However, I don't believe it is suitable for an English class and will give you a `B' for your effort."

"Mrs. Cantrell, is this an English class or lessons in censorship? I think my work is at least very relevant in utilizing the current slang of the day," I said, although a bit more forcefully as usual.

"Paul, if you wish to discuss your grade, please see me after class."

Metal shop brought more lessons in the real world when one of the boys made a comment about how ugly he thought a girl who had brought a message to Mr. Herne at the opening of the class.

"Johnson," Mr. Herne called out in a loud booming voice, once the girl had left. "Front and center. Now." Johnson shuffled to the front of the class to face the teacher.

"Now Johnson here has a problem, don't you, Johnson?"

"No, sir. I mean, yes, sir. I don't know, sir."

"You don't know?" Then saying to the rest of the class, Mr. Herne continued, "Does anyone know what Johnson's problem is?"

Silence. We all knew not to get involved in this type of discussion.

"Well, I'll tell you. Johnson has an eyesight problem. He thinks what just walked in here was not pretty enough for him. Isn't that right, Mr. Johnson?"

The kid named Johnson stared at his feet and mumbled something.

"Men, let me enlighten you. There are no ugly people, only poor eyesight. So in order to help improve Mr. Johnson's eyesight, I am going to allow him to wear these glasses for the rest of the class," Mr. Herne said, handing Johnson a pair of very dark welders goggles. No body laughed. Mr. Herne continued, "Fellows, we all have our fun in here and even tell a few jokes, but I will not tolerate hurtful and insipid remarks made to any guest in this room. Now let's go to work." Mr. Herne probably had never read Emily Post, but he was sure long on good old-fashioned common sense and decent manners, which he always found time to try to instill in us.

****

The end of January found the frame and engine ready for a road test. All that was required for this test was weather conditions of least thirty-plus degrees and dry. Not normal for this time of year, but I had faith that the Gods of high speed would smile on me. Sure enough, I got the bright sun shiny day only it happened to arrive on a school day. All I could think about the entire morning was the test drive, and by sixth bell, I could resist no longer. I cut Biology and quickly thumbed home.

Exchanging my school clothes for the warmest clothes I could find, I headed for the garage and a date with excitement and apprehension. Without wasting any precious fair weather, I fired up the now souped-up engine which had, in addition to the speed equipment I had gotten from old man Crifield, a fifty thousand volt coil and dual point distributor. I studied the sound of the idling four-banger, which was music to my ears, trying to familiarize myself with its every sound for reference after the test run. Since there was no body, or floor board for that matter, to attach an accelerator to, I had to rig a piece of bailing wire to the throttle linkage on the carburetor. It wouldn't really work like a gas pedal, allowing only full throttle or a fast idle, but it should serve the purpose of the test. I sat on a board with no back support, poised my left foot on the clutch and my right foot as near to the brake pedal as possible and eased the bomb down the driveway.

My plan was to drive to the area of streets across Section Road that were circular by design, thus avoiding having to stop and turn around. On the way over I rolled the car from one side of the road to the other, all the while watching the frame for any signs of stress. The quick steering was perfect, a result of the lengthened pitman arm. It took less than one full turn for lock to lock. At the entrance to my "test track", I doubled clutched into first gear, listened to the engine, took one more look at the frame welds, and grabbed the makeshift throttle. The instant I yanked on the wire the tires spun, and the bodiless car rocketed forward almost causing me to lose my grip on the steering wheel. The force of this sudden acceleration was so great I couldn't lift my foot to depress the clutch, and by the time I had let go of the throttle cable, the car was half on the grass shoulder of the road. Holy shit, I could get killed, I thought, as I lined up for another try. I wished I'd rigged a kill switch to the steering column. It was too late now, and I'd come too far to give up at this late stage. I was determined to test until something broke or everything proved okay.

Calming myself after the near disaster, I gripped the wheel with renewed strength and felt a rush of adrenalin as I dumped the clutch while tugging at the cable. This time I held the little beast in a straight line. I reached about fifty in second gear and noticed the main frame section was bowing out, but the front end was very stable and I pushed on, taking the first turn on rails. It hugged the road like paint. Now I was sailing down the short, flat straight to the second turn where I applied full power half way through and promptly spun out, narrowly missing a tree. This was like, crazy man! I loved it!

On the back straight I gingerly doubled clutched the long shift rod, that came directly from the top of the transmission, into high gear. Now in third and at a higher speed I could clearly see the frame bowing out. Time to take it home, one run was enough for now. I patted the drive shaft, only inches from my butt, which was only six inches from the ground, and said aloud, "Nice run, Willie—I love you."

I headed straight for the garage, but once inside I could hardly push the clutch in because I was shaking so much. No sooner had I got the engine shut down than Mom opened the door from the house.

"Paul have you lost your mind, driving that, that death machine?" She cried.

"Ah, come on Mom. I had to test it didn't I?" It was really cool and it really cranked, Willie would have loved it!"

"Oh, I don't know, I just don't know. I don't want to lose you, and what do you mean Willie would have loved it?" Do you mean your brother, Willie?"

"Yeah, he loved speed."

"Do you think about your brother often, son?"

"Yeah, sometimes," I said, knowing I didn't want to talk about it. Mom had calmed down quite a bit and now softly said, "What do you think about...about your brother?"

"I don't know, just stuff that we used to think about, you know stuff that kids think about."

"You never told me."

"You never asked me, and besides, there's nothing wrong with thinking about him is there?"

"No, of course not, Paul. Now come over here and give your mother a hug."

"I can't. I 'm still shaking too bad."

"Oh Paul, really now. Promise me you won't do this again."

"Well, not today."

"I'm going to have to tell your father," she said, as she went in the house.

She never did, or at least I never found out about it. I sat there contemplating the test run until the cold from the open garage door exceeded the heat from the engine, and I was forced to walk, on rubbery legs, to close it. There was no time to rest on my laurels. I had to begin designing a new cross member to keep the frame from bowing out as new words to "Maybellene" flashed through my mind:

"Nothin' out-run my hopped-up Crosley,
and I caught Kathy baby at the top of the hill."

I got to the thumbing spot early the next morning and waited anxiously for Jimmy to show. As he appeared, I shouted, "Man you should'a seen the little Crosley run. I took it out yesterday and in nothing flat we were doin' over fifty. It really fuckin' cranked!"

"Oh, that's where you went. I heard you cut last bell."

"Yeah, it was only Biology and I've already flunked it anyway. No question I'll be taking it again in summer school."

"Well, we'll drive together 'cuz I'm flunkin' algebra," Jimmy admitted.

"At least we won't be lonely. Man, you should'a seen the car run. I can't wait to put the body on and get it finished."

"You mean you drove it without any body, just like we towed it to Roselawn? You're fuckin' meshug, you know that!"

"Me? Shit! I'm not the cat who stole his daddy's car and almost rolled it doin' over sixty on Ridge Road."

"Ah come on man, that was over a year ago and besides I didn't almost roll it." Jimmy said, defending himself.

As a car slowed to pick us up, we decided to do something together Friday night in order to celebrate the recent event and to commiserate our forced summer plans. It was after school before we got a chance to talk again.

"Hey, daddy-o, you got anything lined up for Friday night," I asked.

"We might be able to go with Goldstein 'cuz he told me he isn't going out with Natalie on Friday. He didn't have any idea what we could do other than a movie or something., How about you? Got any ideas?"

"I think the Keynotes are playing at the Drift Inn, but we might have a problem getting in without at least one of us being eighteen."

"We could go to Shuster's. They don't check IDs there."

"I don't know. I don't want to sit around and drink beer all night."

"Why don't I talk to Goldstein again, and we'll just pick you up Friday night and take it from there," Jimmy suggested.

They picked me up around seven.

"What'ya say Auer. I heard that you've got your car almost finished." Louie said, as soon as I slid in the front seat next to Jimmy.

"Not exactly almost. I've still got a lot of work to do. I'm shooting for my birthday, in March, for a completion date."

"Okay, where do you pussies want to go; after you both put a buck in the gas tank," Louie ordered.

"Talking about pussy," Jimmy said. "Let's cruise Madison Avenue. Maybe we'll get lucky and find some strange stuff."

"It'll be strange alright. Anything other than your fist would be strange," Louie said. We all laughed.

"What happened to Natalie? I thought you two were as good as married," Jimmy asked Louie.

"That bitch said she was going to a slumber party and then told me to stay away. Can you beat that?" It was alright for Louie to call her a bitch, but let anyone else say it and they were instant dead. Natalie had become one of the most desirable chicks in school, partly because Louie was going with her, but mostly because she was very good looking.

After an unsuccessful attempt at trying to pick up girls in Covington we hit on the idea of taking in the show at the GAYETY. The "G" was the last of the live stage and strip-tease joints in the City. As young impressionable teenagers, we always went in groups of at least three for fear of being accosted. The theater forever appeared to be filled with winos, derelicts, and queers that seemed to gravitate to the bright lights of the stage like flies to a fire in a garbage dump. Once inside the dimly lit old theater we seated ourselves inconspicuously to one side. The show was already in progress with some blond, who didn't look too bad, down to her pasties and G-string. Somebody in the crowd yelled "put it back in the mud" which brought a little laughter from the surprisingly large contingent of gawkers. When the house lights went up for the short intermission between acts, someone behind us, on the other side of the room, stood and yelled, "It's Woodward night. All for Woodward stand up and holler." We stood along with at least ten other guys, and cheered. Then a group from Norwood tried the same thing, but there were only a handful of them, thus it was established that is was officially Woodward night.

As order was being restored, but before the lights went back down, I was sure I saw George Baker with some of his fellow members of the football team in the gang who started the school cheer. George was the brother of one of the Knights, and I hoped he knew the lines that I had recently heard at a jam session as I shouted out, "Who'll carry the midnight mail."

George knew, answering, "We'll carry the midnight mail."
"What about the Indians," I continued to shout.
"Fuck the Indians," came the reply.
"You'd fuck an Indian?" I asked.
"We'd fuck a chicken!"
"Why you foul (fowl) fuckers," I finished.

We received a rousing laugh form the entire audience. The "G" was about the only place we could get away with stunts like that. Even the stand-up comics didn't use that kind of crude language, having to rely on innuendo to get their point across. These vaudevillian leftovers also doubled as hawkers during the intermission selling everything from kaleidoscopes showing semi- naked ladies to candy and gum. Dressed in a crumpled hat and baggy, out of date, stained trousers, held up by wide suspenders, they were the essence of sleeze. Their opening gag made our night.

> Comic #1: "Hey. You got a banana in your ear."
> Comic #2: "What'd you say?"
> Comic #1: a little louder - "I said you got a
>   banana in your ear."
> Comic #2: louder still - "What'd ya say?"
> This went on, both shouting as loud as they
> could, until comic #2 finally yelled, "I
> can't hear you...I got a banana in my ear!"

It brought the house down.

The strippers weren't really very pretty or young and they only stripped down to their G-string and pasties, but it was one of the rites of passage into manhood that we somehow forced ourselves to endure. Sexually arousing it was not. I mean who could get excited knowing there might be a pervert seated next to you? Besides, the last thing we wanted was to be caught with a hard-on, which would be totally uncool. I'm sure everyone of us would be beatin' our meat in bed late tonight while fanaticizing about the dancers we had seen on stage, but for now being cool was, well, being cool.

Impatient to get to Mt. Vernon Frisch's and flaunt our exploits, we left after seeing most of the strippers at least once. Mt. Vernon Frisch's Drive-in Restaurant, was the place to be if you were Jewish and from either Woodward or Walnut Hills. It was to us what Carters' was to the hot rodders and Silverton Frisch's was to the gentile crowd. Within an hour we had performed the banana in the ear routine so many times that even the waitresses, while taking orders, were cupping their ears in mock submission to the new craze. By Monday morning the whole school would be doing it and only the three of us and the cats from the football team that were at the "G" with us knew its origin. It was our inside joke, which made us feel like BMOCs when our classmates, both girls and boys, emulated us, thus lending an air of respectability to the seedy jokesters from the burlesque show.

If that was the high point of Monday then the low had to be the issuing of report cards. The only "A" I got was in metal shop, the rest being "B"s and "C"s except for the "F" in Biology.

I knew I was going to flunk and I had been working harder since the beginning of the new grading period, but seeing that letter in print was very depressing. Not that I gave a shit about the subject or even the grade, but because this "F" might keep me from getting my license on my sixteenth birthday. Now along with all the other fears of failing the driving test, not having the car done, or worse, having the car turn out uncool, I was facing summer school. Who needs this science crap anyway? I wasn't going to be an scientist or a doctor and I had enough shit to worry about that was more important like, well, like just other shit. They ought to start kids in school earlier, like maybe at two or three and then by the time they were teenagers school would be over and we could be doing more interesting stuff. Shit!

In addition to the high school problems, I was now going to school on Saturday and Sunday in order to be confirmed. It really bugged me to have to waste this precious time studying religion, of all things. I mean, what the fuck, I wasn't going to be a Rabbi either. But, among my peers, it was sorta the thing to do—at least for me. I didn't want to be a total outcast, so I didn't put up much resistance when my parents insisted I go. These teachings in the theory of God and the Jews' position in the world, were actually lessons in history which I found quite interesting.

With all this pressure to bring up my grades, to study for religious classes, to do my chores at home and to still finish my car, I had all the worries that plague any teenager. Fears of pimples growing out of control, being the only virgin at the tenth year reunion, getting hard-ons in class or just saying the wrong thing at the wrong time. To top it all off I had to find time and space in my mind for the important stuff like cars, parts of cars, names of cars, engine sizes, horsepower, current hit songs and their artists along with always being aware of trying to act cool.

The bad news came at dinner that night when I presented my report card. No license until I had passing grades in all subjects. That meant the earliest I could expect to take the driving test would be two weeks after my sixteenth, when the next grading period ended. I would be mortified, to use my sister's favorite word, unless I could keep the exact date of my birth from my friends. More pressure. The fact that I was fast approaching the driving age had not escaped my father— nothing much did—as he announced at dinner that same night, "Paul, if and when you get your operator's license, I am going to allow you to drive the Ford. I looked at the Crosley you've been working on for the past year and though I'm sure it will turn out to be a fine example of your skills, it will not be suitable for everyday driving, especially without a top."

"You mean the '56? What will Bobbi drive? Are we going to have to share it?" I said, not trying to sound ungrateful or pushy.

"I'm going to buy her another vehicle."

"Yeah? What kind?" I said, showing interest in my favorite subject.

"If you're here on Saturday, I hope to bring it home then."

"Is it new? What make? Does she know?"

"Bobbi hasn't been told, so not a word, and I'm not going to say another thing about it until Saturday."

Saturday morning I got a ride to religious class with Judy Bloom and her Mom. She was looking even better than when she stopped by my garage way last summer when I was working on the sports car. As soon as I get my license I'd have to check her out a little closer. In class that day we studied the story in the Torah, the one about Abraham and his trip to the land of Moriah where he was to sacrifice his son Isaac as a burnt offering. I didn't believe it, but I wasn't going to start an argument in that class.

Sitting at the top of the circle in the driveway when I got home was a brand new 1958 Corvette. I hurried to check it out. Much to my dismay it was a "glider", however, automatic transmission or not, it was still a Corvette. I got in and started it up, studying the gauges displayed in the cockpit. I revved the engine, daydreaming of what it would be like to actually own one of these. Well, anyway, one with a four-speed stick.

The old man and I took a ride out in the country to help break it in during the early evening hours. We didn't talk much, but then he was never long on conversation—just the usual questions and orders. Of course, on the other hand, he did leave me alone. I guess he believed that the best way to raise children was to present a good example. And that he did. I never heard him swear, abuse my mother, lie, cheat, steal, display prejudice or even condone any of these weaknesses. I wasn't sure if his methods were working because I sometimes used the vernacular of the low life to describe certain events, though never in the presence of ladies. I never lied and the only stealing I had done was a few pieces of lumber to build tree houses many years ago. Oh yes, and a work bench. Cheating? Well, maybe I had copied a few assignments in school, but I didn't have any prejudice due to the many friends of different backgrounds I had already cultivated.

Later that night I found BB drinking a Coke in his '35 at Carters'.

"Long time so see," I said, climbing in out of the cold.

"Yeah, no shit. I've been keeping my nose to the old grindstone. Between work and this damn night school, I haven't had time to see Janice or work on the '49 or anything. What have you been doing besides pounding your puddin'?"

"Hey, man, the Crosley's almost ready. All I've got to do is put the body on and paint it. I'd have been done sooner, but I've been going to religious school on Saturday and regular Sunday school on Sunday for my confirmation."

"Oh yeah? I was confirmed, it was a pain in the ass," Big Bart said.

"No shit. I didn't know you were Jewish."

"I'm not. It was a Catholic confirmation.

"Catholic, eh, you believe in ghosts and stuff?"

"Naw, I'm an agnostic, asshole." BB said.

"Now I always knew you were an asshole, but I didn't know you were some kind of fancy asshole. What's an agnostic?

"Auer! One of these days I'm going to kick that smart ass of yours," Big Bart joked. "An agnostic is one who doesn't necessarily believe in God, but doesn't necessarily not believe either," BB said.

"Hey that's cool. It's sorta like cover your ass on both sides. If, when the time comes and there is a God, then you can say, `Hey man I never said I didn't believe in you'. And if there ain't no God then you can say you were cool all along, right?" I said.

"Well, that's sorta the way it goes if you want to look at it that way."

"Tell me about this night school, is it interesting? This isn't a Joe college kind of thing, is it?" I asked.

"Hell no. Everybody in my class has a full time job of some kind and, man, is it hard. High school was a piece of cake compared to this."

Sunday afternoon the old man and I took the Vette to Bobbi at Miami and brought the '56 back. Even old four eyes seemed excited that his girl friend had a Corvette. It was a very boring trip. The old man never went over sixty and he wouldn't let me listen to rock & roll on the radio. I enjoyed the trip back more because we were then riding in MY car.

The first day of spring came and went without any fanfare. I was sixteen, and my car was done except for the paint. I decided to take one final shakedown run before painting in case any major changes were required. Friday after school, the day after my birthday, weather permitting, would be the first day for a test with the body on, license or no license. After a brief warm up and a check of the recently installed gauges, I headed for my test track. Now, with a seat to hold me and an accelerator pedal I could really see how it would handle. This time when I dumped the clutch, I easily kept control as the little bomb shot down the straight-a- way. At turn number one I changed down into second and pushed the car through on rails not ready to try a full drift. Turn two was the same though I took up the entire width of the road. Accelerating into the back straight, the mufflerless exhaust produced an ear splitting pitch as the little four banger turned upwards of nine-thousand RPM.

The thought of disturbing any of the people living in all these houses on this normally quiet street never occurred to me, at least not on the first trip around. The only negative observation I had made was that the engine seemed to flatten out well before it should. Maybe the stock carb was not enough for the hot cam. At the end of the first run, I was enjoying it so much that I decided to go again, this time trying for a little more speed in the corners.

Heading into turn one, I tried what I had only read about; the four-wheel drift. Just before the apex and at about forty miles per hour I jerked the wheel hard left which, as it should, started the front end sliding. At this attitude, if I did nothing else the car would plow off the road. If I backed off the gas, I would spin out. However, I forced myself to do what I had read about; I opened the throttle full sending the little sports car into an actual four wheel drift, if only for a second, because I over-corrected and did a complete one-eighty right in the middle of the street. It was exhilarating. Here I was doing what I had only dreamed about doing and doing it with a car I had made. I got straightened out and headed for turn two where I was determined to master the drift.

This time I got it right only, unknown to me at the time,

old lady Fritz, who lived just past turn two, had had time to get her broom ready when she heard me start my second trip around. Now here I was, coming out of a controlled slide with no place to go other than into a tree or right past the edge of her drive where she stood, broom in hand. She was either crazy or had more faith in my driving than I had because the line I was taking was going to put me within inches of where she stood. She didn't budge and as I got to within swinging distance, she gave a round house swipe at me, knocking the tiny, single Plexiglas windscreen loose from its retaining bolts. I ducked and didn't get hit, but I could hear her screaming something as I backed off to reach third gear further on down the street. Enough of this shit, I better get home.

I hadn't been home long enough for the engine to cool down when the police pulled up. I approached the open window of the scout car just as Officer Bloomfield was saying into the mike, "Twenty-one, two-seven the Auer residence."

"Two-seven, Twenty-one. Advise the subject if I catch him racing that thing, he's going straight to Juvenile," came the voice over the radio.

"Twenty-one, okay," Officer Bloomfield replied.

Oh shit, I was in big trouble now. I could just see my chance of ever getting a license fly right out the window.

"Paul? It's Paul, isn't it?" The uniformed cop asked.

"Yes sir."

"Maybe I better take a look at this thing you've been terrorizing the neighborhood with. Is that it?" He said, nodding toward the garage.

"Yes sir," I said, still not believing I should get too familiar with him by calling him by his first name. I stood over to one side as he walked around my pride and joy which was squeezed between the '56, and the work bench—the one made from stolen lumber. Maybe they were still looking for the thief, I thought, as sweat began to form on my forehead. He didn't say anything for the longest time, just peering into everything. Finally, the officer reached back to where his handcuffs were. I looked out the door at the woods. I could run and hide in one of the old tree houses, and when it got dark, I could thumb to Texas or someplace, anyplace. Thoughts of prison raced through my mind as he casually hitched his up his pants and said, "Did you build this yourself?"

"Yes sir," I replied with a voice that sounded guilty as

hell.

"Pretty good. I wish I'd had been able to so something like this when I was younger. You've got quite a place here, with that work bench and all."

He did know! Now the axe is going to fall. If I made a break for it, he might shoot me. I had visions of my body lying spread eagle on the driveway. I wondered if the bullet in my back would hurt more than the falling on the blacktop. I suddenly had an over powering urge to fess up, but my throat was all choked and I couldn't speak. Lucky Willie. Death has got to be better than life in prison.

"Can I take a look at the engine?" Officer Bloomfield asked, without noticing my total silence. He reached for the leather straps that held the hood down while I hurried to assist, still unable to talk. Shit, maybe the parts I got off old man Crifield were stolen, This is crazy. I've got to get hold of myself and start acting cool. I grabbed the straps on my side of the car and helped the officer lift the hood.

"Looks like you've done a lot of work on this, fellah," the cop commented, admiringly. Silence. "I'll tell you one thing, Paul. You're pretty cool. There's no question that this engine has recently been run, I can feel the heat from here, and there's no doubt in my mind that this is the car Mrs. Fritz described as almost running her down. However, since I didn't see you driving it and you have had the presence of mind not to admit to anything, there's nothing I can do other than let you know that if we catch you, it'll be a citation at least. And if Sergeant Prince catches you, well, you heard him on the radio; he'll haul your sorry ass to Juvenile Hall. Is that clear, son?"

I couldn't believe my ears as I stroked my chin and throat, feeling the blood returning and my head clearing. "Yes, sir," I said, in a normal voice.

"I'm not going to give you a ticket or even tell Prince, but I would like to know, just for the sake of truth: How fast were you going around that corner at Mrs. Fritz's? She said you were going at least fifty, but I don't think any car could go that fast around that narrow corner."

"You mean no matter what I say, I won't get into trouble?" I asked still not believing my good fate.

"That's right. I just want to know for my own information."

"Well, I don't really know as the rod doesn't have a

speedometer, but I'm sure I was going at least forty, sir."

"You can cut that `sir' bit too. The official investigation is over. I'm impressed. Your car looks like it should be something you can be proud of, and from what you tell me and what Mrs. Fritz said, it must handle better than anything I've seen."

"Thank you. Do you want me to fire it up so you can hear it?" I offered, but still afraid to call him by his first name.

"Maybe some other time. I better get back on the air or the Sarge will come lookin' for me himself." I followed him to the cruiser and listened as he called in.

"Twenty-one, two-six."

"Two-six, Twenty-one. Were you able to catch the little whippersnapper?"

"Negative. Subject vehicle was in garage, and I was unable to determine who the driver was." Tony hung the mike back on the dash and said, "Look Paul, you better take it easy here in the Village. Even a dog knows not to shit where he eats, if you know what I mean."

"You're right, Tony, I'm sorry. I'll try to keep my testing to the strip."

As the cruiser drove away, a wave of exhaustion swept over me. My emotions had been on a wild roller coaster, and I was too whipped to think about anything, even the flatness of the engine at high speed. I went inside only to be questioned by my mother.

Later that night I went back into the garage and picked up the spare carburetor base, in order to take it to school on Monday. I planned to bore it out in Metal Shop to see if that would improve the top end. The other problem I faced was finding someone to paint the car. The first name to come to mind was that of Denny Bishop, a fellow classmate and member of the rival Cam-lifters Hot Rod Club. Denny's reputation with a paint sprayer was well known. Though I had never seen the car he was building, I had heard it was perfect, body wise.

Monday I learned that I had pulled my six week grade in Biology up to a "C" and thus insured my chances of getting a license when the report came out in two weeks. In Metal Shop, Mr. Herne said he would help me set up the Cincinnati Mill to bore out the venturi. He didn't believe my idea would work either, citing some of the same reasons BB had argued with me about.

At lunch I found Denny, on the "ramp", the only place

smoking was allowed on school property. "Hey Denny, how's it goin'?" I asked taking the fag which was dangling from his lower lip. I hadn't smoked much in the past, but now that I was sixteen I had begun to smoke more. It was cool to have a pack of Luckys in a shirt pocket or rolled up in the sleeve of a T-shirt. Besides the "ramp" was THE place to be during lunch period and to be there and not smoke was, well, just plain uncool.

"You know a quarter will break you of that habit," he said, taking his cigarette back.

"I'm cool, I got some coffin nails in my pocket, but I only have a minute. I need to ask you a favor," I said, again reaching to bum a drag from his weed.

"A Knight needs a favor from a Cam-Lifter? This must be my lucky day."

"Everyday could be a lucky day if you joined a real hot rod club," I said, continuing the good natured joking.

"Well, hurry up and tell me what you need before you smoke the whole thing," Denny said, taking back his fag.

"Okay, okay. I've got the Crosley all finished except for the paint, and I'm wondering if you could possibly lower yourself to do a paint job for a Knight."

"You got the part right about having to lower myself. The question is do I want to sink that low."

"You prick. How 'bout Saturday afternoon and as a special favor to ya, I promise not to tell anyone when I dust you off; if you ever get that duce of yours running."

"Right again. You won't tell anyone because you'll never beat my flathead."

"Anytime. Now how 'bout Saturday? Can you make it?"

"Yeah, I'm sure I can. Just have the paint and thinner there," Denny confirmed.

"Okay, see ya Saturday. Thanks , and I'll tell the rest of the Knights that you Cam-Lifters aren't a bunch of pussies, like everybody says," I said, backing away as Denny flicked his cigarette butt at me.

Saturday I cut my religious class in order to get one last sand job on the body. Denny came over around one, driving a 1948 Lincoln V-12 with his compressor, spray gun and lines stuffed in the trunk. In less than three hours the little sports car was finally finished. It really looked neat with its Ferrari style low open mouth front end and its rounded smooth fenders that were higher than the hood. There were no bumpers or headlights and only one small plastic windscreen on the driver's side that was barely higher than the steering wheel. The brake lights were from the original Crosley and were frenched into the rear fender that turned under at the bottom. The black wall tires, mounted to the hub-cap- less silver painted wheels, contrasted nicely to the deep red of the freshly painted body. There was no chrome or extraneous moldings anywhere on the car to cause air drag or otherwise disturb the lines of the plastic body. The doors were even glassed over, which not only added strength to the body, but also gave an unbroken line for the entire side of the car. It was determined early on that doors would not be needed because the car was so low that stepping over the side into the cockpit was no problem at all.

The following Friday the report cards came out. No sweat. Mom promised to take me to take my drivers test on Saturday, which turned out to be a breeze. All my nervous worrying was for nothing. I took the test in the '56 and afterward Mom bought me a tank of gas, saying that I would have to learn to exist on my allowance and what I could earn on my own for any future fuel. There was a light mist and the streets were wet so I couldn't take the sports car out for its first legal run, but my heart wouldn't have been in it. I had something else to do. Something I had been thinking about for a long time.

After dropping Mom at home, I headed for the gates of the United Jewish Cemetery. It took me a while, but I located the family plot near one of the many roads that twisted through the old burial grounds. I got out in the cold drizzle and stood at the foot of Willie's little marker. A flood of memories and dreams that would never be surged through my mind. I started to speak, in a low voice, just in case someone might be listening. The words, disjointed like my thoughts, sounded surrealistic even at a cemetery.

"Willie, I did it. I wish you were here. Why did it have to happen? I didn't even get to say good-by. We had such good times together, and now we could be really having a ball. I got the body done, but I know you could have done a better job at the finish work. I cut your name into the frame, actually I welded it in. It hurt Willie. I hope you didn't have any pain. I got hurt when Kathy broke up with me, but it was a different kind of hurt. I still think of her, but the pain is gone. I think of you sometimes and wish, I wish I could somehow change things, anything to have you back. Sure I've got a lot of friends, but it just isn't the same as having a brother. Willie, I'm sorry too for all of the dumb things I did to you when we were kids, like the times I teased you in front of that girl and called you a sissy. I know it hurt your feelings, and I am sorry. I'd do anything to get you back, give up my license or even my car. The car, Willie really looks neat, and you'd be thirteen now and we could go to some out of the way place where I could let you drive. Mom talks about you sometimes and so does Bobbi, but Dad never does. You know him, he doesn't ever say anything. Bobbi's not such a bad sister, even though she always called you her baby brother. She's going with this guy, Old Four Eyes, I call him, but he's not such a bad guy. The old man got her a Vette, and now I'm driving the '56. It's really cool and we'd be driving to school in it instead of having to thumb. I hitch hike with Jimmy Cohen, you remember him, that skinny kid with the blond hair. He lives in the old Stewart place now and is my best friend, I guess. I know one thing sure, Willie, when I get married and have a kid I'm going to name him after you. I mean I'm going to name him Willie not William after old Uncle Will, but just plain Willie. I've been going to religious school to get confirmed, and I don't know about all that God and stuff, but I wish I knew how to pray. If I did I'd say a prayer for you, I guess. I don't know Willie, I don't even know if I believe in God. I do remember one part from the service we were reading the other day in Sunday school. It went something like: Our Father, our King, hear our prayer, and then was followed by some requests. Well, if I could ask for a prayer I would: Our Father, our King please take good care of Willie or I'll...I'll kick ass when I get there, if I ever get there, wherever there is. Ah Willie,I don't guess I could kick God's ass, but you know what I mean. I hope you're okay, wherever you are. I know if you were here and just becoming a teen-ager, I would be able to help you. I miss you Willie and I'll be back to see you, keep cool, man...So long Willie"

I looked up to see if there was some kind of sign, but the heavy clouds didn't change. I got back in the '56 and revved the engine one time for Willie before slowly driving away.

AFTER WHILE CROCODILE

CHAPTER 10

Having a car—make that two cars—and a drivers license was, well, just the most. I logged tons of miles on the old '56 in the next few weeks in addition to maybe a hundred or so on the Crosley. The little sports car was running like a champ, especially since I had installed the bored out carburetor on it. It was such a relief to be able to drive to school and not have to worry about rain and stuff. Even religious school wasn't so bad, particularly since I was giving my neighbor, Judy, a ride. She was one good lookin' chick and I would definitely have to find a way to go out with her if I could get her away from her steady— some big animal that played football for Walnut Hills.

On Saturday, the week after I finished setting and adjusting the new carb, Denny showed up to retrieve the spraying outfit he had left behind in case we had to do any touch up. He was a master with the spray gun and none was needed. He was in his '32 three window coupe that had been chopped and channeled with a dropped front axle he had done himself. The engine, a flathead V-8 Sixty, was small but still over twice the cubes as mine. "Looks pretty good, the paint job I mean," he said, in joking a manner, as he walked into the garage.

"Yeah well, it runs just as good. It eats flatheads for breakfast!"

"Shit! That little roadster couldn't pull the rag off a sick whore," he said, continuing to needle me.

"First of all it's not a roaster, it's a sports car, governor, and as such will not only out corner you, but will run circles around any flathead," I boasted.

"Yeah, if you really want to get pulled we could do it right now, chicken shit."

I had to think a minute. Never having ridden in his rod, I wasn't sure just how fast it was. In fact, I didn't know anyone who had, so I really didn't know what I was getting into. If I raced and lost, it would be all over school and Carters'. I was sure I could beat him off the line, but the top end could be doubtful as the Crosley was geared very low. So if we raced on a short stretch of road the race would be mine.

"Okay, schmuck. How 'bout that new road off Section, you know, where they're going to build all those new factories," I said, trying to set him up for a short run.

"You mean right down there in Roselawn?"

CIRCA 1957

"Yeah, it's four lanes of new concrete and there won't be any traffic at all on a Saturday."

"It's not a full quarter mile is it."

"It's probably very close," I lied. "We can run from where Summit comes in back to the stop sign at Section," I said, confidently

"Hey, dad, I don't know. That's the city and we might get caught," Denny whined, starting to back down.

"Okay, chicken heart, but let it be known that you're the one who backed out. I don't want to hear any bull at school Monday."

"Alright, daddy-o, let's do it."

We lined up side by side in the middle of the new road, surrounded by construction equipment and new factories. I raised my hand and, over the loud roar of the engines, said, "When I drop my hand for the third time we'll go! Okay?" Denny nodded his agreement.

Checking for cops and traffic, I raised and lowered my hand shouting, "ONE! TWO! THREE!!"

The little Crosley shot out to an immediate two car lead and held it all the way through second. Settling into third gear, I glanced over my shoulder and could see my lead of now over three car lengths was rapidly decreasing as the big duce coupe gained on me. Just before the '32 pulled even with my rear end, I began braking hard for the traffic light that was fast approaching. Denny roared past and then clamped on his binders sliding to a stop at Section. With a nervous and quick look around to see if we had attracted any cops, we pealed out for home. Once back at the house the endless argument began about who beat whom. The race, the first for the sports car, was by all accounts a successful one with nothing broken, no arrests, and a win, at least according to my version.

Monday it was back to the same old grind, school seven days a week. However, there was a light at the end of the ram tube. Confirmation would be in two weeks and then the following week my sophomore year would end. After that, two weeks of freedom before having to start summer school. The "C" I got in Biology in order to get my license was the only "C" I earned all year in that subject. Jimmy had gotten his license, but now had to work in the family business everyday after school, so we didn't even get to ride to school together. I missed not having him to talk to, with only homeroom to catch up on all the latest bullshit.

The best thing to come out of the confirmation class was the introduction to Elaine Horwitz. I really hadn't paid much attention to her with all the other stuff I had going, but now that the end was in sight and I had a license, I decided to ask her out. The opportunity to talk to her alone didn't present itself during the Saturday class, and I had to wait until Sunday. During Torah study I saw that she had asked to be excused from the room. I waited a few minutes and also asked to be excused. The timing was good. As I came out she was just walking back down the hall toward the room.

"Hi Elaine, can I talk to you for a minute," I said, hoping my fly was closed or I hadn't just sprouted a giant pimple or something.

"Sure Paul, and you can call me Laine; everybody else does."

"Okay, Laine," I said, with a smile, thinking it sounded a little too familiar, but a good sign." I just wanted to know if you might want to go out with me sometime?"

"Well, ah gee, I don't know. When?"

"I don't know. How 'bout tonight? I said, pissed at myself that I didn't have a plan ready. Schmuck!

"Oh, I couldn't do that. It's a school night."

"Oh yeah. Maybe next Saturday night then?" I said, leaning against the wall and trying to keep my cool.

"Where were you thinking about going?" she asked still in a very formal tone.

"I don't know maybe we could double to a movie or something." "I'll have to see. I think I'm doing something with my Mother then. Will you ask me at school tomorrow or Tuesday?"

"Where can I find you?"

"You have that shop class just before lunch don't you?"

"Yeah. How'd you know that?" I asked surprised that she knew while I turned slightly to feel if my zipper was up.

"I have Spanish right across the hall that period, and I've seen you go in there."

"Okay, I'll talk to you then. I guess we better get back in class now, don't ya think."

"She let me open the door for her, and we walked in together. I never heard another word the teacher said for the rest of the class as I rolled our conversation around in my mind.

CIRCA 1957

She didn't say she'd go out with me, but she didn't say she wouldn't either. And she knew that I had a class next to her which meant she had been at least noticing me. Shit, this might be alright. I had to talk to Jimmy and see if he wanted to double.

I stopped by Jimmy's store on the way home to get an early line on his plans for next Saturday. Jimmy was in the back taking inventory when I arrived and after the customary greetings to Mr. Cohen and some of the other employees I knew, I found Jimmy hard at work. "What's goin' on, man?" I greeted him.

"You're just in time. Hand me those boxes. What brings you over here?"

"Well, aside from the fact that I haven't talked to you for fuckin' years I just wanted to know if you would like to double next Saturday night. I might have a date with Elaine...Laine Horwitz."

"Oh yeah. She's not too bad lookin'. How'd you get a date with her? I didn't know this was be kind to animals week." Jimmy joked.

"You asshole. You can get your own boxes," I said, pulling back the box I had started to hand him.

"Aw come on, hand me the damn box. You know I was only jackin' you off about being animal week. Actually it's ugly week and you look like you've been beat with an ugly stick," Jimmy continued to joke.

"Well how 'bout it, schmuck? Think you can get a date?"

"Seriously, I don't think you'd want to double with me next Saturday. My Uncle Jim promised to take me to Flo's."

"Oh yeah, your sixteenth birthday present. Are you going to get around the world or just a straight blow job, you lucky bastard."

"So where are you going to take her?"

"Shit, I don't even know if I have a date with her. I asked her this morning and all she said was that I should ask her at school on Monday. She said something about having to go with her mother on Saturday. Shit, I don't want to go out with her alone for the first time. It's always hard to find something to talk about on a first date. Hey, I've got an idea, why don't you take Laine out and I'll go to the whore house with your Uncle Jim?"

"Fuck you. Just keep handing me those boxes." Jimmy said.

"Talkin' about fuck, how are you and Gail getting along?

Are you getting any?"

"Not yet, but I'm working on it." "Maybe a little stink finger?" I queried.

"Maybe. Which is sure more than you've been getting."

"Yeah I know, I know. I think I'm coming down with that rare and almost incurable male disease," I said.

"Yeah? What's that?"

"You mean you've never heard of the rare and infamous, Lack- a-nookie disease?"

"Yeah, and I think I've got a permanent case of it. This Gail can tease your balls off. Saturday night she had me so worked up that I pulled my cock out and had to start beatin' off while I was fingering her with my other hand. She wouldn't let me do it, but she did finish jackin' me off. I think next Friday night will be the night."

"Friday! You mean you're gonna shtup her on Friday and then on Saturday night get a blow job at Flo's?" I asked, with a look of mock astonishment.

"Yeah, what's wrong with that?" Jimmy answered with a grin.

"Well nothing really. You can't wear the thing out."

"Shhh, here comes the old man," Jimmy said, in a whisper.

Mr. Cohen called back to us, "What are you two schnooks doing back there? It's time to close the store already. You vant I should go to the poor house in the time it takes you to count a few lousy boxes. I could hire a goyim to shlep the boxes faster than the two of you."

"Okay Dad. We're almost done. We'll be right out."

"Oy vey, he's still not done. Hurry up already. You vant your mother to have a heart attack, worrying why we're not home by now?"

Jimmy looked at me and said quietly, "Don't say nothing about Gail in front of the old man."

"Okay, but why? Surely he knows you date girls?"

"Oh he knows alright, and he even knows I date Gail. But if he knew what we did, he'd kill me. She's the daughter of one of his friends. This friend's father and my grandfather came over on the same boat together. So he'd kill me if he knew I was gonna shtup her, ya dig man?"

"What kind of flowers do you want—for your funeral. I think it's only right that I disclose your dishonorable intentions to your father, especially since you won't double with me Saturday night," I said, with mock seriousness.

"You cocksucker. When I'm dead, who're you gonna get to double with then? Now don't even joke about this to my old man," Jimmy pleaded.

Laine agreed to a date on Saturday, when we briefly got to talk between classes fourth bell, this being the only time our paths crossed at the huge school. She told me that I would have to meet her parents, which was okay by me, as this was the first time she would be allowed to date a guy with his own car. Crazy. She didn't have a license and wouldn't be sixteen until September, so she hadn't been anywhere other than with her family or sorority sisters in STP. Sigma Theta Pi was jokingly referred to by the boys as "Small Town Prostitute" and was associated with the chapter at Walnut Hills that Bobbi had belonged to. It was decided that we would go to the Jewish Center on Summit Road which was having a social, just to make a good impression on her parents. Eight o'clock sharp I rolled the '56 into the driveway of the four family where Laine said she lived. After a quick check in the mirror, I walked to the building tucking my blue sport shirt into my school pants and wiping the tops of my penny loafers on the back of my pants legs. I was greeted at the door by Mr. Horwitz. "Come in young man, Elaine will be ready in a minute," he said, motioning me in with a fist full of newspaper.

"Thank you, sir," I said, in my best manner, as I followed him into the living room.

"Elaine tells me you built an automobile. Did you drive it here tonight?"

He said "automobile" like it was a real car, a Ford or Chevrolet or something. I almost laughed when the thought of my car being built, like in a factory. "No sir, I can't drive it at night. It doesn't have headlights. It's mainly for racing."

"Racing? Where do you race? Are you old enough to race?"

"I'm only old enough to race on the drag strip. You have to be twenty-one to race SCCA." I said, starting to feel a little more at ease.

"SCCA? What is that another kind of race?"

It stands for Sports Car Club of America and is the only official sanction for sports car races." I said, getting up as Laine walked in. She had done something to her hair and was wearing a light colored dress that was tied to make her waist look like I could reach around it with my fingers. The dress cinched so tight that it made her breasts look like they were straining to get out. She was wearing flats and when standing next to me didn't come to my chin. I wasn't aware of any lull in the conversation as I stood there ogling her until her father spoke again. "Well, Paul, tell me, what does your father do?"

"Oh Daddy, that's not very nice," Laine said, as she grabbed my arm leading me to the door.

"You kids be home by midnight and drive careful now," Mr. Horwitz called after us as we walked down the steps.

"Honestly, my father's impossible. What kind of questions was he asking you in there?"

"He was just asking me about my car; said you told him that I built a car. Only he said automobile, not car, like it was some official vehicle made in a factory."

"Well, it is an automobile even if it wasn't made in a factory, isn't it, Paul?" Laine asked, coming to the defense of her father.

"Yeah, well, anyway how did you know I made a car, a sports car to be exact?"

"It was in the school newspaper. I can read you know. When can I get a ride in it?"

"Hey, this is really cool man. We haven't been on a date five minutes and already you're planning our wedding," I said.

"Wedding? Who said anything about a wedding?"

"Well you might as well plan it. I thought we were going to the Center."

"Can't we take the sports car to the Center. Hell, I thought you'd like to take it out, Laine swore.

"What kind of language is that for a nice Jewish girl?"
"Hell is hardly a bad word. Does it shock you that I might be more of a tomboy than a lady?"

"I looked at her as we stopped at the end of the drive, waiting for traffic to clear. "You know Laine, you're alright for a chick."

"You're all right too—for a guy."

Our eyes met and for an instant I could see past the cyan iris deep into her dark pupil: I could see a future.

"Okay. If you really want to go to the Center in style, but we'll have to hurry 'cuz there's only about an hour of daylight left. You sure you want to do this?"

We headed straight for home where, after introducing

CIRCA 1957

Laine to Mom and finding her a jacket, we were on our way. The realization that this could be an important event crossed my mind as we headed down Section, the cool evening air blowing full in my face. I glanced at Laine, her hair tied tightly with a scarf, and noted, with pleasure, how the force of the wind was making her tits stand out even more prominently against her dress.

This would be the first time the Jewish kids, for the most part, would see my work, and I hoped it would make a favorable impression. I'm sure many of them believed I was not only a rebel, but a greaser to boot. Not having joined a fraternity—a Jewish fraternity—and conforming to the image of a Harry-high-schooler did have its disadvantages.

My fears were eased when we pulled into the parking lot and were immediately surrounded by a mass of kids. No sooner had I shut the engine off and Laine had gotten out, than Lou Goldstein pushed his way through the crowd, dropped in the passenger seat and ordered, as only Louie could, "Take me for a ride, Auer!"

Okay, I thought, as I restarted the engine, if it's a ride you want, I'll show you I can be just as tough. We pulled out onto Summit and at once made a sharp left into Edgemont, which presented a series of "S" bends that I took in a straight line. In the final turn before exiting the tree lined streets, I pointed the car at the apex of the turn and induced the under steer setting up a four wheel drift, the engine screaming in second gear. The little bomb came out of the bend only a few feet from a parked car and then slammed to a stop at the entrance to Section Road. After the briefest of stops, I spun the tires heading toward the heart of Roselawn. Now on the straight approaching the chicane at Reading Road, I built the speed to over fifty on this mostly residential street. It was then that I became aware of my passenger again, having had my full concentration on the task at hand. Without any conscious thought, I surreptitiously unscrewed the large retaining nut holding the steering wheel to the keyed shaft. All the while I could hear Louie screaming, over the sound of the straight pipes, to slow down. As we got to within a few hundred yards of that final "S" bend I yanked the steering wheel off and extended it over to Louie saying, "Here, you drive!" Not wanting to take my eyes off the road I couldn't look at his face, but I'm sure there might have been a look of real fear, just maybe.

We headed straight for home because it was starting to get dark and exchanged the Crosley for the '56. On the way back to the Center Louie said,"Auer, you're alright." It was a good feeling. I had been accepted, just like that, and without having to compromise my non-conformist ways, I felt, for the first time in my life that I was a member of the tribe.

Back at the Center, Louie praised my driving and handiwork, even telling of my "nerves of steel" by my removing of the steering wheel at at high speed. Laine was a little miffed that I had run off and left her, but I didn't care. Besides, it was good to keep women a little off balance and not let them take control. What else should she expect from a fucking rebel, anyway?

We hung around there until it closed and then, like the rest of the sheep, went to Frisch's for a coke. We headed for her home about eleven, after a quick pass through Carters' to let the hot rodders check out my new chick. We hadn't talked much all night and now that I was walking her to her door I tried to think of what to say, a line or something. "Say, by the way, I don't know if I told you or not, but I like your hair the way you have it fixed."

"Thank you. It's called a flip and I had it done only this morning."

"Is that its natural color? Are you a real blond?"

She stopped half way up the stairs to the apartment and looked me in the eye, "There's only one way you can find out for sure, isn't there?" she said, with this sorta shit-eating grin on her face. It caught me by surprise and I was at a loss for words. Now she had me in my place. Fuckin' women you never know where you stand with them or what they're going to say next. With guys, you could always know what they were thinking, all you had to do was ask and they would give you a straight, no bullshit answer. When we reached her door, she said, "Don't you want to know how?"

I had regained my cool now and replied, "Just like the Indian, I know how."

"What Indian? What are you talking about?" Laine asked.

"You didn't hear about the Indian standing on the street and every time someone walks by he holds up his hand and says, `chance'."

"No, I haven't heard that one. Is that all there is?"

"Well, finally some guy stops and asks this Indian `why

103

do you say <u>chance</u> every time someone walks by. I thought Indians were supposed to say <u>how</u>.' and the Indian says, `Me know how, me want chance'."

Laine sorta smiled, but she didn't say anything. It was my turn to have the shit-eating grin. With the return of my self confidence, I took her hands in mine, saying, "I'd like to see you again—would you like to see me again?" I studied her eyes looking for the same feeling I had had earlier, the look of a future. I was quiet, the mood was right, and the only sound was that of my own breathing. I held my breath while slightly increasing the pressure on her hands. Laine smiled, and then with the look and sound of pure innocence, she said, "I'll see you in Sunday school tomorrow, won't I?"

The mood was broken, she had done it to me again. I said, "That's not exactly what I meant."

"I know what you meant," she purred, moving ever so slightly toward me and leaving her lips parted.

I knew I could kiss her, but two can play this game. "Okay, see ya tomorrow," I said, as I opened the door to her apartment for her.

The next two weeks were a killer, with confirmation and exams all crammed together. By the time it was over I was ready to crank up the merry-go-round, at least for the two weeks until summer school began.

On the last day of school George Baker, the football player, and I agreed that a celebration was in order. Now George wasn't very big, especially for a football player, but he was a fighter and could be just plain mean and tough. He was one of those kind of guys that could, and did, put cigarettes out in the palm of his hand. I had seen him do this on one occasion, just before he sucker punched a guy that had been riding him. George wasn't this way with his friends, only strangers or cats that were looking for a fight. He could take a kidding as well as anyone and was very jovial most of the time. Though he was in the largest gentile fraternity, he was more of a loner, like me. He had a sorta devil may care attitude about him at all times, even when he was kicking ass.

No sooner had I pulled into Baker's driveway on Saturday night, than George cam running out the side door and hopped into my car saying, "Quick man, peal out or I'm a dead man!" I slapped reverse and, without looking, backed into the street just as Abee came running out the same door yelling something.

"What was that all about?" I asked once we were safely down the road.

"Shit man, all I did was try to put the make on my brother's girl. You'd think I was trying to steal his car or something," George said, obviously still excited.

"You asshole. He'll be waiting for you when you get home. Fuck man. Even a dog knows not to shit where he eats."

"I give a shit. Besides, he'll get over it, especially since he needs me to help him tow the Olds to the strip Sunday."

"Okay. Where are we going. I'm ready for a beer."

"Yeah, that sounds cool, man. Take this stocker to the Gypsy Inn. I got served there the other night and if the same bartender is there tonight, he might remember me."

"Crazy man, but will he remember me?"

"Don't sweat it, daddy-o. The trick to appearing older is to always order your drinks by name. It makes it seem like you've been drinking long enough to have acquired a taste for a certain brand. Just watch me and do as I do," George stated in a worldly manner.

George was cool, I had to hand it to him. He walked in the bar like he owned the place and immediately struck up a conversation with the bartender, ordering a Hudepohl draft in mid-sentence. The bartender looked at me and as cool as I could be, I said, "Make it two." Man, we're both cool!. We drank a few beers and shot a game of pool to relax before deciding to move on. I mean, men of the world didn't sit around the same bar all night. We had to go places and breathe beer in the faces of our not so worldly friends.

The first stop was Silverton Frisch's which we took our time getting to because George, the worldly one, advised me to drive very carefully so as not to attract the attention of any cops least they smell the brew. The drive-in lot was so full of cars and people, being the first day of summer vacation, it took us almost an hour just to drive through. We saw a lot of kids and a lot of them saw us. It was cool. I thought I saw Kathy in one of the cars filled with girls, but I wasn't sure and I couldn't park to find out. Anyway, she was history and Laine was better looking. However, for one brief instant I though, if she suddenly called to me telling me how she had made a terrible mistake, I would chuck it all and gladly run to her. I could just see it all now; my car door left standing open in the middle of the crowded lot, horns blowing as we rushed to each others arms. I was going mushugga again. Would I ever get her out of my mind?

The same scene greeted us at Mt. Vernon Frisch's, so we headed back to the Gypsy Inn and more beer. By midnight we were feeling no pain and while engaged in a game of pool some drunk kept bumping into George while he was shooting. The first time it happened George just ignored it, but the second time this guy with a big beer belly nudged him, George asked the cat to please watch where he was going. Beer belly, with a cigarette dangling from his lower lip, looked George up and down and being about a head taller than George said, "Fuck you, buddy." Now that was the wrong thing to say. I knew it and George knew it, but it was for sure old beer belly didn't. Baker reached up and took the cigarette from beer belly's mouth and began grinding it out in his hand. I knew what was coming next, so I got a firm grip on my pool cue in case things got out of hand. Old beer belly started to say something while he balled his fists, but George hit him with a right to the stomach and before beer belly could double over, George caught him with a left to the chin. The big lummox collapsed on the spot, his legs buckling under him. We heard tables and chairs moving in the back of the bar and some guys were getting up, so without finishing our beer we cut out. Not bad for a kid that was only a year older than me and just under six feet. The summer was sure starting off with a bang.

Sunday, for the first time, I took the Crosley to the drag strip and pulled trophy, being the only car in H/Modified Sports Car. All I had to do was make one qualifying run and one trophy run to win. That night I called Laine and made a date for next Friday night, telling her that we were going to hear a new rock & roll band. She wanted to know more, but I said it would have to be a surprise. If I told her the truth she might not want to go. We were going to take in the Drift Inn, a bar with a dance floor that would be featuring the Keynotes.

Bobbi came home from college that week and before I could even ask, told me that I could not, as in never, borrow the Vette. I didn't offer any argument. I mean how could a sixteen year old with two cars complain.

After picking Laine up for our date, we decided to stop for a coke because it was too early to go to the bar. BB was taking curb service in the old '35 at the rear of Carters' lot and we joined him.

"Long time no see," I said, climbing in the back seat behind Laine.

"Man, you leave the doors unlocked in this neighborhood and there's no tellin' what might crawl in, and I wasn't referring to this lovely young lady," BB laughed.

"It's good to see you too, Bart, and I'd like to introduce you to this `lovely young lady', but ladies don't usually want to meet lowly flathead cats," I said, getting my put down in.

"Well, this lady does. Hi, I'm Laine, Laine Horwitz and are you two always like this?"

"Only when—"

"Shhh, listen. Turn the radio on," Laine said, before I could finish speaking. A car had pulled in next to us, its radio playing:

"If you knew Peggy Sue
then you'd know why I feel blue
about Peggy, 'Bout my Peggy Sue hoo hoo...."

"There ain't no radio," BB said.

"No radio? What kind of car is this?" Laine cried.

"What do you expect from a flathead—"

"Shhh, then be quiet. I want to hear the song," Laine cut me off again. When the tribute to Peggy Sue was finally over, I asked, "Why is that song so important?"

"I just love Buddy Holly. I'd do anything for him."

"Well, tonight you're going to hear a cat that's better than Buddy Holly," I said, with an air of authority.

"You two going to the Drift Inn tonight?" BB asked.

"Yeah. You goin'?"

"I don't know. I'm going to stop by Janice's and see what she wants to do."

"Hey man, I've been meaning to tell ya—the other day I jerked a flathead with the Crosley. Tore him a new you know what," I proudly exclaimed.

"That might be, but you'll never jerk my '49."

"At least mine can make it to the end of the quarter."

"Hey you two, stop this constant banter and tell me about the Drift Inn. What is it? Some kind of joint?" Laine interjected.

"Joint would be nice, but let's not judge a book by its cover," I said, trying not to laugh. And then trying to change the subject, I asked BB, "How'd night school go? Are you gonna make it?"

"Yeah, no sweat, but it's going to be a long haul. By the way, are you done with those drill bits you borrowed?"

"Oh yeah, I forgot. I'll bring them over tomorrow. Now I know you don't want to hear this, but since I bored the carb out it runs better than it ever did. It really screams, man."

"Crazy, man. Now I suppose you think you're an engineer?"

"Well—anytime you need a little technical help I'll be glad to assist."

"You cocky little punk. I'd give you an engineering job alright, if this young lady wasn't here. Now why don't you be a good little boy and put an egg in your shoe and beat it."

We got to the Drift Inn while there was still enough light to see the run down conditions of the old neighborhood. I saw some of the guy's cars and felt secure that at least we weren't alone. Laine made me come around and hold the door for her and as she climbed out, I couldn't help noticing the side of her bra covered cabongo through the opening in her sleeveless blouse. Man, I'd bet they'd taste good I thought, feeling a little touch of lack-a- nookie coming on.

Upon entering the dimly lit dance hall we were at once accosted by the bouncer, wanting to see our IDs. Pushing Laine ahead of me, I said to him, "We're with the band, man."

He blocked our way saying, "Where's your instruments, fellah?" Continuing to push Laine ahead, I became miffed responding, "She sings. Now where's our table! Please."

It worked. We went over to the corner table, near the tiny platform that served as a stage and sat down next to Sharon, Frank's girl. The place was even worse than I had imagined with its old scarred wood tables and chairs surrounding a little empty space of linoleum they called a dance floor. The walls had plaster patches on them and the ceiling had pipes and wires running all over the place. The few customers scattered around the joint emulated the place nicely, band table excepted.

Little Mike, playing the guitar, was just beginning to belt out "Tough Enough Baby" , while Isky strummed his stand up bass, Jack blew the sax and Frank squeezed the accordion. Laine leaned over and said in amazement, "The guy that's singing is in my English class. His name's Mike something."

"Yeah, and the chick sitting next to you, Sharon, also

goes to Woodward. Do you know her?"

"No. I didn't know he did this. He's really good!"

"See, I told you this would be better than Buddy Holly."
She gave me a look like, man, what did I know.

When the band took its break we were almost worn out
from dancing and the excitement of being a part of the action. At
the intermission, Laine went over to Little Mike and they talked
and laughed, about school and stuff, I guess. I hoped anyway.
She came back to me and said that Mike was going to dedicate
the next song to us. She was really having a good time—the sloe
gin fizzes we were drinking didn't hurt either. I wasn't having
such a bad time myself, really beginning to like this chick. She
fit in so well no matter what we did or where we went.

Back on stage Mike announced that the next song was
being dedicated to, he almost said classmates, which would
have given away our ages, but caught himself in time to say,
"That good lookin' blond in the corner with ole what's his name."
It got a little laugh as he began to sing the Monotones big hit:
"Book of Love".

Laine and I got up and slow danced, so close that half
way through the song I clasped my hands in the small of her
back and she put her arms around my neck. I thought about
reaching down and holding on to her buns, like some of the other
cats were doing with their chicks, but was afraid she might not
like it. As Mike crooned I tried to envision if our dating could
become a book of love and when I could begin chapter one by
telling her I loved her. When the music stopped, we were still
standing pressed to each other. Little Mike said, over the
microphone, "Alright you two, the music is over." Laine turned
red, but I thought it was cool.

"If this isn't any fun maybe you'd rather go out in the car
and listen for Buddy Holly songs on the radio," I teased Laine as
we sat down. She got a little grin on her face and then reached
over, grabbed my shirt and pulled me closer, kissing me softly
on the lips.

It was after eleven before I could finally tear her away
from the place. She had to be home by twelve-thirty and that
didn't leave us much time to make out, assuming of course, she
would.

I headed across town with Laine sitting right next to me,
my arm around her, driving with my left hand. Maybe these
automatic transmissions weren't so bad after all. We didn't talk

much, being content just to listen to the rock & roll on the radio and snuggle. I heard the DJ say it was eleven-thirty as we pulled into Roselawn Park, stopping in one of the unlit areas. Shit, less than an hour, I thought, switching the key from on to accessory, and all in the same move, putting my left arm around her, searching for her lips with mine. We kissed and hugged, as I planned my next move, in order to rearrange my cock which had started to become hard in an uncomfortable position. The slight break allowed Laine to begin a protest.

"Paul, we really shouldn't be doing this. This is only our second date. Can't we just talk?"

"I don't want to talk, I want—" She put her hand on my arm to stop me, as I recognized the deep velvet tones of the Monotones coming over the car radio as they started in on chapter one of what was sure to be "our song".

We listened, looking into each others eyes, hearts pounding, knowing that this was truly meant for us alone.

Before the song ended we were back in an embrace and this time I slid my hand from her back, around her side and onto her firm, hand sized breast. She didn't panic or anything, but she did push at my hand with her elbow before breaking and saying in a whisper, "Paul, please don't."

Don't!! Shit, she must be kidding. Don't is a word that ain't in the vocabulary of a sixteen-year-old with two cars, a drivers license, and a chick on his arm! I pulled her to me, but she turned her head and began telling me, "Oh, Paul. I want it to be so right. I've liked you for a long time, and I don't want to spoil it. Can't we just kiss? Please, I want you to respect me I want to be friends with you a long time."

I took a deep breath, "Elaine, I really like you and I don't know, I just can't help it, and what do you mean you've liked me for a long time? We only just met a few months ago, didn't we?"

"Well yeah, but I've watched you and wanted to go out with you since the first time I saw you."

"Yeah, when was that?" I asked, my ego soaring.

"Oh, it was long ago, way back at the beginning of school. You were just standing in the hall, talking to that shop teacher, and I don't know, you just looked neat. Like you were all grown up and talking to Mr. what's his name like you were equals, or something."

"Yeah! Mr. Herne is pretty cool," I said, trying to put the make on her again. She resisted only long enough to say, ""We haven't even gotten to chapter one yet."

I didn't get to cop much of a feel, but it was still nice. After a long good-by at her door, I headed for Jew Frisch's to try to find Jimmy. The place was packed as usual and I joined a group of Sigma's to see if they had seen him. The only Phi Ep's I could see were in the back of the restaurant, and I couldn't get to them. Gerry, who I used to swim on the team with, told me he's seen Jimmy earlier, but he didn't know where he was now. I placed an order for a coke just as Jimmy walked in. He came over saying, "Hey man, I've been looking everywhere for you. I drove through Carters' and Silverton Frisch's and just all over. I've got to talk to ya."

"Well, here I am. So talk," I said.

"Not here. Meet me at Section and Farm Acres, Okay."

"But, I just ordered a coke, man."

"Fuck the coke, this is serious."

"Okay, Okay." And turning to Gerry said, "Ask the waitress to cancel the coke, will ya?"

Jimmy was already waiting for me at what used to be the lower fields of the old dairy farm. I got in his car saying, "Alright what's so damn important?"

"Well, you know that chick, Gail?" She told me she thinks she's pregnant. What the fuck am I gonna to do? I don't want to marry her. Maybe I can join the Navy," Jimmy cried, beginning to spill his guts.

"Slow down, man and first of all you don't join the Navy. If anything you join the Jewish Navy."

"If you mean the Coast Guard? That's what I meant."

"Check. Second, how could she be pregnant? The last time we talked you hadn't even gotten into her pants yet."

"Yeah, well truthfully we've been doing it for about a month now and she said she was supposed to start her period last week and didn't."

"Why you little fucker, you. Been slippin' it to her all along. Didn't you use a rubber?" I asked.

"Well, sometimes I did, but at least one of them broke. What am I gonna to do?" Jimmy pleaded.

"Look, the first thing is to find out if she is really knocked up. Girls sometimes are just late, you know."

"Yeah, I know, but what if—"

"If. If my aunt had balls she'd be my uncle. If, shimiff! Do you love her?"

"I don't know. I don't want to get married if that's what you mean."

"Has anybody else been shtupping her?"

"Hell no! I was the first. She hasn't even looked at another guy since I've been going with her."

"A real cocksman. They won't put you in jail for too long. What is she, fifteen or sixteen?" I joked.

"This isn't funny, prick. What about you and the blond chick you had a date with tonight?"

"Laine? She loves me, what else."

"You gonna get a little? I hope you do and you get her knocked up. Then we can be in the Coast Guard together."

"You putz. You'd wish that on your best friend? Now lets get real. The best thing for you to do is to find a doctor in the yellow pages and then after school pose as man and wife and get a test. Tell the doctor that you just moved here from some other city and you just want a test. It can't cost more than fifteen, twenty bucks. Right now we both need some sleep. Call me in the morning and we can work on this some more, Okay?"

"Yeah, I guess you're right. Thanks," Jimmy said, starting his engine.

Laine and I went to the strip Sunday in the '56. I got pulled on the first elimination run. She told me she thought she might be falling in love, and I told her that I was scared to fall in love. We talked a lot and I let her know what had happened with Kathy. She was very sympathetic. In fact, while I was pouring my heart out to her, she was running her fingers through my hair and kissing my neck—and all this in broad daylight with people standing around. It was a good line, I'd have to remember that. Maybe something good would come out of that affair after all.

I called Jimmy from Laine's when I took her home and he related that Gail had started her period this morning. He also told me he was going to find some salt peter and never go out with girls again, ever. I didn't believe him for a minute.

Laine and I saw each other every night, and some days too, the entire next week. We got into some pretty heavy petting which she enjoyed as much as I did. I thought I was going to get some the night I had her bra loose and her slacks open, but a cop drove up and shined a spot light into the car. She seemed real scared after that and told me she didn't want to have her first experience in the front seat of a car. She didn't think it was very funny when I said we could always get in the back seat.

AND THE BAD GIRL SAYS, "ITS GOT TO BE HARD—"

CIRCA 1957

CHAPTER 11

Monday...Summer school...Fuck...and was it ever hot in that old building. I didn't get to see Laine much because classes started early and I had a twenty-minute drive on top of that, so I had to get to bed earlier than usual. On a whim, I bought Laine the new song, "Oh, Boy!" by Buddy Holly and the Crickets, for which she couldn't thank me enough. I also bought "Book of Love" at the same time, but I didn't give it to her. During the third week of school Laine told me her mother was going to Chicago to visit her sister and since her father left for work before seven, I should come over before school. She said she'd leave the door open and I should just come in. I asked her if she was going to fix me breakfast and she said, "Something like that." Women, you can never get a straight answer from them. But, it was agreed that I would come over the next morning.

I parked on a side street near the apartment house and out of the neighbor's sight. I had the Monotones record with me as I knocked on the door which opened to my touch. I pushed the door open further and, not seeing anybody, called for Elaine. From somewhere in the apartment, I heard Laine say softly, "Close the door and come back the hall to the left."

A little nervous, I did as instructed and found myself in her bedroom. Laine was still in bed with the covers pulled up around her neck. Holding the record behind me I asked where her record player was. With a quizzical look, she nodded toward a pile of clothes in the corner. I put the record on, setting it on repeat and turned to face her. Her look of 'what's this all about' changed to a warm smile as soon as she recognized the song.

"Paul, do you love me?"

"It says so in the "Book of Love", Laine."

She propped herself up on one elbow and, threw off the covers, saying, "Well, hurry up and hop in."

Wow. She had a perfect body. I stared at her tits that stuck straight out, not all droopy like most of the broads in the girly magazines, and she had a patch of blond, real blond hair! I couldn't get my clothes off fast enough. By the time I was stripped, my pecker was standing up straight and ready for action. Crawling between the flowered sheets, Laine said, with eyes wide, "Wait, I want to look at you. I've never seen a real man before. I didn't know they got so big. The pictures in our health book don't look at all like that! Is it going to hurt? Oh Paul, I love you so much please don't hurt me."

"I love you, Elaine but, let's not talk now. I slid in and was already starting to worry that I might come before I ever got it in—or worse—it might go soft. We kissed. She started to breath hard and fast, but kept her legs together as I ran my hand over her entire body. Before the record began its second play she suddenly said, "Paul, we really shouldn't be doing this. What if I get pregnant? Don't you have something to put on?"

"No. You don't have to the first time. This is the first time, isn't it?"

"Yes, of course, what kind of a girl do you think I am, anyway?" I tugged at the pillow.

"Paul, will you still love me after you get what you want?"

My dick had gone soft and I was already late for school. Fuckin' women. You can't figure 'em.

"Ah Laine, you're just one big PT. Now my nuts hurt, and if I miss school today , then I'll only have one more day that I can miss. If I really get sick and have to skip two days, legally, I'll lose the whole year and no PT's worth that," I said, getting really pissed.

"What's a PT, and I'm sorry. I've just never done anything like this before."

"PT means prick teaser and I don't need that. My nuts already hurt."

"What do you mean by that"

"Well, if a man gets very excited and doesn't get his rocks off then he gets what they call, lover's nuts. Your balls hurt real bad. Like mine do right now."

"I'm sorry Paul, but I'm scared that you'll break up with me and not respect me when it's over. I love you so much."

"Oh baby, I love you now and I'll love you forever. Like the song says in chapter two,`We're never, gonna part' but, if you keep this shit up we will." It was time to go for broke. If she was just playing with me I wanted to find out now. I'd be the laughing stock of Jew Frisch's if she went around and told how she teased me so. Starting to get out of bed I continued, "Laine, I've got to go to school, but I'll be back tomorrow morning and if you really love me...have the door open. If you want to call it quits now that you've made a fool of me, then leave it locked, and I won't bother you again. It will break my heart, but I'll always love you."

I had really put myself into a corner. I mean I did dig this chick, but if she didn't put out, I would be forced to break up with her, which was better than being made a fool of, I thought. At any rate, I resisted the overpowering urge to call her, deciding to play the hand I had dealt myself.

Everything went as planned except that she had on PJ's and panties. Why a chick would have that stuff on knowing what's coming was beyond me. The big fellow had just started to throb when she started again, "Paul, do you love me? I mean really love me? I have to know. I'm giving you something I wouldn't give to anyone else. Oh Paul, I love you more than anything in the world. Paul, tell me we're doing the right thing," she pleaded, as she hugged me.

"Oh Laine, I love you more than anything else and this is the only way I can really show you. I'm not much good with words and stuff. I just love you, and only you."

She kept hugging me so tight that I had a hard time getting her clothes off. I sure didn't want to waste any time feeling her up when the real thing was staring me in the face. I rolled her on her back and went to put it in. Man, if the guys could see me now. It wouldn't go in! I shoved the big blunt tool hard against where I thought the opening should be. Shit! Now what's wrong. All sorts of thoughts flashed through my mind. Maybe I was too big; what if there's something I had to do first to a virgin? I knew girls were supposed to have a membrane or something that was supposed to break on the first time. What if I can't do it and I go soft and the guys find out? I could just hear them now as they taunted me "Auer can't do it, Auer can't—" I forced her legs apart with mine and took my hand, using my thumb as a guide I found the hole. It wasn't all wet like I thought it should be. I shoved hard hoping to get it in before she changed her mind or wanted to do that bullshit love talk again.

"Paul, Paul please don't hurt...OH!!"

It was in. I pushed hard as she clawed at my back. Wow! I started to come on the first stroke and raised up on my hands to look at my cock sliding in and out of her, man I was fucking a real pussy now. I glanced at her face and though her eyes were shut tight, I could see tears running down the side of her face. Why would anyone cry over something like this I wondered. Who cared?

It was over before I had time to even suck on her titties or anything. Shit, I've been able to prolong it more with my own hand. I didn't give a shit though, I'd done it! Jimmy didn't have anything on me now. Well, the blow job he said he got at Flo's, but...maybe....

I lay still, my breathing shallow and fast. I wanted to lay there forever.

"Paul, honey, is it over?"

Pushing myself back on my haunches to look at my first real live snatch, I felt like a real man.

"Why are you grinning? And what are you looking at?" Laine said, while trying to pull some covers over her.

"You're beautiful. I just want to look. Let's just lay here, and in a while, maybe we can do it again," I said, softly and sincerely, as I reached to caress one of her cazotskis.

"No. You've done enough. Now let me get up. There's stuff running out of me. I've got to go to the bathroom." I laid down next to her trying to suck on a tit while she struggled to put covers on us. It was futile. She just wanted to hug. After a while she asked, in a whisper, "Was this the first time for you too, Paul?"

"No," I lied.

"It wasn't??? Who have you done this with before?" She demanded incredulously.

"Hey, a gentleman doesn't talk about these things," I wisely protested. It was one of the smartest things I'd ever said. Now she was sure that I wouldn't ruin her reputation by blabbing our love story all over Frisch's, and it cemented the fact that I was very worldly and knew what I was doing.

Laine insisted that I skip school so she could fix a big breakfast for me. She seemed to really want to do that, like we were playing house or something. I gave her my Spiedel ID bracelet, with my name engraved on the outside and a place for a picture on the inside. I had just gotten it as a confirmation gift, and really didn't want to wear it because of all the machinery I was around. We were officially going steady, but that didn't earn me enough brownie points to get any more nookie, so we played 'old married couple'.

With her snuggling next to me on the couch after breakfast, I got an inkling of what wedded bliss might be.

"Paul? What are you going to do after school...I mean after college? Are you going to become a doctor or lawyer or something?" Laine asked with interest and sincerity.

"Hey, I don't even know what I'm going to be doing

tomorrow. I'll probably just end up working for my father's company. What I'd really like to do though is to build and race cars. There are some cats out on the west coast who are making really big money setting up some of the fastest machines in the country. I don't think I want to go to college; it's just `Harry-High-School' turned into `Joe College', if you dig what I'm saying. How, 'bout you? Are you going to go to college and start a career?"

"I guess I'll go to college, but I don't want to be tied to some job or profession all my life. I mean a job and career are fine, but it's no substitute for marriage, is it? At least that's the way Mrs. Simpkins, she's my Home Ec teacher, puts it. A girl just can't have a career and a family, it's just impossible. Who would take care of the children and who would cook the food, clean the house, do the laundry and all that stuff?"

"You mean all you want to do is get married and have a bunch of little rug rats?" I asked losing interest in the game. It had begun to rain and I hoped the windows in the '56 were closed.

"Well, I'd like to travel and do other stuff, but mostly I'd just like being married...to you and raising our kids. Wouldn't it be neat if we were married now and—"

"And could practice at making babies all day," I finished for her. "Let's, just pretend we're married and it's bed time," I continued, reaching for her thigh.

"Not now, Paul. You made me bleed and I it will hurt if we do it again. Besides, that's not what married people do all the time."

Could life be any better? All summer long it was an endless string of one or more of the following daily events: Sex with Laine (well maybe it was only once a week, alright a month...so it was only two more times the whole summer, but it was good), Coney Island, drag strip, beer at Shuster's, beer at the Gypsy Inn, Carters', Jew Frisch's, Silverton Frisch's, working on cars, drive- in movies, jam sessions, Moonlight Gardens, swimming, cutting grass and doubling with Jimmy, now dating a chick named Judy, who was always popping her gum which drove Laine bananas.

FEELS GOOD OUT TODAY. THINK I'LL LEAVE IT OUT.

CIRCA 1957

CHAPTER 12

The first day of school was met with mixed feelings. It would be good to mingle with old friends and see how some of the chicks had developed, but now that I was a Junior I couldn't take shop any more. My entire schedule was taken up with college prep courses that the school counselor had insisted I take.

I met Jimmy in the parking lot at Swifton, and we walked up the front circle together toward the usual groups of kids spouting the latest put downs. Before being surrounded by the throngs, I told Jimmy that we had to talk, I had problems. He suggested we meet on the ramp at lunch. We approached the first gang, all Phi Ep's, to hear. "Hey Auer, Cohen's lunch box is open." Laughter, as I looked around to see what was so funny. Somebody, noticing my confusion, said, "Your fly's open." More laughter as I looked down to see that it wasn't. I laughed with them as I offered my hand to the wise guy, saying, "Shake the hand that shook the king." He took my hand as I added, "Now shake the king," motioning toward my crotch. This time I got the laughter.

Somebody started telling a joke when the laughter subsided. "Hey, did you guys hear the one about the kid who's mother caught him jackin' off and told him if he didn't stop he'd go blind?...The kid then asked his mom if it would be okay to do it just until he needed glasses."

"That's a true story, isn't it Allen?" Much laughter.

"Ah, eat me man, I'm a jelly bean", the kid named Allen responded.

"Man, that's so old the first time I heard it I laughed so hard I kicked the slats out of my cradle."

"Hey you guys, no shit about this one; Ivan Bromowitz was caught wackin' off by his mom. Seems he fell asleep with his hand on his cock and his mom walked in on him."

"Isn't he the cat who could beat off ten times in an hour?"

"Naw that was—"

I drifted away toward the COS's and punched George in the arm, saying, "Hey, you big hood, you been taken ugly pills again."

"Your mother wears combat boots, Auer. What the fuck have you been up to?"

"Hey, I've got your combat boots hangin' right here, pussy." There was some playful fisti-cuffs and more of the same

121

friendly banter, in addition to the usual conversations about whose pants we'd like to get into, until the bell rang.

I found Laine in the front hall and walked her to her homeroom. We would only have one class together, but our lunch period was within ten minutes of each others, so we could spend some time together. That could also be bad if I wanted to talk to other chicks at lunch. Nothing's ever simple. Already I had problems, that's why I wanted to talk to Jimmy. Laine looked good, she always looked good. Today she had on a sleeveless blouse that I could practically see through, a big wide belt and a skirt that hugged her nice firm ass. The sight of her aroused feelings of desire that I had to suppress lest I get a stiff one while standing in the hall.

"Hi, honey. Where have you been? I've been waiting, like hours for you," she said, as I approached.

"Hi good lookin'. I was outside looking for you," I half lied.

We both laughed.

"Honey, walk me to my room, will ya?"

Taking her hand and starting down one of the almost three miles of halls I said, "Okay, but please don't call me 'honey'. You know now I hate that. It sounds so cheap."

"Alright already. I think it's so neat that we have English together, and we'll also get to see each other at lunch. Will you take me to Pasquale's after school, before we go home?"

"Well, I guess."

"What do you mean, you guess? Don't you want to. I mean we are going steady, aren't we?" Laine began to whine.

"Yeah sure, but—"

"But, what? After school is the only time we can have together. You know I won't be able to go out on school nights. Don't you want to be with me after school, Paul honey? Oh, I'm sorry I didn't mean to call you honey. It's just that I love you so much and Paul is such a formal name. Forgive me?"

"The bells gonna ring. See ya in English," I said, leaning to get a kiss.

"No, Paul. You know I don't go for PDA and besides there's a teacher standing over there."

"Okay, Okay. No public display of affection, but no 'honey' either."

After a quick lunch alone I found Jimmy with a group of guys on the ramp, having a smoke and a good laugh. Naturally

I had to ask what was so funny. Louie explained, "I was just asking Cohen here if he had ever tasted a sweeter dick than mine and he won't answer. Can you beat that?"

"I could beat it if I could find it," I retorted motioning for Jimmy to follow me to a quieter place. Goldstein gave me the finger amid the laughter as Jimmy followed me.

"Hey gimme a weed man. I left mine in the car."

Handing me his fliptop pack of Marlboros, Jimmy said, "So what's so fuckin' important, dad?"

"Dad? Listen daddy-o, the least you could do is have some Luckys or Camels for me to smoke. These fuckin' filters are like suckin' a tittie through a night gown."

"All you wanted is to put down my fags?"

"No man. I got trouble with this chick, Elaine. Like man she's getting too possessive. She wants to be with me every damn minute of the day. And not only that she's already talking like we're gonna get married."

"See I told you. You get her cherry and she'll love you forever, you dumb fuck," Jimmy expounded his wisdom.

"Yeah, I know, I know, but I'm not ready to talk marriage and shit. I mean she has it all figured out how we would have kids and she'd quit school and all that shit, man. I don't want to lose her or anything. It's just that I need a little freedom. Tell me what the fuck I should do."

"Yeah, well the first thing is to be sure you wear a rubber. You're not going bareback are you?"

"Well, sometimes, but that's the other problem. She's starting to cut my water off; says we should wait till we're married. Can you believe that shit! Married! Shit all I want is to get a little pussy once in a while and right away she wants to have kids and get hitched. Fuckin' women."

"Well, the best thing to do," Jimmy said, "Is to just play along with her. It takes two to get married and if you wear protection then she can't get pregnant. You keep tellin' her you love her and all that shit, and if she still cuts your water off, then fuck it, man. You can find another chick. But, she'll always love you and you can always go back if you play your cards right, if you catch my drift."

"Yeah, maybe you're right, but I don't want to hurt her. I really do like this chick and I wouldn't mind being married to her in a few years, I think. Make that a whole lot of years, but there's other chicks I'd like to date too."

Jimmy started toward the door saying, "I've got to get to class. What are you gonna do after school?"

"Fuck, I don't know, she wants me to spend everyday after school with her. Hey, you didn't tell me about that Judy what's her name, the one from Walnut HIlls. How're ya doin' with her?"

"Like later man, I've got to get."

Man, it was like being married. Every day after school that week Elaine and I, and sometimes some of her sorority sisters, went to Pasquale's or the record store, where we could hear the latest 45's in the little booths. I'd always end up taking her home where we'd park in the back of the apartment house and talk and maybe snoof a little, but no petting, for fear of being seen. I told her that Sunday was the regional meet at Beechmont and I was going to race the Crosley where I was sure to get one of the big, class winners trophies. She only agreed to go when I told her that George was taking a date.

Sunday, when I came to pick her up, her father, still in his robe, came down to look at the car I had "made". I don't think it was quite what he had expected saying, "You be careful with my little girl, in this contraptions. She's the only one I've got, young man." He said something else which I didn't hear as I started the engine while Laine climbed in. I was in a hurry to peal out before he or anyone, changed their mind.

No sooner than we were settled in the pit than Isky called for me, over the loud speaker, to come to the timing stand. We walked over while Isky continued to "test" the PA by commenting that cats who race sports cars can't be all bad if they have such fine lookin' chicks. Laine ate it up. Once up in the tower Isky told me, "Man, we're short handed today, so you'll have to work the pit gate."

"Ah, man. Who's going to protect this fine lookin' young thing while I'm on the gate?"

"Why you can just leave her with ole Isky."

"Hey, I wouldn't trust you with my dog," I said, continuing the jesting.

"You don't have a dog, man."

"Now you get the picture."

"Okay, I'll tell you what. The cat from the Enquirer is going to be here to take pictures for the paper and I'll set it up so Laine is the one to hand out the trophies to the winners. They'll probably take her picture for the paper and all that stuff."

I looked at Laine. She was shaking her head up and down with a big smile on her face.

"Man, you got me over a barrel, but I didn't bring my SOTA arm—"

"No sweat, we've got plenty. Now get to work and leave me alone with this sweet young thing," Isky smiled, putting his arm around Laine.

Climbing down the ladder I got the last put down in, "Just remember, ole buddy, what ever you'll be doing to my chick up there, I'll be doing to your rod in the pit, ya dig?"

George and his brother, Abee, driving their D/Gas, '52 Olds got there just in time for the final qualifications. I only had a minute to talk to him, as he passed through the pit gate, "Hey man, how come you're so late?"

"We forgot it was Mom's birthday and we'd promised to take her to church this morning."

"What about your date? I thought you were bringing that little red head?"

"Fuck her. She stood me up. We went by her house and there wasn't anyone there, fuckin' cunt," George swore.

The Regionals were a big success. Isky pulled the C/gas trophy in his '32, the one with the Caddy engine that he had built in my garage. The Bakers lost in elimination, BB never showed up, confirming rumors that he had given up racing, and I got trophy for H/Modified Sports Car. Elaine had her picture taken with each trophy handed out and realized the strip wasn't such an awful place after all. The bad news was that the oil pump failed on the Crosley's final run and the engine seized. Benny's '56 was once again the club's tow truck as he was my only way home.

At school Monday, Laine was the center of attention, her picture having been on the front page of the sports section. Life was good, perfect, except for the locked up engine, no funds to rebuild it with and my continually slipping grades. Tuesday I gave a chick in my American History class a ride home and Laine saw me. She threw the ID bracelet at me when I saw her the next day at school. I didn't want to break up with her, but it seemed that every time we were alone and I tried to just feel her up she'd stop me and we'd end up arguing.

Thursday my parents told me that they thought that I'd been running wild and they were restricting my activities until my grades came up. This came down to no more going out on school nights and no working on the car after dinner. Jimmy was no help as he was having the same kind of troubles, only his parents promised him a Corvette if he brought his grades up. His latest chick, Judy, had also broken up with him. How could everything turn to shit in such a short time, and through no real fault of my own?

Laine didn't speak to me for the rest of the week, but then out of the blue the following Wednesday she came up to me in the front hall, "The new TV season starts tonight. Do you want to come over? Ricky Nelson is going to sing on the "Ozzie and Harriet Show" and "Armstrong Circle Theater" is having a special about juvenile delinquents."   "Are your parents going to be home?"

"Yes. Does it make a difference?"

"No." I lied.

"Okay, be over before eight-thirty. There's the bell. I better go to class.

"Can I carry your books," I said, trying to suck back in.

"Sure." But she said it like she didn't care if I did.

We walked down the hall without holding hands, and when we got to her room I leaned over for a kiss.

"Now Paul, you know—"

"Yeah, but I don't even get any PRIVATE display of affection anymore."

"Well, it's not my fault. See ya." She turned and walked into the room without even a backward glance. Shit, maybe Jimmy was wrong about this cherry business.

I knew I would get in trouble by defying my parents, but I had to find out if she still loved me or was just playing a game. We watched Ricky Nelson, or rather I watched, and Laine swooned. Then we saw some murder mystery on "Kraft Theater", followed by the program about JD's which made me feel a little uncomfortable. But, before it was over we walked to my car to talk.

"Laine, I'm sorry about taking that girl home, she was only a friend, and I do really dig you. Will you ever forgive me?" I whined.

"Oh sure, Paul, there's nothing to forgive," she said, with total detachment.

"There's a Phi Rho dance coming up Saturday a-week, will you go with me?"

"Well Paul, that's so far in advance, I just don't know."

"Okay, how 'bout this Saturday night. We could go to a movie or something. I think "Cat on a Hot Tin Roof" is playing at the Albee?"

"I can't. There's a sorority slumber party, and I told the girls I'd be there."

I grabbed her and put a lip lock on her. She didn't respond. Fuckin'; women. She was as cold as ice—dry ice. Every time I touched her I got burned.

The old man was waiting for me when I got home. All he said was that I was grounded until the report cards came out and then he'd decide what was what. Things weren't going well at all. I needed time to think, and having to go to school in the morning only made matters worse. I wished Willie was here so I could talk to him or have him talk to Mom and Dad. The rest of the week was no fun even though Laine seemed to have warmed up a little now that I was spending my lunch hour with her and taking her home after school everyday again. Because I was grounded, I couldn't take her out Friday night so I used the time then, and on Saturday, to tear down the Crosley engine. It wasn't so bad. Only one journal was scored. It would probably cost me a few weeks allowance, which I didn't have, to get the crank ground and buy a new bearing, but I was sure Mom would lend me the money. The following week the report cards came out and I knew I was in big trouble. Now I wouldn't be allowed to take Elaine to the Phi Rho dance, even after I'd practically promised my future away to get her to agree to go with me.

Taking the report card home made the grounding official. In addition, I had to come home every day right after school, no more taking Laine home or going to Pasquale's. It was unfair. What the fuck does the school—or for that matter parents— know. A man can't race and build cars, go steady with a chick, be cool and study too. It's just too much to ask. I thought of running away, but I was broke.

Friday morning I found Jimmy and George in the front hall bitchin' about their grades. I joined them and we all commiserated together, finally hitting on the idea that skipping school was the thing to do for the moment. It felt good to be telling our friends how they were such suckers to be going to school on this beautiful day, as we strutted out of the building and down the front circle. We decided to take Jimmy's convertible in case it got hot enough to put the top down. George said he had met a chick at a church revival his mother had made him go to, who lived in Lexington. He knew her name and where she went to school but that was all. Maybe this chick had some girl friends and we could all score. It was decided to head south.

We filled up at Kaufman's Cities Service in Roselawn where, Jimmy's dad had a charge, and got a map of Kentucky. It took us almost two hours to get to Lexington and another hour just to find the high school, having to stop and ask directions a few times. Luck was with us as we found the chick George knew at the first class break. While he was reintroducing himself, Jimmy and I walked over to two cute chicks standing by their lockers. Jimmy broke the ice, saying to the one with a pony tail, "Hi, my name's Charlie and this is my brother Billy and we're new here. Is this a cool school, baby?"

"Yes. I guess so," she giggled.

"Do you like to dance?" Jimmy said, continuing to press.

"Yes."

"Are you going steady?"

"No."

"Let's fuck." Her mouth dropped open, she looked at her friend, then, Wham! She landed a glancing blow to the side of his head and then rushed off.

"What'd you say that for, schmuck?" I demanded.

"Well, we don't have a lot of time for small talk. Besides I heard about this guy who always says that to new chicks he meets."

"Yeah, so?"

"So, he get his face slapped a lot, but he also gets laid a lot."

Meanwhile George had started down the hall motioning for us to follow. We fell in behind as he led us into a class room, taking seats in the rear. As soon as class started, Jimmy, with one hand cupped behind his ear, shouted in my direction, "What'd you say, man?" Taking the cue, we completed the banana in the ear routine to the delight of the whole class. As the class calmed down, the teacher took charge. "Who are you and what are you doing in my class?"

I stood, saying, "I'm Billy, this is my brother Charlie, and that's Albert over there. We just transferred in here from Louisville, baby." I got a lot of snickers with the word baby.

"Well! Where are your admittance papers young man," she demanded, obviously flustered.

This time Jimmy stood and, in his best hillbilly accent said, "Sugar, we here ain't got no ad-mittance yet."

"Well! You three just march yourselves right down to the office and get them."

"Shucks, Honey, we ain't never learned how to march and besides we kinda like it here."

The class was now totally out of control with kids standing in the aisles to get a better look at us and laughing out loud. The Teacher, who must have been at least sixty, tried to speak again but finally gave up and walked out the door. As if on cue, George now stood, walked to the front of the class, raising both hands high to call for order. Everyone's attention was riveted on this intruder as he waited for total silence before slowly saying, "I think it is time for my brothers and I to ...make like a hockey player ...and get the puck outta here." We beat it to the door to the sound of more laughter, dragging George with us as he began singing the Woodward fight song.

"Hail to Woodward, cheer for Woodward High,
Proudly wave our banner to the sky,
We have the spirit...."

We didn't stop until we hit the first little restaurant in Paris. It was a welcome break to relax, only George became pissed when he realized that he hadn't had time to get his chick's phone number. We assured him that we didn't think she would want anything to do with him after our little Cincinnati style humor. It only made him madder. The ptomaine parlor was so sleazy looking that we all had what we believed to be the safest thing on any menu, grilled cheese and a coke. To appease George, and let him take out his frustrations, Jimmy let him drive.

Taking U.S. 27 North, which was better road than U.S. 25, and with George driving we were making good time roaring through one little burg after another. Coming out of Cynthiana we hit a stretch of three lane road. George decided it was time to see what the big Imp would do, pushing the needle to over a hundred, windows open and the canvas top ballooning high over their struts. No sooner had we pulled to a stop in the next town than a cop pulled next to us. We had never seen him. He leaned over, rolled down his passenger window, motioning for George to do the same. The cop car was a 1957 Chev with no markings and the unmistakable sound of a two-seventy engine loping under the hood. "Say boys," the cop began in a slow southern drawl. "Ya'll goin'a mite fast back there weren't ya?"

George didn't know what to say. Nobody did. The cop continued, "Now I'll tell ya what I want 'chew to do. Ya'll just turn that there machine around here and follor me back to the Court House. I rightly believe the Judge jest might want to have a talk with ya'll. Ya hear?"

George acknowledged the command as politely as possible, and we began the trip back to Cynthiana. Following the cop, we ran through our options. We could try to out run him by turning off at the next intersection, claim one of us was sick and we were trying to get to a hospital, or claim the gas pedal stuck. As the miles rolled by, we realized that anything we tried would be just plain dumb.

The Court House, and its inhabitants, were right off a "Saturday Evening Post" cover. It looked like Norman Rockwell had made the whole thing, with its giant stone construction, dark woodwork and big white, globe-shaped light fixtures that hung from the high ceilings. The clerk and bailiff were both rosy cheeked and bright eyed, one wearing bib overalls, the other a short vest over his huge belly. The Judge looked like a hold-over from the "Grapes of Wrath", with his fat unshaven face, a cigar in the corner of his mouth and big wide suspenders stretched over an ivory colored under shirt which partially covered his hairy chest. As the officer ushered us into the court room, a middle aged woman hurriedly got down from the Judge's bench where she had been sitting and walked out the back door, straightening her skirt as she went. The officer spoke as the Judge swiveled around in his high back chair to face us, "Yer Honor, these here boys was ah goin' faster than the duly posted legal speed limit."

"How fast were they going, Ernie?" The Judge asked.

"Don't rightly know, yer Honor, but I was ah goin' a mite over ah hundred and twenty and I was ah barely catchin' 'em. Had to chase 'em plum to the light at the County Road."

"How old are you boys and why aren't you in school?" Demanded the Judge.

"We're all about sixteen, sir, and we didn't have school today, George volunteered.

"No school? Where in tarnation do you go to school. This ain't no holly-day, is it?"

"No sir. We're from Cincinnati and it's a teacher's day."

He bought it. So far so good.

"Well, if you want to plead guilty and pay the clerk a hundred dollars you can drive real slow outta here."

We huddled only to discover that all we had between us was twenty two dollars and change. George, now the official spokesman stepped forward, "Your Honor, all we have is twenty dollars between us, but if you'll let us go we'll send the rest of it as soon as we get home, honest."

"No, that won't do. Do you have a driver's license, son?"

"Yes sir," George said, producing his permit.

"Ernie, was this the boy who was driving?" the Judge asked, taking the license from George.

"Yes sir, your Honor," replied Officer Ernie.

The Judge removed the cigar from his mouth, belched and, still studying the piece of paper in his hand, said, "George Baker, eh. Well Mr. Baker, I'm going to keep this here license and this Court will expect you back here, with your parents, on Monday morning at ten o'clock sharp, to answer to the charges against you. And you better bring a hundred dollars. Now is that clear?"

"Yes sir!"

"Okay. Now Ernie I want you to escort these young boys to the town limit, and I also want you to radio ahead to the State Police post that they're coming through."

Having to drive the speed limit got us back to Cincinnati just before four. We decided to stop at Laine's to see if she knew whether we had been found out for skipping. I went up alone and as soon as Laine saw me she threw her arms around my neck hugging me tight and telling me how glad she was that I was okay. When she finally backed off enough to catch her breath, I learned that her parents were not home so I went to the window over looking the driveway and yelled for the other guys to come up. She threw her arms around me again, telling me that she had heard on the radio after school of an auto accident involving some kids who had cut school.

"Oh Paul, I don't know what I would have done if it had been you. I was just worried sick. Hold me and tell me you still love me."

I wished the other guys weren't coming up the stairs. Damn, bad timing, I thought, as I told Laine I loved her. We were still embracing when Jimmy and George walked in.

"Alright you two love birds, break it up." Jimmy said.

"Well, did we get caught," George insisted.

"Oh, I'm sure you will be. It was all over school that you guys skipped. What's going to happen to you?"

"Shit, they'll probably kick us out for three days, and I'll never see that Corvette," Jimmy moaned.

"Man, the only thing that will save me is the football team, I hope," George said, a look of anguish on his face.

Laine looked at me, wondering my fate. I couldn't say anything. The thought of being grounded for life just when she was coming back to me was too much. Nobody spoke for a few moments until Laine, in her usual happy-go-lucky voice said, "Hey, you know that Sharon, the one who was at the Drift Inn that night?" and without waiting for an answer, "Well, she quit school today. She told me she's pregnant and is going to marry that Frank fellah, the one who plays in the band." Nobody was in the mood to hear somebody else's good news, but Laine continued anyway, "She's already showing, but she said that Frank works for his father in some kind of business and they're going to live in the Swifton Apartments. It's so romantic isn't it, Paul?"

I didn't want to go home yet; it was time to put some kind of plan into action. "Say Elaine," I began, "can you go out tonight. I don't feel like being alone."

"Yeah, sure, but do you think you'll be allowed after today? I thought you were grounded anyway."

"Well, I'm just not going to go home, at least not until they're all asleep. What I want to do is wash up here and then have Jimmy drop me at my car, come back here and pick you up, then maybe get something to eat at Carters' or Frisch's. I hope you have some money, I'm getting a little low."

"That's okay with me, but why don't you stay here for dinner, and then we can go out if you want. My mom would love to have you, I'm sure."

"Okay. What time is your mom coming home? Do I have time to get my car first, or should I clean up now?"

"She's shopping and won't be home for at least another hour. Let me get a coat and I'll go with you." The big delicious meal after such a heavy day lulled me into a false sense of complacency. I was so sure of myself that I even told Laine, and in front of her mother yet, that I would pick her up for the frat dance tomorrow around eight-thirty. I was convinced that I would be allowed to go as Mom had hinted that I might get a reprieve from my punishment for this dance. We left the apartment after watching "Death Valley Days" on TV, and just rode around for a while, ending up in Robinson Park in Pee Ridge.

We made out some and talked some, but I was starting to feel the strain of the days events, which I had to relate to her. After a half hour or so of this on again off again snoofing, I was able to get her bra unsnapped with one hand, a feat that prompted the question of how I learned to do it. I didn't tell her that I had studied one of my sister's bras to learn how the hooks worked a long time ago. I was getting pretty horny, but every time I would slide my hand between her legs she would push it away. I was slowly getting pissed. I mean if this chick really loved me why all the hassle? Finally, I whispered, "Laine, baby, I love you and I need you. Please. I want you and I want to touch you and love you. Loosen you pants, please."

"Oh Paul, I don't want to. What if something happens?"

"Nothings going to happen. What could happen? We love each other and that's all that should matter."

"I mean what if a cop comes or something?"

"Cops don't come to this park," I said, with authority.

She unzipped her slacks. I probed her with my finger. She began to breath hard as I raised her sweater to kiss and suck her now bra-less breasts. I pushed her slacks down further and whispered, probing deeper with my finger, "Lets get in the back seat.

"No, Paul, please let's not."

"Come on, Laine. What's the difference, my finger or me? I need you now. Everything else is crashing down around me. I love you Elaine."

"Paul, what happens if I get pregnant? Will you marry me, like Sharon and Frank?"

"Oh, you know I would, Laine. I love you more that anything, I wouldn't let anything happen to you, I'll always be here, I whispered as I nuzzled her neck."

"Oh, Paul, I...part of me wants to and part of me doesn't. Can't we just do this?"

"Oh, please Laine, I've got to."

"No! Now let's stop right now," she said, sitting up straighter and pushing my hands away.

"You don't really love me do you? You're just using me

for your own pleasure aren't you? You're kicking me when I'm down."

"Oh Paul, I'm sorry, I just don't know what to do."

"Well, I'll tell you what not to do," I said, pulling away from her and starting to get pissed again. "You can stop all this PT shit. I can't take it. Now we haven't done it in a long time, and tonight I need it. It's not like that's all I take you out for." My cock had started to get soft. It was now or never. I roughly pulled her to me an kissed her hard on the lips while pushing her pants all the way down. She resisted again saying, "Paul, I don't want to."

"Come on Laine I have to, now take off those damn pants."

She didn't move. I started to slink away almost whining I said, "Please, just this once."

"Oh alright, but hurry up in case someone comes."

She said it matter-of-factly, like she was doing me such a big favor. Well maybe she was. My dick was only half hard and she wasn't responding at all. She just lay there with one leg over the edge of the front seat and her head wedged between the arm rest and the back of the seat. In too short a time, I knew I wasn't going to get my rocks off. I tried until I became exhausted from the effort and the day's events, finally collapsing on top of her, the smell of our sex filling the inside of the steamed windows.

"Well, are you done?" she broke the silence.

"Yeah."

"Did you?" Too tired to answer, I slowly raised up and struggled to pull my school slacks up. I hooked her bra for her as she wriggled back into her slacks. As I started the engine, I said, "I like the way you smell."

"Why thank you, Paul. It's Windsong."

I gave her a little shit eating grin. She thought for a moment, flushed, and said, "That's disgusting, Paul. I thought you meant my perfume."

"Well, it is your smell and all I said—"

"I know what you said," Laine emphatically stated as she rolled down her window.

"And in answer to your question, no, I didn't, thanks to you. A man's not like a girl. He just can't do it by just opening up his legs. It takes stimulation. Next time we're not going to argue about it."

"What makes you think there's going to be a next time?"

"If we get married, then there'll be a next time for sure."

It might have been a draw, but I got the last word in anyway.

She didn't want to go to Frisch's for fear that some of her friends might see her and guess what we'd been up to, so we stopped at Carters' and had a coke with Benny and Carole. They hadn't heard about Sharon and Frank, so Laine filled them in. It was almost midnight when I dropped Elaine off and headed for home.

I didn't know what to expect when I got home, but everything was just as I left it in the garage. There were no notes on the bulletin board, in the kitchen or in my room. Maybe things would be okay after all. I lay in bed too tired to sleep, thinking how everything had a good side and a bad side: I pull trophy at the strip, but blow the engine; we have a great time in Lexington, but get caught; Laine lets me do it, but I can't. I longed for the times when I was a kid, the times with Willie when things only had good sides.

IT'S ALRIGHT, ONCE YOU GET PAST THE USED PART

CIRCA 1957

Saturday morning I slept until after ten. After a quick shower and a long time holding hot compresses on a new pimple I went down to an empty kitchen where I found cinnamon bread in the bread box for some toast and some fresh squeezed orange juice in the ice box. I was starting to feel pretty good, maybe things were going to be alright. The old man had obviously left for the plant, and Mom was somewhere upstairs, probably making the beds, for I could hear someone up there moving around. The day was cloudy, but it didn't look like rain so I decided to wash the '56 in preparation for the dance tonight.

Everything in the garage seemed to be just as I left it last night, including the keys in the ignition of both cars. Grabbing the big two bay garage door I gave a heave, but it didn't move. I heaved again. Sometimes it stuck. Still no yield. Looking for the problem didn't take long. A large chain and padlock was securely attached to the upper door and a support beam. The old man, who else. Now who does he think he is locking up my cars like this. Never mind that the titles are in his name, a mere technicality. I didn't have time to get pissed, I needed a plan. I could pack some clothes and call Jimmy. Naw. I could take my Mother's car. Naw, she'd get mad and he'd have me arrested. Shit, I'll just get the hack saw and cut the damn chain. Fuck 'em, I'll show them they can't cramp my style.

No sooner had I gotten the saw in place than Mom opened the door from the house, "Just what do you think you're doing, young man?"

"I'm taking my car out for a ride and you better not try to stop me." Man I was hot and getting hotter with every stroke of the blade.

"We'll see about that. Now put that tool down and come in the house at once," she demanded.

I kept sawing as she shut the door and went back into the house. I knew she was going to call the old man, but in a few minutes I would be on my way. The saw blade broke. Damn! It took forever to find another and it was a used one at that. Back sawing again I heard a car pull up in front of the garage. Shit, no doubt it's the old man, I thought, peering out the window. Worse—it was a cop car and the old man's Cadillac right behind it. I was trapped. Throwing the hack saw at the door in disgust, I sat on the trunk of the '56 to await a tongue lashing.

CIRCA 1957

Of all the cops, it had to be Sergeant Prince following my father into the garage. The old man picked up the hack saw, looked up to the chain and said, accusingly, "Look here officer, he's ruined the chain!"

Sergeant Prince examined the evidence, then slowly turned to me saying, "Looks like malicious destruction of property to me. Did you do this, son?"

"Yeah, so what. It's my saw, and it's my car."

"Whose cars are these, Mr. Auer?" the Sergeant asked.

"Both of them are mine, officer and Paul didn't have my permission to take them or cut my chain."

"Guess we can add Grand Theft Auto to the charges too. What do you want done, Mr. Auer?"

"Take him away."

I couldn't believe my ears. What is this shit? Didn't these guys know I had a date tonight, and I had things to do!

"Hey man, wait a minute I haven't—"

"Shut up kid and hold your hands out," the big cop said, producing a pair of handcuffs.

As the copper practically dragged me out of the garage, I caught a glimpse of my mother, who I was sure would come to my rescue. I looked at her with the most pitifully pleading eyes I could muster, expecting her to be wringing her hands with sorrow in her eyes. No soap. Even she was on their side. The look on her face was one of you-got-what-you-deserved as she stood with hands firmly planted on hips.

The police station was very new and modern with recessed florescent lights and all blond wood trim, including the big panel that held the radio speakers and various dials and switches. Without a word from anyone, I was placed in one of the contemporary chrome and canvas chairs right outside the Captain's office. The Sergeant went into Capt'n McDaniel's office, closing the door behind him. By the time I had cooled down and decided that surrender was better than confrontation the Captain had worked up a good head of steam. The door to his office slammed open, and he sorta bulled his way across the squad room, where he emphatically opened the front door. Then, without saying a word, he strode over to where I was sitting, removed the handcuffs, pulled his revolver from its holster, opened the cylinder to check if it was loaded and, with a with a deep authoritative voice, said, "You want to run, punk, well, go ahead, the door's open." I didn't move. I didn't even breathe. "Well, what are you waiting for?" he continued. "Go ahead and run. Because just as soon as you step out that door, I'm gonna fill your sorry ass full of holes, kiddo." Shit, this was big time. I wasn't gonna fuck with these guys. Besides my wrists hurt from the cuffs and I had to pee. There should have been heavy deep music droning in the background, like in a movie, but all I could hear was the reality of my breathing and the occasional crackle of the police radio. I had never seen the head cop like this before. I wondered what happened to the nice Capt'n who always brought Santa around on Christmas and had held me on his lap when I was a little kid. He must have gotten old and cynical. Surely it wasn't me who had changed!

Realizing that his prisoner wasn't going to make a dash for the open door, this officer in charge, turned to the Sergeant saying, "Take him to detention and if he tries to escape, shoot him!"

The cuffs went back on and I was again manhandled into the waiting squad car. I was close to tears, but I sure wasn't going to let them have the satisfaction of seeing me cry. On the way to 2020 Auburn Avenue, the detention center, the sergeant lightened up a bit, trying to talk to me like a father. "Son, if I may borrow a word from the Yiddish language, nobody goes through life without a little tsouris. Do you know the word? Do you know what I mean?"

"Yes sir, I'm sorry. What's going to happen to me now?"

"Well, I guess they'll lock you up and give you a hearing on Monday."

"Oh man, you mean they won't do it today?" I wailed still having hope that something could be salvaged from this black day.

"No, the Judge doesn't hold court on weekends. Why? I'll bet you had a date tonight didn't you?"

"Yeah, and she'll probably never speak to me again, now."

"Oh, she will if she's worth keeping. Does she live in the village?"

"No sir."

"Well then, I probably don't know her or her folks. But, I do know your parents and they are fine people, who only want to bring you up right. I know about your little brother, and maybe his loss somehow caused this to come to a head today. We cops aren't as dumb as some of you kids think we are. I know that you've been pretty much doing what you damn well please for a long time. Maybe your parents weren't as strict with you for fear of adding to your unhappiness over the loss of your brother. This has probably been a long time coming, and if I'm any judge of kids, I'll bet your grades aren't what they should be either."

"No sir, I'm not doing too good there."

"So now, after all this time of doing it your way, they're finding out it's not working, and now they're only trying to get you back on the right path."

"Yeah, well, they didn't have to have me arrested, did they?"

"Oh, this isn't like a real arrest. This is only Juvenile Court. Here they try to help you so you don't become a real criminal and end up in adult court later. This is more like your father asking his friend, the Captain, to do him a favor and help straighten you out."

We rode the rest of the way in silence, but just before the officer got out to come around and open the door for me, he said, "Paul, I'd like to give you a little advice that you can take anyway you want. It's been my experience that if you show remorse and make an honest effort to obey your parents, everything will work out alright. You've got your whole life before you and this is only one short period of it. I know you kids all have a hard time seeing beyond next week, but believe me, things are better if you learn to play by the rules."

He made a lot of sense, but I was still pissed and I don't believe I even thanked him when he left me. I had a lot of thinking to do. Things were confusing and I didn't know which way the merry- go-round was turning.

Welcoming me into the "Twenty-Twenty Club" was an older gentleman who almost apologetically told me I would have to be put in one of the solitary rooms because they were full up in the regular cells. The room was small, tiny compared to my room at home, with only a iron railed bed and a overhead light fixture with was covered with wire mesh. It wasn't like a real jail cell as it had a steel door with a small window instead of the customary bars. In fact the only bars at all were at the main entrance. The whole place was very quiet and subdued. I was glad to be alone where I could think out my problems.

At meal time I was ushered out of my cell and in to a large room where my fellow inmates and I were allowed to talk and smoke. Most of the kids seemed like just regular guys, but some were real hoods with their ball point pen tatoos, duck tails, and constant sneers. I talked with one of the tougher looking cats who told me that he had been there for six weeks on a charge of joy riding and he was prepared to stay there until he was eighteen it he had to. He said they weren't going to break him. From that conversation, and others, I learned that for first-timers all you had to do is break down and cry, and they'd let you go. That seemed to fit in with what Sergeant Prince had said about remorse.

Monday I was bored stiff and ready to come home. Two days of nothing to do but beat my meat and carve Laine's and my initials into the metal door with my belt buckle. The hearing with a referee, my mother, father and me went well, once I told of my sorrow and promised to be a good boy. I got off with a six month driving suspension, partly because I had a few moving traffic violations that had never come before the court. The good news was that the referee told me that if I kept my nose clean for the next three months, I should come back and see him and he might reduce my sentence. From the "Twenty-Twenty Club" I rode with my parents to Woodward for a conference with the Vice Principal. My sentence there was a three days suspension. I learned we had been caught only because a teacher, late for school, had seen us driving away from Swifton as she was pulling in.

During the next few days I tried catching up with my studies while reflecting on my situation. The only conclusion I could come to was I needed to talk to somebody who could help me through the next few months. Thursday, my first day back at school, I got permission from my study hall teacher to leave class to talk to Mr. Herne. I found him with his class, busy at work, but he said he could give me a few minutes now or I could come back after school. I jumped on the chance to talk after school when we would have no time limit even though it meant that I would have to thumb home. Jimmy, my only ride to and from school, wouldn't be able to wait as he now had to go directly to work after school every day as well as Saturdays. I told Elaine during lunch that I thought it would be better if she dated other guys, since I wouldn't be able to take her out unless we doubled with someone else. She said she loved me and would wait forever if she had to. Somehow it didn't make me feel any better. I mean, I really liked her, I think.

Mr. Herne was in his office which was nothing more

than a glassed in corner of the large shop area. I walked in, placed my books on his desk, removed a four jaw chuck and a set of collets from the chair and sat down with a sigh.

"What's wrong, hot rod? That Crosley finally give out?"

"That too," I said with a smile.

"Oh, this sounds bad. What can I do for you, son?"

He let me ramble on for almost an hour, as I told him of my confusion and problems. I related how I felt about Laine or how I didn't know how I felt, and how I should have joined a fraternity, but how on the other hand I was proud that I had so many different friends. But then, I didn't have any real close friends, like the frat brothers seemed to be. I don't know if I made any sense to Mr. Herne, but he let me talk until I couldn't talk anymore.

"Paul, you've got a good head on your shoulders, and I'm sure you believe that. What you might not believe is that you're no different than any other teenager, now or at anytime in the past. Everybody goes through times when they don't know which way to go, and everybody has the same fears and worries you have. Maybe not all at the same time and in the same manner, but we all have our doubts and troubles. The thing that sets you apart from many of the others, is that you're smart enough to seek help at a time when you're confused. I only wish I had more time to help you, but I'm just a shop teacher, so the best I can do is give my personal philosophy of life and hope you will be able to understand it and gain from it. This ideal has served me well and has been a code I have lived by and applied to most every problem I've encountered. Basically, I believe that the secret to life, or the key to happiness and success, is the positive ability to adapt to change. That's all it is. If you can adapt to changes you'll no doubt face in the future, then you'll do okay. If you won't or can't adjust your life style to the changes...you'll most likely experience a lot of problems and turmoil. Son, there are just some things that you can't change in life, so the smartest thing is to learn how best to live with them. Take, for example, when your little brother died: That was a change that you couldn't do anything about, so you had to adapt to the fact that he wouldn't be around any more. Do you know what I'm trying to say, Paul?"

"Yes sir, I think I know. It's like my parents are making new or different demands on me and it's I who has to adjust or adapt to the change if I want things to go well for me."

"You've got it. Now, I know it's easy to see and say, but the hard part is to be able to actually adapt. Do you follow that?"

"Yeah, I guess. I know what I should do, but doing it is the hard part. Right?"

"Well, yes. It's not just doing something. It's a whole mental attitude of how you face problems. Let's suppose, for instance, that you have a girl and she breaks up with you. Now you could beg and plead with her, you could throw a tantrum and kick and scream, or you could cry and get drunk, swearing never to talk to a girl again. None of these things will make the girl like you again or restore things to the way they were. You've experienced a change and if you adapt to it, you can go on about your life by learning from the incident and thus preparing for the next inevitable change, that of acquiring another girl friend."

"I see. And on the flip side, if I'm not happy with my present girl, then why should I hang on to something that is bound to change. I should accept the fact that things have already changed and I should break clean instead of living in the past."

"That's the idea, but just be sure you understand it's the positive ability to adapt to change, that's important. A negative ability to adapt to change, like throwing a tantrum when your girl breaks up with you, will do you no good. It must be a positive change to really get the most out of life. Now get the hell out of here, I've got papers to grade. But come back and see me again."

"Okay, Mr. Herne, and thanks. I feel better already, sir."

The stuff Mr. Herne had said made a lot of sense and I made up my mind that I would at least adapt to the fact that I had to bring my grades up and I was going to do as my parents wished; at least as long as it was reasonable. As to Laine, I figured I'd just let things go and see what happened believing that she'd always be there if I needed a date or something. If I got interested in another chick, well, I'll just have to see what happens.

It sure wasn't much fun with out wheels. Sometime in the middle of December one of the guys in Phi Rho asked me if I would be interested in becoming a honorary member of their fraternity. I was really honored and accepted at once. I never did find out what their reason was for extending the invitation, but it really didn't matter. They were all a bunch of pretty good guys whom I had known and hung around with since beginning at

CIRCA 1957

Woodward in the eighth grade. That was a much needed high point of this dreary period. Even Laine was impressed, wanting to know if I was going to get a frat jacket so she could wear it. That was good enough reason not to buy one. One club jacket was all I needed.

Christmas vacation was spent rebuilding the Crosley engine with some of the money I got as gifts. New Year's Eve was a stag at Jeff Hoodin's, one of my new frat brothers. Some of the seniors brought in a case of three-two beer and we all got drunk, or pretended to. It took a lot of three-two to get drunk even for a sixteen year old. Laine was P.O.'d that I didn't take her out to dinner and a show, but my heart wouldn't have been in it. Besides, I didn't have that kind of scratch left after paying to have the crank turned and to buying new main bearings.

The end of the semester yielded a report card that secured good times, at least for the next five months, and also was three months into my driving suspension. I paid a visit to the Referee at Juvenile Hall, report card in hand, and he returned my license after a stern lecture. Man, I was free again! It was time to celebrate and cut loose from the monk-like existence I had been living for the past ninety days or so. Having to hitch hike home from the "Twenty-Twenty Club" with a valid operators licence in my pocket was, well, sacrilegious.

I called Jimmy at his store as soon as I got home, "Hey Pussy, I got my license back and I'm ready to let it all hang out. What say we do some serious drinking Friday night?"

"Yeah, I could sure use that. My old man's had me working day and night and now I don't think I even have a date for this week end."

"What do you mean you don't think you have a date?"

"Well, there's this chick I've been trying to go out with, only her mom won't let us," Jimmy said.

"What kind of shit is that? You're not trying to fuck her mother, are you? Who is she, anyway?"

"You don't know her, she goes to Miss Daughtry's and she's not allowed to go out with Jews."

"Yeah, well fuck her. Meet me at Frisch's, eight o'clock Friday night and you can cry on my shoulder all night, okay"

"I guess. What are we going to do? Get some of Arnold's home brew and go to the drive-in?"

"Hell no! I've got better plans. Some of the Phi Rho boys, who are always a step ahead of you Phi Ep's, have discovered a little bar in Newport that will serve mixed drinks without asking for ID, man." "Sounds cool to me. I guess I could lower myself to go slumming with a few Phi Rho's," Jimmy said, getting in his own put down.

With a promise to be home by midnight, I headed for Frisch's. I could have picked Jimmy up or he me, but it was always better to have your own car in case something came up that required it. By eight-thirty I had finished a coke and realized that Jimmy wasn't going to show, so I drove to Jeff Hoodin's house to pick him up, as promised.

After adjusting our eyes to the dim light of the Midwestern Bar and Pool Room, we located brother Ronny Lowenstein at a back table, already well into a bottle of Hudey. The Bar was dirty, dark, filled with loud hillbillies and country music. Our apprehensions were eased when Ronny introduced us to a few of the locals he was sitting with. Lowenstein knew some of the sleaziest guys ever.

"What are you cocksuckers gonna drink?" Lowenstein demanded once we were seated.

"We'll match what ever you drink," Hoodin stated like a real man.

"Okay, you candy-asses. "Honey," Lowenstein called to the waitress, "bring some shots of Jim Beam with a Hudey chaser all around." Lowenstein, obviously in charge, continues, "Me and Elmo here, do this all the time. Don't we Elmo?" The hilljack seated next to Ronny, nodded. "Auer, I heard you held your own New Year's so let's see if you can drink the real stuff."

The thought flashed through my mind. How do I get myself into these situations? But the die was cast. I just couldn't back out of a challenge to my manhood now.

The first straight slug of whiskey I had ever had— served in a tiny shot glass—almost made me choke, but I was able to keep from making a fool of myself with a gulp of beer. I had heard that straight whiskey gave you a warm feeling all over, but it only made my ears hot. Subsequent shots went down much easier. Either I was one hell of a drinker, or the drinks were watered down. I chose to believe the former by loudly proclaiming "Bullshit" when Lowenstein suggested that they might be. We put away ten of these boilermakers apiece before Lowenstein fell face down on the table. I looked at Hoodin, who hadn't finished his tenth and wasn't about to. "Wha' say Sheff, wanna hit the road?" I slurred.

"Think you can drive, man?" he mumbled without really caring.

"Fuck, I can drive blind-folded. You scared pussy?"

"Shit. Not me. Les get the fug outta here."

We walked slowly through the bar, taking care not to bump anyone lest a fight begin over a drunken stumble. It's a little unclear how we managed to make it to Frisch's. Once there, I told Jeff, slumped against the passenger door, that he better not puke in the car. Not feeling so hot myself, I walked to the back of the lot and stuck my finger down my throat. It worked and after a hot cup of coffee I began to feel almost okay again. A little before midnight, Jimmy pulled in, alone, in his big Impala.

Approaching his car on still unsure legs, I said, "Hey, prick. What is this, national B.F. week?" Where were you?"

"Hey, man I didn't buddy fuck you. I told you I might have a date. Did you guys go over to that bar in Newport?"

"Yeah, who'd you go out with, that cunt from the girl's school? The one that doesn't like Jews?"

"Yeah, she snuck out. And it's not her who doesn't like Jews, it's her parents, asshole."

"Well, did you get any, schmuck?"

"No, but I will. I got my finger wet and was she ever hot! We were in Mount Storm Park and a cop came. Then I had to take her home. Let's get a coke man, I'm dying."

"I can't. I've got to get home, it's almost midnight and I promised Mom I'd be home by twelve. Listen, Hoodin's in my car, passed out, so you've got to take him home or I'll be late."

"Ah, man. Why are you gonna stick me with him?"

"Haven't you heard asshole? It's fuck your buddy week," I said, getting in the last dig.

We found Hoodin, who had somehow regained a portion of his facilities, sitting on the pavement, feet out in front of him, leaning up against the fender skirts, and singing in a loud, drunken voice:

> "Oh, walkin' down Canal Street
> knockin' at every door,
> God damn son-of-a-bitch
> I couldn't find a whore.
> Well, finally I found one,
> and she was tall and thin,

God dam son-of-a-bitch,
I couldn't get it in.
Well, finally I...."

The next week was just like any other week, until Wednesday. Actually, it happened on Tuesday night, but by Wednesday morning the whole world knew. Buddy Holly, Richie Valens and the Big Bopper died in a plane crash. The date, February third, Nineteen hundred and fifty nine, would eat like battery acid in every teenagers heart. None of us had ever experienced any real unifying tragedy or death of such a public figure. We had never known war or the death of a President. Nothing catastrophic had ever occurred in our lifetime. Until now. It was devastating.

A pall had fallen over the entire school. There were kids, mostly girls, crying on each others shoulders and walking around in a daze. The songs these masters of our passions sang not only entertained us, but they told of our innermost feelings. They knew how we felt—they knew what we dreamed—they were us and we were them. They said in song things we couldn't express by ourselves.

At lunch I went over to Swifton and bought a sympathy card which I mailed to Laine because I knew Buddy Holly was her favorite. I saw her in the hall before fifth bell and all she said, through tear stained eyes, was a plea to try to understand. I understood. I remembered the night at Carters', in BB's radioless '35, when she made us keep quiet so she could hear "Peggy Sue" on the radio of the car next to us. I understood. Only I was thinking more of Willie.

KOOKIE, LEND ME YOUR COMB

CIRCA 1957

CHAPTER 14

March brought Spring, my seventeenth birthday and more good news, sort of. With the coming of the grass growing season I was informed by my father that I would be expected to take charge of all outdoor maintenance. It seems that old Bill Schatzel, the Company's gardener, had suffered a heart attack during the past winter and would no longer be able to do the work. Previously, I had been paid the exorbitant, to hear my father tell it, rate of seventy-five cents per hour for any work done in helping Bill cut grass at the Plant. I wasn't paid for cutting grass at home since that was part of my chores, for which I received an allowance. Now I had the old man over a barrel. I demanded, and got, the manly sum of $1.25 per hour! This was no small job as the factory was situated on twelve acres of land, half of which was lawn and half was rough field that had to be cut with the farm tractor. The residence was only about two acres of lawn, but required a lot of trimming especially around the pool. Both locations had many bushes and hedges that had to be shaped regularly. This was my first chance to really make some money, but I didn't know what to do with this new found wealth, so I just decided to save it and see what happens. However, I did visit Auggie at the Auto Shack and purchase a chrome air cleaner for the '56 with some of my birthday money, just so it wouldn't be entirely stock. I mean even BB had a racing air cleaner on the old '35! I could have bought spinner hub caps, but I figured by now the red and white ford was well known by friends and the police alike. Not only had my identity been well established by my cars, but I had been recognized by some of my peers as a man who knew how to handle the wheel.

My first realization of this reputation became evident when Howard Richards, a fellow frat brother, called upon me to show him how to take corners. He had just gotten his first car, a 1953 Dodge sedan, and stopped by the house after school with his request. Hard, as he was nick-named by some of the hillbillies he worked with at his after school gas station job (because that's the way they pronounced Howard), was a genuine nice guy. He was short, a little pudgy and had an impish look about him that induced chick's mothering instincts. He never had trouble finding a date, but getting past first base was his biggest problem. He reminded me a little of Willie.

After a short inspection of his set of wheels—he had

already taken the hood and trunk ornaments off in preparation for a future nose and deck job—we went for a drive. I pulled the rather awkward handling tub onto Fair Oaks Drive and immediately reached about forty-five after a speed shift to second. Approaching the corner in front of the mail boxes I put the right front tire on the edge of the berm, gave the steering wheel a sharp tug and poured the coal to her. The big sedan didn't exactly go into a four-wheel drift, but it did slide enough to end up placing us perfectly right in front of the stop sign. We drove through a few other side streets as I explained and demonstrated the basics of car handling while my student hung on to the arm rest. The whole thing didn't take more than half an hour because he had to go to work. Even though I didn't have the opportunity to watch him drive, he assured me that he understood the principles and would be back another time, after he had a chance to practice.

It wasn't fifteen minutes after he left that Mom called to me that Howard was here. I hadn't heard him drive up, but there he was, standing at the front door, his car no where in sight.

Hard walked into the room, white as a sheet, with a big gash on his forehead and collapsed on the bed.

"Hey man, what happened? Where's your car?" I asked, totally bewildered.

"Well, it sorta went off the road."

"What do you mean, sorta? Where is it and what happened to your head?"

"Well, you know that big tree just past the mail boxes? It almost killed me. I was just trying to go around the corner like, like you did, and wham, the next thing I know I'm stuck in this tree," Hard moaned.

"Are you okay? Do you want my Mom to fix your head?"

"Naw. Let me rest here a minute and then maybe I can wash up and we can go look at the car."

"How bad is it? Do you think it will run? Should I get a chain and try to pull it out with the '56?" I asked, still firing questions at him.

"I don't know. Give me a minute and we'll go look at it."

As Hard finished cleaning up, a police car pulled into the driveway. We went out to see. It was the young officer, Tony Bloomfield.

"You fellows know anything about that Blue Dodge

wrapped around the tree at Section?" The officer asked.

"Yes sir, it's my friend's," I said, motioning toward Howard.

"Figures. I didn't think I'd have to look very far. We had a report of a similar vehicle racing through the Village about an hour ago. You guys wouldn't know anything about that, would you?"

"No, wasn't us." Hard smiled.

Hard drove down with the cop and I followed in the '56. The Blue bomb was a total. He'd hit the tree head on and wiped out the entire front end and his life savings in a single instant. But, it really wasn't as bad as all that. The gas station he worked for sent their tow truck at no charge, and Hard did have insurance.

As the weather got better, the grass grew and I was now spending all my non-school hours cutting. Even when it rained, I had to use that time to clean and repair the equipment. I was sure socking away the scratch, but I didn't have any time to spend it.

At the rate it was piling up, by the end of the summer, I would have three maybe four hundred in cash. My dreams of what to do with the money bounced from dropping a bigger engine in the Crosley to customizing the '56 or taking a trip somewhere. That was my problem. I never knew what I wanted to do.

It seemed that some guys knew what they were going to do for the rest of their life, from the minute they were born. They had their whole life planned out. Some of the frat brothers knew what college they were going to, what they were going to study, who they wanted to work for, where they wanted to live and even who they were going to marry. I didn't know whether I envied them, resented them, or felt sorry for them. At least whatever life brought me would be a surprise. Jimmy was like that. He knew that all he had to do was get passing grades in school, take the easiest classes at Ohio State, where he wanted to go, and upon graduation he would marry a Jewish girl, even though he dated a lot of shiksas, have a couple of kids, join the country club and live in Amberley Village. He had even known what fraternity he wanted when he was in the seventh grade.

In the seventh grade I didn't know whether to shit or go blind. I was glad that I was only seventeen, and had plenty of time to decide what I wanted to do. I knew I could go to college,

CIRCA 1957

just as Bobbi had done, or I could go to work for the Company. My father had always told me that someday the Company would be mine, but that didn't really excite me when I thought how he worked a seven day week. He never did anything for fun, and I sure as hell didn't want to get into a rut like that. Whenever my mother would complain that he wasn't spending enough time with her and the family, he would whine about how hard he works so we can enjoy the finer things of life. He always left the impression that if he didn't go to work everyday, the whole thing would come down around us and he'd be driven to the "poor house." I didn't really believe him, but I didn't give a shit either. Mom always said that his work was his hobby, and that's all he wanted to do. I guess it would be neat to get paid for working at your hobby, but I couldn't see me doing it all the time. I mean even if somebody paid me to build and race cars, I don't think I could do it seven days a week forever. Maybe my old man was tired of what he did, but didn't know what else he could do. I doubted it, but what did I know.

During the next Knight's meeting I learned that a custom car show was going to be held in Columbus on the upcoming weekend. I mentioned this to Hard and Jimmy in school the next day, and Jimmy picked up on the idea right away, saying that his cousin had been after him to come up for a visit. It seems that she and some of her girl friends were going to have a slumber party at one of the girls' houses in Bexley, Saturday night. It sounded perfect. We agreed to leave around seven in the evening because all of us had to work that day. The plan was that we'd go directly to the house where the party was to be, which Jimmy promised to call and get directions to, and stay the night telling the girls we didn't have any money for a hotel. Then, Sunday morning we would take in the car show and be home in time for dinner.

Friday the rumor went around Woodward that Ivan Kaplan and some of his Sigma's had cut school yesterday and had made it to Columbus in two hours flat. I found Ivan on the ramp during lunch.

"Hey Kaplan, I heard you made a rather quick trip yesterday."

"Yeah , the ole Chevy was running fine. Why? You thinking of trying to beat the time?" He asked with a cock sure smile.

"Oh no. I don't think I could match your skill. But, just

for the record, where did you time it from and to?"

"We left here at eight a.m. and pulled to the stop at High and Broad at exactly ten in the morning."

"What were you guys doing up there anyway, and did you see any cops on the way?" I asked, trying to collect information.

"The only cop we saw was in Washington Court House, but he had his hood up in a gas station as we rolled through. We did get awful lucky though. For some reason there just wasn't any traffic."

What'd you do, go up to visit some of the guys at Ohio State?"

"Yeah, we checked out Blinky's new frat house, and man, was it ever cool."

I didn't think he was lying. A hundred and ten miles in a hundred and twenty minutes wasn't unrealistic. Maybe we could better the mark. He already held the record to Dayton, so I was determined to at least give him a little competition.

Saturday I finished cutting the grass I hadn't gotten to Friday after school and even found time to install a new set of plugs in the '56 before ringing out for the day. I figured that since the old man owned the car, the least he could do is pay for the time to put the plugs in. Somehow, I forgot to tell him. Just as I got home, George stopped by in his "new" '51 chev that he was planning to chop the top on.

"Hey, Baker, you still driving without a license?" I asked.

"Naw man, didn't you hear?" The stupid judge mailed my license back to me. Can you beat that?"

"No shit! That'd been me they'd have come up here and got me and I'd still be in the slammer. Did you ever tell your old man?"

"Are you crazy, Man? Fuck no, I didn't tell him., He'd have killed me dead!" George exclaimed.

"You lucky bastard. You never had to pay any scratch either did ya?"

"Not a damn nickel. Anyway, why I stopped over is to see if you wanted to toss a few cold ones down tonight? I've got a hungering for some Hudey."

I gave George my regrets, explaining the Columbus trip, which was now only an hour away. But we did agree to go together to the strip for the opening meet, which was scheduled

CIRCA 1957

for Sunday-a-week.

After a quick shower and the performance of my now twice weekly ritual of shaving, I slipped into my Harry-high-school clothes and splashed on a little Old Spice. The chicks in Bexley might not dig Levis and a T-shirt, so I wanted to look sharp. At dinner, I told Mom and Dad that I wouldn't be home until tomorrow because Jimmy's cousin had insisted that we spend the night with her family. Their only comment was to be careful. Yeah sure, did they think I would take foolish chances?

The clock on the Roselawn Center Building showed seven-ten as we, Hard riding shotgun and Jimmy in the back to watch for cops, headed north. Traffic was light as we sped out State Route three, weaving in and out of the few cars that got in our way. Luck was with us as we hit the first stretch of two lane highway just outside of Montgomery. A long line of cars was ahead of us, but nothing was coming the other way as I pulled over the center line flooring the gas pedal. Locking the Ford-a-matic in passing gear I shouted, "Pick a number from one to ten."

Jimmy yelled back, "Nine."

"Count 'em," I said, as we started to pass them all.

We got to eight before we had to duck back in behind the lead car, an old Studebaker. When the path was once again clear we shot around the Studebaker and leveled off at ninety. The Ford was running like a charm. Hard was invaluable in knowing when to pass on the right in the little towns that we roared through. He seemed to sense the power of the little V8 in relation to the allotted passing space. Our luck was still holding. We had only caught two stop lights so far and hadn't even seen a cop. It was just getting dark when we came out of Washington Court House and hit the long straight, flat stretches that were the last leg. Traffic was still very light and I held the car at ninety for miles on end, not even having to slow in order to pass what cars got in our path. All except one.

For the longest time there was a set of tail lights that we were barely gaining on. Maybe it was a State Cop, trying to clock us from the front. Too late now. We pressed on. A few miles out of Grove City we caught him. It was a '58 Plymouth Fury that had slowed down to see if we were the law, I guessed. When he slowed I tried to pass. No way. Within a mile we were nose to tail at a hundred and fifteen! The most the '56 had ever done before was about one-oh-seven, but riding the slipstream of the Fury we could go as fast as he could without even having to hold the gas pedal to the floor. But every time we tried to pass and hit the full force of the wind, even at full throttle, the little Ford would slow down and then we'd have to fight to get back in the slipstream. It was like this all the way to Grove City, where the Plymouth turned off with a wave of the hand. Now it was the home stretch. We hit High Street and Hard noted the time at eight fifty- two, but we still had a few miles to Broad Street, the center of town. Traffic picked up and we caught a few lights. It seemed agonizingly slow after the high speed we had been used to. Finally, Broad was in sight: Time—nine o'clock sharp! one hundred and ten miles 110 minutes!! Let 'em try an beat that! We were all ecstatic and a little relieved too. Being part of history was worth every risk and cold sweat that went with it.

The dangers in this type of driving never seemed to be as great as they probably were. It's not that we weren't afraid of dying, but that we really didn't believe we could be killed. Oh sure, we'd all read about other teenagers killed in auto accidents, and the police and our parents always preached to us about how dangerous it was to drive fast, but we never actually knew anyone who was killed in a car wreck. Even some of the books we read gave the illusion that fast driving would be rewarded, such as in Henry Gregor Felson's Hot Rod. The teenage hero of that book builds and races his car on the streets only to be caught and punished. Never mind that. The real message that comes across is when the local cop, who knows the hero is a better driver, turns the wheel of his scout car over to the kid for a high speed mercy run to a distant hospital. It would never happen in real life, but that didn't stop us from fantasizing about it. Even teenagers had a little bit of Walter Mitty in them. Besides, the modern State highways, with their wide, two lane, smoothly paved surface and generous gravel shoulders were far safer that what our parents generation had driven on.

HOW'S YOUR BIRD?

CIRCA 1957

CHAPTER 15

It was almost ten by the time we found Jimmy's cousins house in the East suburbs of Columbus. The house was one of those big two and a half story jobs with a large tree shaded front lawn on a street you just knew was packed with similar estates, but couldn't see because of all the foliage. The half circle flower bed lined drive was filled with cars—all late models. They were obviously well-to-do. We parked in an inconspicuous spot on the street and walked up to the pillared front porch and knocked on the wide, solid white door. Familiar sounds of rock & roll music blasted us, as the door opened revealing a cat that looked like he played linebacker for the Bears.

"What do you guys want?" said the bruiser.

"Ah, I'm looking for my cousin, Diane Cohen,": Jimmy squeaked.

The door opened a little wider and a second bruiser filled that opening.

"These guys trying to crash the party?" Asked bruiser number two.

With glimpses between the two brutes, as they shifted from foot to foot, we could see lots of girls and almost as many guys.

"No, man. We just want to talk to his cousin. Would you please ask her to come out," Hard volunteered.

"Bruiser number one turned to bruiser number two saying, "Tell Diane to come out." Then turning to us, he added, "We'll give you five minutes, no more. Understand, punks!"

The bruisers looked at us and we looked at our shoes while running over escape plans in our minds. Nobody said anything until Diane came to the door, dressed in an oversized football jersey.

"Oh hi, Jimmy. I really didn't think you'd come, but I'm glad you did. Would you like to come in?" Diane asked, as soon as she got to the door.

Jimmy brazenly stepped between the bruisers, saying, "Well, ah, we just sorta decided to drive on up and we were hoping to stay the night so we can see the car show tomorrow. I didn't know the whole football team was going to be here to welcome us."

"They're all nice boys. Now come in and get a coke or something."

Once inside it was worse. We were surrounded by bruisers, so we only stayed about an hour before cutting out to find a place to sleep.

Back downtown we bought a couple of six packs of three-two to relieve the night's tension while we looked for a cheap hotel. A big neon sign advertising rooms for three dollars caught our eye. It looked a little seedy, but at least it was affordable. We parked on the street and followed some painted up broad wearing heels that were so high she had trouble walking up the stairs. The guy she was with was a stumbling drunk and had to hold onto her for balance. It was almost comical, but we didn't laugh. Who knows, maybe the guy had a knife or something. The desk clerk handed the whore a key with out any exchange of words and then turned to us. "Can I help you boys."

"Yes sir," I said, laying three dollars on the counter. "We'd like a room for the night." "That'll be three dollars each, fellahs."

"Wait a minute. We only want one room and the sign says three dollars for a room," Howard said, jumping in.

"What are you guys? Wise guys or something. Now pay up or get the fuck out before I call the cops."

We paid. He gave us a key from one of the little slots behind the desk and in a non-stop monotone said, "Your room's on the third floor in the middle, the baths at the end of the hall, keep quiet and don't leave any trash."

"Bath! You mean there's no bathroom in our room?"

"That's right, boys, only one bath per floor," the clerk said, with an air of obvious distaste. We started across the old broom swept and stained wood floor, stopping only to ask, "Where's the elevator? Sir."

"What the fuck do you guys think this is, the fuckin' Hilton? There ain't no elevators. The stairs are to your left around the corner."

We walked up the three flights, Hard still carrying the bottles of beer under his coat, laughing softly as Jimmy made comments about the clerks IQ and obviously dubious parentage.

The room—well, it certainly couldn't be mistaken for a suite at the Hilton, not that any of us had ever been in a Hilton—was, like the lobby, broom clean. There were two beds, a dust covered dresser and a overhead light fixture hung from a chain. It was hot, but we couldn't figure out how to turn off the steam radiator so we raised the roll up blind and opened the dirty window.

It must have been after midnight when Hard, now feeling no pain from the beer, exclaimed, "Man, I gotta to piss like a race horse and I'll be damned if I'm going to use some cockroach infested public bathroom when I'm paying for my own room." With that he walked over to the open window and proceeded to let it all hang out. Before he was finished, we could hear shouting from the street below. We all peeked out and saw some guy standing next to a cab, wiping his bald head and scream up at us at the same time. "You drunken cocksucker, I'm gonna kill you." No discussion was needed. We beat it out the door and made for the bathroom, where Hard ducked into a stall and Jimmy and I stripped off our shirts in preparation for a shower. We could hear "piss head" stomping the halls, calling for the "cocksucking pisser" to come out. Somebody else came out in the hall and told him if he didn't shut up he'd throw him, the cabby, out the window.

Sunday we awoke to a cold rain. After a hot breakfast in a greasy spoon near the hotel, we found the Memorial Hall where the car show was to be, only to discover that it didn't open for two more hours. Four cups of coffee and the Sunday paper later, we finally got to see the car show. Boy, was it a disappointment! There were only a few real hot rods scattered among the new cars displayed by the various dealers from the area. We were on the road home within the hour. The trip wasn't a total waste. We did set a new speed record, and we had the experiences of the hotel to brag to our friends about.

I called Laine as soon as I got back and she read me the riot act because I was spending all my time with the boys when I wasn't working or putzing with my cars. She calmed down enough to ask me if I still loved her, and all I said was, "Yeah, sure," and she hung up on me. I couldn't figure it out. Here I told her I loved her—well, same thing—and she gets mad and hangs up. Women, there's no pleasing them. I thought about calling her back, but I was really beat and didn't feel like a big scene or anything. All I wanted was a little sympathy and maybe some praise on my driving ability, and all I got was a hassle and demands to profess my love.

Monday, after school, I saw Louie and two chicks hop into his old Chevy. The one was Natalie, his sometimes steady, but the other was new to me and very good looking. I hustled over, "Hey Goldstein, haven't you heard, it's against the law to have two good lookin' chicks at the same time in a six banger?"

"Maybe you'd like to try to take one of them off my hands?" Louie the tough said, only half joking.

"Well, if it wasn't for this one little fact, Goldstein, I'd drag you out of that car and give you a sound thrashing," I said, with a big smile on my face.

"Yeah. What's the one thing?"

"Fear! Just plain old cold fear," I laughed.

"Auer, you're crazy."

"No. I'm sane. Only a crazy man would attack you, Louie."

"You got a point there, now what's this going to cost me?"

"Just an introduction to that lovely lady seated next to Natalie."

"Well, why didn't you say so instead of coming up with these cockamamy stories about the law and stuff."

"Hey, the laws true. I wouldn't lie about a thing like that."

"Auer, I can't stand any more. I'll introduce you if you promise to leave me alone."

"Okay. But only if she'll consent to allow me to drive her home, or where ever she's going."

With a deep sigh of capitulation, Louie said, "Donna, this is Paul Auer, Paul, this is Donna Diamond. Now can we go?"

"Hi Donna," I said

"Hi Paul, it's nice to meet you."

"Can I give you a lift somewhere?" I pressed, as Louie started the engine.

"You are fast. Just like they said," Donna replied.

"Wait." The car started to back out of it's space. "You can't leave after saying something like that," I pleaded.

The car stopped. I walked around to the passenger side and leaned in. "I'd really like to get to know you. Can I give you a lift?"

Donna looked at Natalie, who just shrugged her shoulders.

"Okay. It really is out of the way for Louie, if you don't mind. And besides, I'm sure they'd rather be alone anyway."

She was a knockout. Her hair was a deep red and sorta long, but all curly, not curly like a kid's, but big curls that wound and turned all over here lovely head. Her complexion was on the dark side, like mine, and she had a nice set of cabongos that rode up high under a tight yellow sweater.

"I'm not going to try the old line about where have you been all my life, but how come I haven't seen you around school before?" I said, as we walked to the '56. "Well, we only moved here about a month ago. Daddy works for P & G and they just transferred him here. You live in Amberley don't you?"

"Yeah, and how'd you know that and what else do you know about me?"

"Just that you're fast and live in Amberley."

"Fast? Well, I do drive some fast cars," I bragged knowing that's not what she meant.

"That's not the kind of fast I was referring to."

We reached the Ford, and as I opened the door for her, I felt excitement when she brushed past me to enter the car. I walked around to the driver's side as she leaned over to unlock the door for me.

"Aren't you afraid to be with a `fast guy'," I said, as the engine caught on the usual first crack of the starter.

"I can take care of myself, and besides, you're kinda cute."

"Cute? That's for puppy dogs." I swung the five-six out of its place and realized I didn't know which way to go.

"Where're we going?" I asked, seeing a large group of kids cross the street toward Swifton and hoping that Laine or one of her friends wasn't among them. I had told her that I had to go right to work after school. She was still mad and had wanted me to take her home so we could talk.

"I live in the Village, too, on Lamarque."

On the ride home she told me she was only a sophomore, lived with her mother and father and little brother, who she said was a brat. This was their third and most likely the last move for the Company and that Woodward was the biggest, and so far the best school she had attended. When we got to her one-story ranch in the newer section of the Village, I asked, "If you're not busy Saturday night I'd like to take you some place."

"Where would you like to take me?"

"Is that a yes or a no?"

"That depends on what you had in mind."

"Well, we could go to Miami U. in Oxford if you wanted."

"Oxford? Where's that? We only just met and right away you want to take me out of town. You do move right along, don't you!"

CIRCA 1957

"It's only about thirty miles away and I thought we'd go there and visit my sister, who's going to be a senior there next year."

"Can I let you know tomorrow? It sounds like fun. Is that where you want to go to college?"

"I don't know. It's too far away to plan. Geez, I won't even know what I'm doing Saturday night until tomorrow."

"You're something else, Paul. Now I have to go in. I have scads of homework to do," Donna said, opening the door.

"Wait. Before you go why don't you slide over here so I can give you a small token of my appreciation for your consideration of being my escort this weekend."

"What? A token. You mean a Kiss?" She asked incredulously.

"For starters."

"You really are fast. I haven't known you for even an hour and you're ready to make out."

"Well, I didn't want to disappoint you. Besides, I want to know what kind of girl I'll be taking to meet my sister. You don't think I want to take some little tramp up there who kisses every guy she meets. Do you?" It was my turn to act incredulous. She got out of the car and, with a look of puzzlement on her face, said, "I'll be in room one-forty for homeroom tomorrow if you want to stop in."

I drove away thinking that my new plan of how to handle women would be to "keep em guessing". Man, she was totally confused. I also thought about my other problem, Laine and the fact that she wanted to go out Saturday too. I didn't want to lose Laine, at least not until I've got a new girl.

I found Donna in her homeroom the next morning and she said okay for Saturday night, but I would first have to come in and meet her parents. Man, I'd have kissed her parents if she wanted me to. She got better looking every time I saw her. Today she had on a tight navy blue skirt that showed off her perfect buns. When the bell rang I let her walk into her room so I could look at them before heading to my homeroom.

At lunch I ran into Laine on the ramp. She was just pulling a Kent from her purse. I lit hers before lighting my Lucky, trying to think of some way to get out of Saturday night with her.

"Oh, Paul, guess what? Peggy, you know, Sharon's sister, called me last night and invited me to a baby shower for

Sharon. She's due any time now. Isn't it exciting. I've never known anyone who was our age and was going to have a baby," Laine told me, exhaling smoke through her nose.

"Oh yeah. I heard she and Frank finally tied the knot."

"She told me they got married by a J.P. in Kentucky, and Mike was their best man and Peggy was the maid of honor. It was a very small wedding, only her parents and Frank's. Well, Mike and Peggy were there too. I think it's so neat."

"Yeah neat. I think they're too young to get tied down."

"Well maybe she is, but Frank's twenty-two and has a good job with his father. She also told me that the band is going to make a record. Did you know that?" Laine asked.

"Yeah, I heard that too. They're going to cut "Pyramid", the one they wrote. On the flip side will be Little Mike singing, "Tough Enough Baby". You heard them both the night we went to the Drift Inn."

"How come you never tell me these things, Paul?"

"I don't know. I guess you never asked."

"Honestly, you men! Do you know Frank very well?"

"Yeah, pretty well, I guess. I helped him do a tune-up on his wagon a couple of months ago and a few times he took me home from the strip and stuff like that. Why?"

"I don't know. I just wondered."

"Say Laine, about Saturday night...I don't think I can make it. Okay?" I said, in the same matter of fact tone.

She threw her head back to toss the hair out of her eyes and looked directly at me. "Why not. Are you going out the with the boys again? I swear I think you're turning queer."

"No. As a matter of fact I 'm going to visit my sister at Miami," I said, returning her gaze.

"Well, why can't I go? I've never been to Miami."

I dropped my cigarette and ground it out with the toe of my penny loafer to avoid her eyes. "You just can't, that's all."

She blew smoke in my face and dropped her weed giving me something else to look down at.

"There's someone else isn't there, Paul?"

Fuck! She knew. How could she know? Without looking up, I said, "I've got to get to class, Laine."

She grabbed my arm and I looked into her blinking and moist eyes, "Ohhh, Paul. How could you do this to me? After what we did. I love you Paul. Who is she? I'm sorry, maybe I've been a little too demanding lately. I'll change. Oh Paul, won't you give me one more chance, like it says in chapter four of our song.

I put my arm around her as we walked up the ramp into the building.

"Hey Laine, nothing's changed. I just can't go out with you Saturday, that's all."

"Can we go out Friday. I was going to baby-sit for the people across the hall, but I'll get out of it if you'll take me out, Paul"

I knew there were tears running down her face, but I couldn't look, "I can't, Laine I promised some of the guys."

She pulled away from me as we reached the main hall and walked away without looking back. I didn't feel so good. I wished it was Kathy who was walking away. Fuck it. I had other problems. Now I just had to make it with Donna, or I'd be without a chick for the summer.

I called Bobbi that night and she said she would be glad to have me and a date come up for the evening. There was toga party planned at one of the fraternity houses, but we could come dressed in school clothes. I thanked her as she gave me directions to the frat house. Around eight that night a white Corvette pulled up in front of the house and blew the horn. Now I knew it couldn't be my sister, because I had just talked to her long distance. I went out, only to see Jimmy sitting behind the wheel of the brand new Vette.

"Hey man, is it yours? Did your old man finally break down and buy you one?" I asked with excitement.

"Sure did and he's going to get a hard top for it by next winter too."

Peering inside, I said, "Ah man, it's a glider. Wouldn't he get you a stick?"

"Naw. You know my mother has to be able to drive it too."

"Well, take me for a ride. Has it at least got two-fours?" I said, sliding into the red bucket seat.

"Not a chance, but I have plans to add them. She'll never know."

"Neat man. If I ever get a chance to drive my sister's car we'll have to tear one off."

My Father was waiting for us when we returned from a short ride to Frisch's. He looked the car over saying it was just like Bobbi's and then asked me if I wanted one too. I didn't even have to answer, Jimmy did it for my by saying, "I think you better check your father into Longview, he must be going meshug." The old man just laughed and said, "We'll see who's meshug."

After he went in the house, Jimmy said, "I wonder what he meant by that? Maybe he's going to get you one."

"I doubt that. It's his standard answer to everything."

After Jimmy left I called Hard and George to tell them about the new Vette on the block. George told me he was still planning to go to the strip with me Sunday and that he was going to run his '51 in E/Stock, even though the "stocker" now sported a mild cam.

Friday night Jimmy and I made continuous trips through Carters', both Frisch's, and even cruised Norwood Frisch's trying to pick up girls. We had the top down and heater going full blast because it was only about fifty out. We struck out but it was fun trying, especially in a new Vette.

Saturday was cool and cloudy with the constant threat of rain. I got all the grass cut that had to be cut and was finished around four which was shift change at the plant. They were now on two shifts working six days a week. As I was putting the mower away, one of the younger pressmen stopped in the garage on his way into work. He had on sun glasses, a sweat shirt, jeans and sandals on his feet. His hair looked like he hadn't been to a barber in some time and he had a short beard. I nodded to him as he came in, not knowing his name though I had seen him around the press room before. He was in constant motion. His hands were always moving, his fingers snapping while his shoulders seemed to be moving in a short of twitch.

"Hey, man, like how's it goin'?" he said, upon entering.

"Okay, I guess. Are you arriving or leaving?"

"Like, man, I'm always arriving. Like it's cool, ya dig?"

"Yeah, I dig," I said, wondering what kind o cat this was.

"Like man," he said, while snapping his fingers. "Like, have you got a pliers or something, man? Like, my battery cable is like loose, ya dig."

I fixed his battery terminal on his old '51 Buick that looked like a garbage dump inside while he rummaged around in the glove box. As I slammed the hood, he came up to me with a small leather bag in his hand. "Like, man, do you want some, like grass, man?"

"Grass?" I questioned.

"Yeah, man, it's good stuff. Like, I grew it myself."

"What is it? Marijuana?" I had heard of the stuff but never seen it.

"Like, yeah, man. It's pot."

"No. I don't think so, man. Thanks anyway."

"Like, man if you ever want some. like come on over to my pad and I'll like give you some, okay man. And thanks for fixing' my heap, man."

Maybe I should have taken some of his pot, but there was something about him that spelled trouble—the kind of trouble I didn't need. Anyway, I had learned a few new words and actually talked to a real beatnik. From what I'd heard and read, I guess that's what he was.

When he went into the factory, I walked over to his car and looked it over to see what else I could learn about beatniks. On the front seat was a pamphlet entitled "Howl and other Poems" by Allen Ginsberg. I reached in through he open window and tried reading it. It was weird shit. I didn't understand what the cat was trying to say and I gave up rather quickly. It was almost five and I still had to finish putting away the equipment and give the '56 a quick wash job.

After dinner I showered and shaved noticing that my face was almost clear of pimples. It was a good sign. I put on my best school slacks, a white button down shirt that Bessie always ironed so neatly and then rebuttons the three little collar buttons. Over the shirt I pulled on one of those Fabian sweaters, the ones that were all fuzzy and soft. At eight o'clock I pulled up in front of Donna's house. While waiting for the door to open, I reminded myself not to ask any dumb questions, remembering my embarrassment the first time I met Kathy's Mom. Mrs. Diamond opened the door just seconds after I rang. "Hi, I'm Paul Auer and I'm here to pick Donna up."

"Oh yes, I'm Donna's mother. Won't you please come in. Donna will be down in a minute. Oh, isn't that silly of me, she can't come down. This is the first ranch house we've lived in and I just can't get used to having the bedrooms on the same floor as everything else."

We entered the living room, where I was introduced to Mr. Diamond, a kindly looking man dressed in white shirt and tie. Looking up from the newspaper he was reading he asked in a friendly tone, "Now tell me son, where is it you two plan to go tonight?"

"We're going to Miami University in Oxford, Ohio, sir. It's about thirty-five miles from here and we're going to a party with my sister."

"Does your sister attend Miami?"

"Yes sir, she's in her third year."

"Where is this party and who's going to be there?"

"We'll be meeting Bobbi, that's my sister, and her fiancee at a fraternity house where the party is."

A boy of about ten, with a baseball mitt on, had entered the room. He waited until I finished speaking, before saying, "You're Paul aren't you?"

"Yes. What's your name?"

"I'm Artie. I know you're Paul 'cuz DD's got your name written all over her math tablet."

"Well, I hope she spelled it right. Do you like to play baseball?" I asked, stooping down and reaching for his mitt. "Can I see your glove, Artie?" He handed the mitt over with pride as I continued, "Say this is a really good one. A Stan Musial model. Is he your favorite?"

"Yeah, I guess. We didn't have a baseball team in Denver, but now that we're in Cincinnati I'm going to be a Redlegs fan."

"Well then, who's your favorite on the Reds team?"

"I guess I like Ted Klususki the best.

"Yeah, he's one of my favorites too. They call him the Big Klu."

"I know and I'd love to go see him someday," Artie sighed.

Donna walked into the room, her deep red hair bouncing as she smiled at me and then bent over to kiss her father. I stood up and handed Artie back his mitt as Donna said, "Artie go away and stop bothering my guest. Why are you such a brat?" She said it with a meanness that I wasn't used to. Artie hung his head and started to shuffle out of the room.

"Artie," I said, "maybe I can get some tickets and we can go to a game sometime, okay?"

"That would be neat-o," he said, without lifting his head or looking back.

"He's such a brat," Donna, mentioned again.

"I thought he was a pretty nice kid," I said.

"Well, you don't have to live with him. Come on let's go."

"What time are you two going to be back?" Mr. Diamond

asked, as I helped Donna on with her sweater.

"What time would you like us back, sir," I replied.

"Would midnight be in line?"

"That's fine with me, sir. I'll have her home by twelve. Good night, sir, Mrs. Diamond, it was nice to meet you both."

As soon as we got in the car Donna asked, "What did that little creep brother of mine tell you? He's such a brat" I didn't like what I was hearing. It seemed more than sibling rivalry.

"Good evening to you too, Miss Donna," I said, with a smile.

"What's that supposed to mean?"

"Well, since you haven't even said hello to me yet, I thought I'd try to start again. How come you're so hard on your little brother? He seems like any normal kid to me."

"Well, he's not. He's always into my things and he's Mom's favorite and he's always pestering me and my friends. He's just a brat and if he told you anything about me, I'll ring his little neck." I decided not to tell her what Artie had told me. Maybe she was just having a bad time at something else, and Artie had set her off. Maybe, but that didn't explain why he slunk out of the room like he did. It just didn't look right. Well, it's not my problem. Besides, we were going to have a good time tonight and I didn't want to begin it with an argument.

As we dropped off the ridge toward Reading Road from the northern end of the Village, I pulled the Ford-a-matic into intermediate and listened to engine back off through the blown out muffler. It was music to my ears. We took Reading north to one-twenty-six, turned west past the Lockland Highway and on out through the northern parts of the county to the junction with U.S. Twenty-seven. Once settled onto the highway, Donna kicked off her shoes and sat with her feet up on the seat and her back to the door. In response to my questions, she told me of her life in Denver and how she missed her friends. She said she'd had a boy friend back there who didn't show up to say good bye on moving day and she was hurt but didn't want to talk about it. She also told me how proud she was of her father because he was now a vice president of Procter and Gamble. She thought P & G was the best company in the world and made the best products ever. It almost sounded like a commercial. With the air of superiority she asked what my father did.

"He's with the Progress Litho Company, you know, the plant on Section Road just across from Gibson Art, at the railroad tracks."

"What does he do for them."

"Well, he , ah owns it."

"Oh, I see," she said, no longer smug. Are you going to work there when you finish college?"

"I don't know what I want to do, but I know I couldn't work for P & G."

"Why not? It's the best there is," she said, getting defensive.

"Oh it might be at making soap, but they don't hire Jews."

"I thought you were Jewish. How do you know that about P & G?"

"It's just common knowledge, that's all."

"Well, I didn't know that and I certainly never heard my father say anything like that. Are you sure about that?"

"Yeah, I'm sure. Does it make a difference?" I asked.

"Does what make a difference?"

"The fact that I'm Jewish."

"No. Not to me it doesn't. Does it make a difference that I'm not?"

"Obviously not, I asked you out didn't I?"

"Does it bother you about P & G, assuming it's true?" Donna inquired.

"No, not really. I realize that there are people and companies out there that have various kinds of prejudices. The Jews have been accustomed to it for generations so we just form our own companies and such. We don't have to buy their soap and stuff, you know."

"A lot of my friends in Denver were Jewish and I even thought about converting one time when they were all getting Bar Mitzva'd, but I didn't. Maybe I was just envious that they were having all those parties and getting presents and stuff. Were you Bar Mitzva'd?"

"No, I was confirmed last year, though."

We rode on a little way in silence, just listening to the radio until I dropped my hand down to the seat where her feet were and tickled them. She giggled, pulled them back and then would thrust them out again, daring me to try it anew. It broke the ice and I realized that she really didn't harbor any bigotry.

We found the frat house without any trouble and were ushered in by some cat dressed in only a bed sheet. In fact, most of the people there were covered in various pieces or forms of sheets. Bobbi and John introduced us around and provided cups so we could drink the Omega's famous "Purple Passion". It was some concoction of grape juice and gin which tasted just awful, but I would never admit it. I had to keep my cool and appear more mature. If "Joe College" thought it was good, then I would have to agree. The four of us were standing around watching the drunks get drunker and the sheets get looser, when one of them came up to Donna and put his arm around her saying, "I can help you get out of those clothes and into a sheet, my sheet, if you want, honey."

Slipping out from under his arm and pressing closer to me she coolly said, "No thanks, I'm fine."

The drunk moved closer, looking her up and down as I stepped back thinking that if he puts his hands on her again, I wanted room to swing. John grabbed his frat brother by the arm and said, "Cool it, Sam. She's our guest. They could put you in jail for what you're thinking. I don't even think she's sixteen yet!"

Sam moved away as John turned to me and said, "Sorry. Sometimes a little booze brings out the worst in people. He's really a great guy. So what do you think of our home, Paul?"

"You've got a nice pad here, John. Do any of these guys smoke pot?

"Pad? Pot? What are you, a beatnik now?" John asked.

Bobbi looked at me with surprise saying, "Paul, you don't smoke pot do you?"

"No, I haven't, yet. Why, do you have some?"

"No! And where did you learn about that stuff?" she asked.

"Hey, I get around. I'm no square you know."

"Well, you stay away from that stuff. Now I haven't told Daddy about most of the things you've done, but if you start using grass, I'm going to tell and that's not all I'll do, little brother."

"Hey, be cool. I only asked a question. I don't dig beatniks, man."

"Well, I'm glad to hear that. There's enough of them on campus and even a few in this fraternity. Yuck."

By eleven the party was getting pretty loud and we had to leave if we were to make it to Donna's house by midnight and still have a little time left for snoofing, if I was lucky. Bobbi walked us to the door and quietly said that she liked my date and to please be careful on the drive home. We walked out to the strains of the Kingston Trio, which was all they seemed to have in their music library.

We hadn't gone more than a few mile when Paul Anka's new song came over the car radio.

"Put your head on my shoulder,
Whisper in my ear, baby,
Just a kiss...."

I slowed down to the legal limit of fifty, put my right arm on the back of the seat and without taking my eyes off the road said, "That's some pretty good advice."

"What is?" Donna said, trying to be coy.

"Paul Anka is suggesting that you put your head on my shoulder. You wouldn't want to disappoint him would ya?"

I turned my head to glance at her and wink. She slid over and we drove like that for miles through the dark country side with only the dim glow of the dash board for light.

A set of headlights that had been gaining on us for the past few miles turned out to be a full-sized Greyhound and was now right on our bumper. I tapped the brake pedal with my left foot without slowing down to let the guy know he was too close. His answer was to turn his brights on and move even closer. Now, U.S. Twenty- seven, for this stretch, was a rather hilly and twisty road with few places to pass, especially for something the size of a bus. I really didn't want to mess with this cat, being very comfortable with a chick on my arm and all, so I ran the Ford up to sixty figuring that's what the guy wanted. In less than a mile the bus was right back on our tail. I took my arm from the back of the seat and placed it on the wheel telling Donna, "You'd better move over. This guy's crazy." I kicked the V8 down into passing gear and quickly increased the distance between us, leveling off around seventy-five. The mammoth bus came up behind again only not as close as we negotiated a set of sweeping "S"'bends. On the next flat I pushed the '56 to just under a hundred with the monster now about a hundred yards back. I knew at the end of the straight was a chicane open enough to see all the way around and down the next straight. If there was no on-coming traffic I planned to lead the bus hard into the turn.

The needle hovered at a hundred, the dashed white line

passed under the car like a ribbon with small dirty spots on it, the bright high beams picking up only pieces of roadside trees, occasional barns, mailboxes and such as we hurtled toward the approaching hard left. I caught a glimpse of the big yellow and black warning sign over the smaller sign with the thirty-five M.P.H. indicating the upcoming bend and its recommended speed. I strained hard to see any on-coming traffic then picked my cut off point and clamped down hard on the brakes while locking the transmission in second. The engine screamed at being over revved, ninety, eighty, I felt the brakes begin to fade, seventy. We approached the apex, I put the left front tire just off the edge of the pavement and opened the throttle full. The little five-six hung tight as I took up the entire width of the roadway, but leaving myself set up for the second turn. Same plan, same action, same reaction. Once safely out of the bend I glanced in the mirror and watched bouncing headlights and a cloud of dust; I knew my mystery adversary was fighting for his life.

I brought the Ford back to the limit and inspected the gauges amid the smell of burnt brake lining. The bus never got closer than half a mile all the way to One-twenty-six where we turned off.

Donna didn't say a word until we stopped in her driveway.

"I'll say one thing, make that two things for you, Paul. It sure hasn't been a dull evening and, and Lou Goldstein sure was right when he said you really know how to handle a car. I thought we were going to be killed. How did you do it? I don't know whether I was more scared of going off the road or having that bus run over the top of us. Were you scared?"

"Well, not at the time, but I'll have to admit that I was a little shaky afterward. Anyway, that's all over. Now it's time for the question of the hour. Do you kiss on the first date?"

"You're incredible! First you almost kill me and now all you can think about is making out."

"Wait a minute. We didn't almost get killed, not even close, and who said anything about making out. All I said was-"

"I know what you said."

"Well? do ya." I pressed.

"No. Not as a rule."

"Okay then. How 'bout the last?" I teased.

"What's that supposed to mean? Is this our last date or

something?"

"I guess that's up to you, Donna."

She didn't say anything and I couldn't see her face in the dark car.

"Miss Diamond. I would like to see you again. Would you like to see me again?" I said, using the same line I had used on Laine.

"Are you always this direct?" she asked.

"Naw, only with people I like. Are you going to answer my question?" The porch light flashed twice.

"I have to go in now. An the answer is yes," she said, opening the car door. At the front door I held her shoulders and moved to kiss her. She turned her head saying, "I told you I don't kiss on the first date."

"Well then, this is our second. The first was when I took you home from school the other day."

"That wasn't a date," she protested.

"In Cincinnati it is. You're going to have to learn about the local rules if you're going to live here."

"You're impossible," she laughed.

"Well, then maybe this is our last."

"Well then," she mimicked. "That's up to you."

I released her as she opened the door to the house. As I turned to walk away she said softly through the screen door, "Will you call me, Paul?"

"So-long, Donna. It's been fun."

It was late and I was tired. Too tired to go looking for Jimmy. I wanted to talk to him of the night's action, tell him about Donna, only there really wasn't much to tell, other than my feelings. Home was only a few minutes away and Jimmy and Frisch's would be an hour or more before I could sleep. I decided sleep was a better idea. It had been a long day.

I lay awake a long time thinking about Donna. I really liked this chick. She was smart, maybe smarter than I was. I couldn't think of her as a conquest, as I had Laine, I liked her too much- -like a friend. But, I didn't want to end up having her as a non- romantic friend. I sure didn't want a platonic relationship like some guys had with girls. The only nonphysical alliance I wanted was like I already had with Jimmy. I didn't understand how some guys could have intimate conversations with a chick and not have the desire to do anything else. Maybe they did.

Sunday, George and I went to the strip and I pulled

another trophy with the Crosley, only my oil pressure was very low and the rear end started to howl on the last run and continued to do so all the way home. Bad news. I wasn't up to another engine rebuild and I sure didn't want to replace the ring and pinion gears. The thought of selling the little bomb crossed my mind, not only for those reasons, but to truly race in sports car competition I would have to wait four more years until I was twenty-one.

I didn't call Donna at all on Sunday, deciding to play it cool. I didn't want to rush things. In fact, by Monday I had come to the conclusion that I wasn't going to ask her out for at least another week just to see how it's going. She was pretty good at the game for a sixteen-year-old unless she didn't really care, because she didn't even hint about a date whenever we met in school. I guess I was hoping that maybe she had had such a good time Saturday night that she'd be bugging me to take her out again. No such luck.

I spent Friday night running some tests and pulling the inspection plate from the third member. The gears looked bad, with a few chips off the ring gear. In addition, there was no question that the oil pump had problems. Oil pressure was very low and the overhead cam was hardly getting any oil at all. A consultation was in order so around ten I went to Carters' looking for some of the Knights. Benny and Harry were inside going over the latest issue of Hot Rod Magazine. After pouring out my trouble to them the consensus was to try some fifty weight oil in the crankcase and pack the differential with axle grease and then try to sell it. The good news was that a used car lot specializing in sports cars was scheduled to open soon on Reading Road in front of the Twin Drive- in. This was going to require some serious thought, because if I was going to sell it, it would have to be this summer. Trying to sell an open roaster any other time of the year was out of the question. The guys also told me that Frank had been in earlier passing out cigars. It seems that Sharon had given birth to a boy the other night. I thought about going to Frisch's to look for Laine and tell her about Sharon, but decided that she'd probably ball me out for not knowing the kids weight, hair color, or name for that matter. Besides, she probably already knew and then she'd think I was just using the information to try to make up to her. It was too much trouble, so I just hung around Carters' going from car to car and booth to booth, talking cars with fellow rodders.

The next week at school I got around to asking Donna for a date for the following weekend. She said she was going out with some of the girls on Friday and had to baby-sit Saturday. When I suggested that I come over while she baby-sat all she said was that she'd think about it and I should call her Thursday night. Man, maybe this chick wasn't so great after all. I mean, by now she should have been jumping at the chance to be with me again. Well, two can play this game. I decided not to call her Thursday, try to avoid her on Friday, and plan something else to do Saturday.

With school almost over and the weather getting warmer some of the guys decided to go the drive-in Saturday night and try to pick up some chicks. Jimmy took the '58. His Dad had not sold it when he got the Corvette so Mrs. Cohen would always have a car around to drive. Four of us met at Frisch's around nine and agreed that George would drive Jimmy's car because it had the biggest trunk and George was the biggest guy. The rest of us, Louie, Jimmy and I, would hide in the trunk until we were safely in the drive-in. This way we would only have to pay for one person and would then get to split that four ways! As we folded ourselves into the trunk, Louie laid out the rules.

"Nobody better cut the cheese."

No sooner had we begun the short trip across Reading Road to the pit than Jimmy started, "Louie, I gotta let one."

"Cohen, I'll kill ya."

"No shit, Louie. If I don't cut one I'll explode."

"You fart Cohen and you're dead."

"I can't help it Louie. Just a little one, please," Jimmy begged.

Just for fun I added, "Wait, I'll light a match."

"You dumb son-of-a-bitch, you'll blow us all to hell," Louie cried, as George hollered for us to be quiet because we were approaching the ticket booth. Once inside, George drove to the back of the parking area and let us all out, Jimmy making the sound of a fart with his mouth as Louie scrambled after him. The night was a total bust. Of the few cars with just chicks, we couldn't even get a friendly hello.

Exam week! One more week and school would be over for the summer. I found Donna in the front hall at school Monday morning talking with a group of girls.

"Hi good lookin", I began.

"I thought you were going to come over Saturday night?"

"Well, I thought you had to baby-sit or something."

"That's right, but you were supposed to call me."

"Can we talk," I said, taking her by the arm and leading her away from the group. "Look, Donna, let's not play games. I would like to go out with you, but I don't want to have to wait around for days while you make up your mind. Either you want to go out with me or you don't."

"I really did have to baby-sit, and I wasn't sure that you would be allowed to come over if my parents weren't home," she pouted.

"Yeah, sure a sixteen-year-old girl can't be trusted in her own house while her brother's home."

"Well, I had to make sure, okay?"

We were both silent for a moment.

"Okay, how 'bout this Saturday night?" I asked.

"I can't. I have a date."

"With who?" I asked incredulously.

"With whom," Donna said, correcting me.

"That's what I said. Who's the nerd you have a date with?" I demanded, getting a little P.O.'d.

"You probably don't know him. He's a boy I just met in my English class."

"Yeah, well, break it! We're going out Saturday night. Okay!"

"Oh Paul, I don't know if I can do that. It wouldn't be very nice."

"Look, you can either go out with him or you can go with me, but you can't go out with both of us. I don't like that game."

"I'll see what I can do. Will you call me tonight?"

"Sure, you better get to class now" I was taking a big chance, but I really didn't want to have to compete for her. Either she dug me or she didn't. I didn't want to waste a lot of time and money to find out she liked some other cat all along.

I squeezed by the exams and didn't have to sign up for summer school this year.

HOW YA HANGIN'?

CHAPTER 16

"Well I'm ah gonna raise ah fuss,
I'm ah gonna raise ah hollar,
about ah workin' all summer,
just to try to save ah dollar.
Well every time I call my baby,
just to get ah date, my boss says,
'No dice son, you gotta work late.'
Sometimes I wonder what I'm ah gonna do, but
there ain't no cure for the summer time blues...."

Nothing, absolutely nothing, summed it up better than Eddie Cochran's, "Summertime Blues". Every teenager of driving age could empathize with the fact that there were now dues to be paid to which there was no appeal. Adults didn't understand—much less care—that a broken date or missed opportunity was catastrophic. It was a real awakening to learn that the freedom of a set of wheels came with certain responsibilities. The carefree summers of our childhood were gone, replaced by the got to dance beat and true to life words of this song.

By Friday exams were finally over, and Donna had agreed to break her date with creep-o. However, she insisted that we don't go anywhere where we might be seen. That was alright with me, as long as he was out of the picture.

That night Hard and I decided to celebrate the coming of summer by "climbing the Vine" after he got off work at the gas station. This procedure, as we had heard, was the task of hitting every sleazy bar on Vine Street. The idea was to start at the bottom, in the Over-the-Rhine area, and have a drink in every bar on the street, until the drinkers reached the top of the hill or passed out. There were so many bars in this four block stretch of run down old world neighborhood that the latter was the most probable. The side kick to this "right of manhood" was that, this being a very tough vicinity, just surviving was made into an exciting but very real challenge.

The first bar, some small dank, and dingy single roomer with only a long, arm-pit-high bar and no tables, provided a confidence builder as we tossed down a cold Hudey. We, of course, didn't return the stares of some of the locals as they surely stared at our "Harry-high-school clothes" and young whiskerless, pimpled faces. Everybody there was at least fifty, dirty and smelly, including the bar tender! With liquid courage in our bellies we swaggered into the next dive, The Swing Bar. This lovely place was much bigger, with a small dance floor and large area filled with tables and chairs on a old and worn smooth wood floor. It, like the previous bar, was dark, more from dirt than lack of light. The walls, where they weren't covered with some beer ad, were a stained yellow as was the ceiling. The high ceiling might have been white at one time but now its molded design, molds which looked like things we had made out of clay back in grade school, was just a uniformly dirty, yellowish off-white.

While waiting for our drinks we noticed three chicks, who appeared to be about our age, seated a few tables over and a single guy at the table next to us. Over the rock & roll, blaring out of the juke box, Hard leaned over to the stranger. "Hey, man, what say the three of us try to pick up on those chick over there. Maybe they would like to dance and then join us at this table. Wanna try?"

The stranger nodded with a smile, showing yellowing teeth and receding gums. Nothing was said as to who would ask whom to dance, it was just a luck of the draw kind of thing. The one I extended my hand to was almost my height and had very white skin, which contrasted harshly with the six pounds of bright red lipstick she had on. Each chick was eager to dance and within seconds we were all shaking it on the dance floor.

No sooner than we were starting to enjoy ourselves when a loud crash was heard. Out of the corner of my eye, I saw a chair flying through the air. Here was some behemoth of guy, wading through tables and chairs, in a direct route for the dance floor. This huge hillbilly, with a two day growth of beard and a belly that protruded from his too small T-shirt, was bellowing from a toothless mouth, "Nobody's gonna dance with my woman!" Now sometimes you get lucky. This time fate had dealt the stranger the losing hand, as it was he who was dancing with the brute's woman. As Hard and I made a quick but quiet retreat for the door, the stranger was taking a pounding in the corner by the juke box. We both knew it could have just as easily been one of us and decided that we had climbed high enough on the Vine for one night. Next time we'll have to be sure to take Louie and George along. We got back into Howard's '57 Chevy, which he had just bought with the insurance money from the accident, and sat awhile to calm our nerves before heading for Carters' and a more docile atmosphere.

Donna stopped by the plant with two of her girl friends while I was cutting grass Saturday morning, but I didn't have much time to talk. Besides, I must have looked like hell with the cuffs of my jeans filled with grass and an tattered flannel shirt over an frayed and faded alligator shirt. Old Bill had always told me to turn my cuffs down so the grass clipping wouldn't catch in them, but jeans without the cuffs rolled up was just plain uncool. She had come by to ask me to pick her up early, so we could see some love story at the Ambassador, but I convinced her that for this date we should go to the passion pit, where there was less of a chance of being seen. Man, I sure didn't want to go to an indoor movie, even if it looked like it was going to rain.

I got to Donna's around eight and found Artie tossing a rubber ball at the closed garage door. I took the ball from him and threw him a couple of pop-ups, along with a few grounders. He didn't miss a one, but I was starting to sweat in the humid, rain threatening air and called it quits.

"Say, you're pretty good kid. Do you play on a team?" I asked.

"Naw, but my mom is going to try to get me on a Knot-hole team this summer. Do you play baseball?"

"Not since I was ten or twelve," I replied feeling like an old man. "Say, how about it if I get some Reds tickets and we go see a real baseball game sometime?" I continued.

"Neat-o. Can you really get tickets?" he said, with genuine excitement.

"Sure. My father's company has tickets for every game and if customers aren't using them, I can get them."

Donna came out and yelled, "Artie, Daddy said to stop throwing the ball against the house. Now go inside and stop bothering Paul, you little brat."

"Hey, easy Donna. He's not bothering me." I still hadn't gotten use to, nor did I like, the way she treated her little brother.

"Well, it's time for him to come in anyway. Are you ready to go?"

"Anytime you are, baby." I said, as I turned to Artie, saying, "Maybe next week we can go Artie, I think the Reds are in town then."

"Does DD have to go too," he asked in a pleading way.

"Go where? What are you two up to. And don't call me

that," Donna demanded.

Artie ran into the house as I walked up to Donna. "Is DD
your nick name? What's it stand for?" I looked at her slightly
parted deep red lips, that were almost the same color as her hair,
thinking how I couldn't wait to put a lip lock on them as soon as
we got to the drive-in.

"It's what they called me back in Denver, and I hate it.
Now that little creep has told you. I'm gonna get him for that,"
she said, with a meanness I had heard before and didn't like.
"Now what are you going to do with that little brat? And what
are you staring at?" She continued.

"I staring at your lips and thinking how I'd like to nibble
on them and run my tongue across those white teeth of yours
and— "

"Paul! Shhh. Somebody might hear you. Now tell me
what you and Artie are up to?" she said, calming down and
getting a sparkle in her eyes and a blush on her cheeks.

"All I told him is that sometimes I can get Company
tickets for the Red's games and if I did, I'd take him. If I can get
some next week, do you want to go?"

"I've never been to a real baseball game before, and I'd
like to go, but not if we have to take Artie."

"Well, if I get tickets I'll have to take Artie. After all, it
was our idea and he seems to love the game so."

"I don't want to stand here and argue with you. Come in
and say hello to my parents so we can go, okay?"

Once we were in the '56 and headed for the pit, I asked
again. "So tell me, what does DD, stand for?"

"It just stands for Donna Diamond, and I don't like to be
called that, so please don't do it. Alright?"

"Okay by me, but I kinda like it. It's cute."

"Well, I don't like to be cute. Cute is for babies."

"I'll bet Artie has a different meaning for the initials."

"What do you mean by that?"

"To Artie, I'll bet he thinks of DD as Dumb Donna. At
least that's what I'd call a sister as mean as you are."

"I'm not mean. It's just that he's such a pest. Now, can
we change the subject?"

We weren't off to a very good start and I was seeing a
side of her that I didn't like but....

No sooner had we parked at the drive-in than it started
to rain. Since the show hadn't started, we were allowed rain

checks. After a pass through the proper restaurant lots we ended up in Robinson park. Not taking a chance of letting her get too comfortable, as soon as we parked, I said, "There's something that's going to bother me all night unless we get it taken care of right now."

"What's that?"

"Come here and I'll show you."

"If you mean a good night kiss, aren't you supposed to save that for the door at the end of the night?"

"Yeah, well if I did that, then I'd be thinking about it all night and wouldn't be able to concentrate on anything else. So why don't we get it over nice and early."

"Paul! I swear, you've got more lines than Carter's has little liver pills!"

I moved over, taking her face in my hands. We stared into each others eyes, I ran my fingers through that dark red hair. We kissed and I nibbled on those lush maroon lips. She pressed into me and put her arms around my neck, but when we broke she pulled away. I sensed not to push the issue so I just put my arm around her and gently pulled her over so that her head was on my shoulder.

"Paul? Have you ever gone to bed with a girl?"

"Wow, you don't beat around the bush, do you? One kiss and you want to know all my secrets."

"Well, I just wondered. Have you?" she said, in a persistent manner.

"You mean in the last twenty-four hours?" I said, trying to joke about it. not knowing what she was up to.

"Now be serious. But if you don't want to answer, then that's alright with me and I'll change the subject."

"Okay. If you want the truth then I'll tell you. Yes I had sex with another girl."

"Who was it?"

"Wait a minute. That question I'm not going to answer. I mean, I'm not the kind of guy that kisses and tells, so that's all you're going to get out of me. Why all these questions?"

"I don't know. I just felt like asking it. Tell me something else. Does it make a difference to guys if a girl is not a virgin? I mean, when they get married. Does a guy expect to marry a virgin?"

"Hell no! Most of the guys I know think that any guy that insists that his wife be a virgin must have something wrong with him. I know I wouldn't marry a girl unless I'd slept with her first. I wouldn't want to get stuck with some frigid chick, if you know what I mean. Why? Why all these questions.?"

"I don't know, Paul. I just like you and I want to know what you think."

She kept a tight grip on my hand as we silently sat, listening to the rain washing the '56, and an old Johnny Mathis on the radio.

"There's something bothering you isn't there, Donna? Do you want to tell me about it?"

"Oh Paul, I don't know." "Well, if something is bothering you, it's always better to talk about it. What is it, are you pregnant or something?"

"No! I'm not pregnant, or something."

She was silent again as I kissed her forehead.

"Paul? Would it make a difference to you if I wasn't a virgin?"

"Naw. Is that what's bothering you? Damn. I thought you had a real problem. Was it anybody I know?"

"Are you joking with me? Please don't lie to me," Donna pleaded.

"I've never lied to you and I never will." I said, as seriously as I could. "If some other guy liked you enough to sleep with you, then it only shows he has good taste. How many guys have there been?"

"Only one, what kind of a girl do you think I am? Oh, Paul please don't tell anyone. I'd just die if anybody found out. Please?"

"Your secret is safe with me. I have no reason to tell anyone else. Was this some guy in Denver, or what?" I asked.

I could feel her head nod against my shoulder. "Please don't tell, will you, Paul?"

"Look, Donna, I'm not going to say a word to anyone and what happened before you met me doesn't make any difference to me and that's the emet."

"The what?" she asked.

"The Emet. It means the truth in yiddish."

With a big sigh, Donna said, "I feel better already. Last night I called Keith, he's the boy in Denver, and he told me not to bother him again. It really hurt. I mean I sorta knew it was coming because he's never called me since I left, and I've written him and called him and everything. But to hear him say it's over, well, it just hurt and now I feel so, so soiled. Are you sure it doesn't make any difference to other guys. You're not just saying that to make me feel better, are you? Please, please tell me the truth."

I turned her toward me and kissed her on the lips. I could tell she was crying and I just held her as she hugged me tighter.

"That's the only way I know how to show you that it doesn't make any difference to me." Maybe that's why she was so hard on Artie tonight, I thought. We just held tight to each other as I softly kissed her neck, thinking about what it must have been like for that lucky stiff in Denver. After a while I continued, "When you feel like a little humor, I'll recite a poem for you that, in a crude way, tells how men feel about things like this."

"What is it? Its not dirty is it?"

"No. Just a little crude. Do you want to hear it?"

I took her silence to mean yes.

"I know a woman who wears red shoes,
she drinks my liquor and she drinks my booze.
She ain't got no cherry but that's no sin,
'cuz she's still got the box that it came in."

"You're right, it's a little crude. I only hope it's true."

"Wanna hear the one about the guy who meets his ex-wife's new husband on the street and says—"

"That's all right. Maybe some other time."

Hey, this was going to work out great. I thought she really dug me and now we shared a secret, which meant that she would rather confide in me than one of her girl friends. I thought of Laine and wondered if she had the same kind of problems. Well, they weren't my problems. Maybe I was a little bit of a heal when it came to Laine, but at least I was a sexually satisfied heal. One thing was sure clear. Donna hadn't forgotten the first one—the guy in Denver.

We made out until it was time to go home. Just kissing and hugging. I never tried to go past first base. The rain had slowed to a drizzle and I had fun practicing my drifts around corners when I took her home.

I found Jimmy at Frisch's and we drove to Farm Acres Drive, where I got into his Vette and we talked. It had been a while and we both had a lot of catching up to do. He was still dating the chick from the private girls school, who was a very steady piece of ass, but he was tiring of her. I told of my past problems with Laine and how things were going with the redhead. I didn't tell him of her past Denver experiences, but I did relate how I felt about how she treated her little brother. Jimmy's opinion was that she might have real problems, but that I should just hang lose for now and see how it went. It was too early in the relationship to worry about such things, was his advice. He was probably right, as usual.

...AN HOW'S YOUR OL' WAZOO

CHAPTER 17

It was still raining Sunday when I finally got out of bed. The old man had already gone to the office and I needed to talk to him, something I never enjoyed. Maybe it was because he didn't offer any compliments or, for that matter, advice. After a big breakfast, fixed by sister Bobbi in one of her kinder moments, I drove to the plant and found my father at his desk behind the usual stack of papers.

"Well, what's on your so-called mind?" he said, in a joking way, as I entered the large office filled with samples of recent jobs tacked to the display board and covering chairs and filing cabinets. I always found it interesting to see these pieces of packaging or products in various stages of completion. Today the most prominent jobs were sheets of whiskey labels that resembled a jig saw puzzle of sorts. I could tell by the color bar at the bottom of the biggest sheet that there was five colors plus gold bronze and at least a dozen or so different sized and shaped labels nested on the huge sheets of paper.

"Nothing. I just stopped by to see my old buddy." I could joke too.

"Old buddy, eh? What's this going to cost me? Did you wreck the car, or are you in need of some money?"

"Well, since you asked...I could use some Redlegs tickets."

"Oh, I see. You want I should supply the tickets so you can take some schlemiels out on the town. Such a big shot you are. When is it you want these seats and how many? Maybe you want I should buy the whole stadium, so you can take all of your hoodlum friends at once. Is that what you want, to see your father in the poor house?"

"No, Dad, I only need three but, if you could spare five I would be most grateful. I'll take them anytime for any game. Of course, day games would mean I might have to miss some work."

"Alright, already. I'll stop my work, the life blood of our Company, and we'll go look. He wants baseball tickets today, who knows what he'll want me to stop my work for tomorrow. You need a haircut. I know I have a bum for a son, but at least you don't have to look like a bum," he continued with his good-natured ribbing.

He got up and we went to the vault to check the status

of the available seats. All ten were there for the Friday night game with the Cardinals.

"So who is this I'm entertaining," he said, handing me five tickets.

"Well, three are for me, my girl, and her little brother, and the other two are for Jimmy and his date."

"Now listen, if some customer calls and wants the tickets you have to give them up, you understand that. The customer comes first."

"Oh sure. I understand, no problem and thanks Dad."

We went back to his office and I helped him sort papers while I told him of the problems I was having with the Crosley. He didn't say anything on the subject. At noon we went to Sands Restaurant for a sandwich, where he told me, "Son, if you want to sell the car it's okay with me, only the title doesn't pass until the check clears the bank. I don't care whose check it is. No exceptions. Is that understood?"

"Yes sir," I said, knowing that his explicit instructions always had to be followed to the `nth' degree.

"Now, if you can keep out of trouble and keep working like you've been on the lawn, then when we buy new Company cars this fall I might get something for you."

"Oh yeah! What kind?" I asked suddenly filled with excitement.

"Now don't get your bowels in an uproar, I said might."

Man things were sounding better every day. I left the old man at the plant and went home to putz around in the garage, there being nothing else doing on a rainy afternoon. Around three, Bobby Pilder, nicknamed, the "Spider", stopped over, driving his parents new Mercury station wagon. It was a mammoth stage coach with the biggest engine available and all the extras. It even had a power tailgate window. We went into the garage to get out of the rain, where the Spider reveled his reason for the visit.

"Hey Paul, I understand that you've had some experience with racing fuels?'

"Yeah, a little."

"Well, Ivan Kaplan has been putting the Merc down by saying that his mom's Chevy can beat it, and I'd like to shut him up once and for all. Only, I'm not so sure the stage coach there could beat him. It's awful heavy and he's now got two-fours, man. Do you think you could mix up a brew of something to give me an edge?"

"Most likely," I said, taking on an air of superiority.

"What would you use, man?"

"Well, I've used nitro-methane before and it's about the hottest stuff there is. It's what most of the double "A" fuel dragsters are now using. Of course, without a lot of experimentation and carb set up, you run the risk of burning the engine up."

"But, will it last long enough to win the race?"

"Oh sure. I would mix the nitro with a little benzol to help lubricate the valves. But to really make it work right, you should enlarge the main jets. I've got a little of the fuel now and we could start today if you wanted."

"No. I don't want to tamper with the engine because if anything goes wrong, then it won't be covered by the warranty, dig?"

"How much are you going to race him for. I mean the fuel is going to cost you at least twenty-five bucks, man."

"The race is for a hundred, but I'd go for free just to beat his ass. Can you get this nitro and do you want the money now?"

"I can get it this week if you give me the scratch."

Thursday night, the scheduled race night, the Spider arrived around seven-thirty. I got out two one gallon cans and we used them to mix the nitro with the benzol. We pulled the hub caps, removed the rear seats and spare tire to save weight, and then drove around Roselawn to burn up any gasoline in the tank. Right on time we pulled into the Jewish Center parking lot for the agreed staging meeting. After agreement on who would act as lookout and who would block traffic from the rear, the entire entourage, including spectator cars, headed for the LTA. We were the last to leave the parking lot, not wanting anyone to see the brew being poured into the big Merc's tank. By the time we got to the divided highway signs marking the start of the quarter mile the Merc was beginning to run a little rough. The Spider had to keep his foot on the gas pedal and the engine racing against the transmission to keep it from stalling. The foot bridge at the end of the quarter was covered with at least fifteen to twenty kids, waiting for the onset of the race. The temperature gauge showed that the giant stage coach was already running hot. The excitement of the moment, combined with the stench of the expelled, burned concoction, was exhilarating and nauseating at the same time.

The lookout at the turn-around, just past the foot

bridge, signaled with his headlights that all was clear. I looked in back and could see that at least half a dozen cars had begun to back up behind our blocker. I rolled the window down, looked at Ivan, he nodded that he was ready, and I screamed, ONE! TWO! THREE!

The huge Merc shuttered for a moment and then pinned me in my seat as we took off after the little Chevy. Bobby had it locked in low range until the engine sounded like it was coming apart. The shift to intermediate produced a solid chirp of rubber. We caught the Chev and passed him a full hundred yards before the foot bridge. The Chevy braked hard at the turn-around while we kept going, headed for the nearest gas station.

After a fill up to dilute the brew, we went back to the Center. The Merc now had a very bad miss and the Spider could hardly keep it running. At the Center some of the spectators swore they saw flames shooting out of the Merc's tail pipe when we passed under the foot bridge. Ivan, having lost face, didn't show up. The victory was ours and everybody was patting the Spider on the back with congratulations.

The next day Bobbi made me a proposition I couldn't pass up. She would let me use her Corvette for my date to the ball game, if I washed and waxed it for her. Man, I could hardly wait. I knocked off trimming hedges in the early afternoon and spent the next three hours or so giving the Snowcrest White sports car a through cleaning. I only stopped long enough to call Jimmy to see if he had gotten a date and to tell him that we would both have to drive, since I was also a Vette driver. I had spoken to him earlier in the week about the plans and he said he wasn't sure if he could get a date because the chick from the girls school was now history. It seems that her mother had caught them in the act and had immediately made plans to have her daughter spend the rest of the summer—maybe longer— with some aunt in Florida. His date tonight, he told me, would be the daughter of one of the store's customers.

I picked Donna and Artie up at a quarter to seven and Artie was as excited as any ten year old could be. Going to a Redlegs game and riding in a Corvette had to be the high point of the summer for him. Donna, on the other hand, was more upset now that she had to share a seat with her brother, let alone have him tag along on a date. I didn't give a shit. I was having too much fun myself. The short train of two identical Corvettes brought a lot of stares all the way to Crosley Field.

We parked on a side street and as we were preparing to put the tops up a little colored boy came up to us and offered to "watch the cars" for a quarter each. Seemed reasonable to us so we just left the tops down. The game was a lot of fun. The Redlegs won and we stuffed ourselves on beer, peanuts and cracker jacks. Artie was now a converted Redlegs fan. Even Donna looked like she was having a good time, when she wasn't scolding Artie for something. He was such a nice kid that if made me uncomfortable when she berated him. It made me think of Willie and how unhappy he would have been if I were the one to belittle him, especially in front of others. The only time I could remember going to the ball game with Willie was the year before he died. Dad had taken us along with two other kids whose father was a customer of the Company. The older of the two, about two years older than I was at the time, played Knot-hole and explained the game to Willie, like I was trying to do for Artie. I bet if Willie were here he would really get along with Artie.

Before heading home we were obligated for the mandatory trip through Frisch's. Hard was there and tried to goad us into a race against his '57, but we knew we wouldn't have a chance. Pulling out of the drive-in restaurant, I noticed the used car lot in front of the Twin Drive-in, that was going to specialize in sports cars, had its grand opening banners strung from light pole to light pole. Their lot wasn't very full and I had visions of the Crosley displayed under the bright spotlights as a real attention-getter. I decided to decide by Monday.

We got Artie home by eleven, and then Donna and I just sat in front of her house and talked. I tried asking her if the reason that she was so hard on Artie was that maybe she was jealous, but she got mad and didn't want to talk about him. I was in too good of a mood, so I didn't push it. It didn't even upset me when she made me put the top up so we could snoof without being seen by the neighbors. Midnight found me at Carters' for a coke with some of the Knights. Sharon and Frank were there and they invited me over to their '57 to see the baby. It looked just like any other baby only I said the usual things about how nice it was and all that bull. Sharon wasn't very glad to see me because I had broken up with Laine—now one of her best friends. I just told her that things didn't work out, but that I still liked her and all. She then started in on a lecture, but I was able to get away.

CIRCA 1957

I talked with BB, who agreed that the time to sell the Crosley was now, if I was going to sell it. He also said he was through with racing for good and was now just looking forward to getting his degree, which was still years away, and settling down to marriage and raising a family. He sounded so old. It was depressing.

Saturday when I got through cutting grass, Mom told me that someone named Donna had called. This was a first; I mean girls don't call guys. I hurried to the phone.

"Hi, baby, what's up?" I asked as soon as she answered.

"Oh Paul, the greatest news. My Mom and I are going to Denver for a visit. We'll be gone a whole month. Isn't that great? And guess what else? We have to go out on the train, but we get to fly back. Neat. Huh?"

I imagined her face all lit up with a big smile of deep red lipstick and extra white teeth with just a little overbite. She sounded so excited that I really couldn't help but be happy for her. Trying to pick up a little sympathy, I said, "Oh swell. Now what am I supposed to do while you're partying it up in Denver? Are you going to see that guy, what his name when—"

"No. I'm not going to see Keith, if that's who you mean. I never want to see him again!"

"What if he came back to you on his knees and begged?" I said, pushing the issue, afraid of what the answer might be.

"No. I don't want anything to do with him. Paul, I won't play games with you, if that's what you're afraid of. So don't worry, okay?"

"I guess. When are you leaving, anyway?"

"That's the bad part. We're leaving Sunday night."

"Can I see you tonight? I'll come right over if you want me to."

"No, I have to pack, but I'm so glad you called. I hope your mother doesn't think I'm too forward for calling. I just had to talk to you and I wasn't sure what you were going to do tonight. What are you going to do tonight?"

"I was going to call and see what you wanted to do."

"Well, I've got to get started packing. I'll miss you, Paul. Will you miss me?"

"Oh, you know I will. Damn a whole month? Will you send me a post card?"

"I'll send you a letter. I don't want anyone to read what I write you. Bye now. I'll miss you."

Shit! Just when things were starting to go good.

Monday morning I drove the '56 to World Wide Motors and talked to them about my Crosley. They were interested and told me to bring it down, and if we could agree on a price they would write a check on the spot.

At home, in the garage, I sat in the old sports car for what might be the last time and reflected on its past. Strangely, I didn't feel sad. Here I had put so much time, money and sweat into this piece of plastic and steel that I thought surely I would have tears in my eyes. All that came to mind was the three hundred bucks I hoped to get. I reached for the ignition and as my hand touched the switch my mind traced each wire connected to it. The thoughts of each part joined together and all the painstaking work that had gone into making this dream. I stabbed at the clutch and traced its linkage, all homemade, all the way to the point where it attached to the bell housing on one side and the frame on the other, next to the spot where I had welded in the name WILLIE. Damn! Now my eyes were starting to get a little moist. Damn. The car came, was transformed and now it'll be gone, and Willie never got to see it- -at any stage. Double damn. I haven't even been to visit him in a long time. Tomorrow. Yeah, tomorrow I'll visit Willie for sure, no shit!

I ran my sleeve across my eyes, twisted the key and listened to my baby sing to me for the last time. It would have been fun to make one last pass at the old "test track", especially past old lady Fritz's, but I wasn't sure the engine or the rear end would take it. On the trip down to the lot, I was pleased that the heavy oil in the crankcase and the grease in the differential kept everything quiet. At the car lot the salesmen all seemed excited with my car. So much so that I told them I was asking six hundred instead of the five hundred I had originally planned to ask. They countered with a bid of three and we found mutual ground at four-twenty-five, after a little further haggling. That was a full one and a quarter more than I expected. One of the salesmen gave me a ride home in a TR-3 and I promised to bring the title as soon as the check they had given me cleared.

Wednesday night I ran into the Spider at Carters'. "Hey, man, how's it goin'?" I said, sitting next to him at the counter. "Did Ivan ever pay you?"

"The asshole, he only gave me fifty bucks, said he figured we cheated somehow. I ought to kick his ass!" Bobby said, obviously still a little pissed off.

"Well shit, you still made twenty-five on the deal and you smoked him off to boot."

"By the way. How much was the nitro? Do you owe me any money?" Bobby fished.

"The total was twenty and change. The rest is for my trouble."

"Why you putz. You're buying the cokes then, prick."

"Putz! Prick! If it wasn't for me you'd have lost the race, but I'll buy the cokes anyway, just to show you what a nice guy I am. By the way, how's the Merc? Did it smooth out by the time you got home?" I asked.

"You didn't hear? Man, the thing barely got me home and the next day it wouldn't even start."

"No shit. Was your Mom pissed?"

"Listen it gets better. I told her it was running fine when I drove it, so we had it towed to the dealer and, get this, they tore it down the next day and called to say all the valves were burned but, the whole thing isn't going to cost a cent. The dealer said it was covered under warranty. Shit, it only had about three thousand miles on it!"

"So your Mom's not pissed at you, eh? You lucky bastard. Who do you want to race now? Let's do it again after they fix the engine. I think if I add more benzol to the brew it'll keep the valves cooler. Want me to get some more stuff?"

"Fuck you, man. Why don't we put it in your '56 this time?"

"No, we can't do that. The Ford's out of warranty."

The summer was starting to drag with nothing to do but cut grass, trim hedges and hang out with the guys. If Donna was here at least I'd have a date once in a while. She had already sent me a bunch of letters, all marked S.W.A.K. on the back, but she didn't say much inside. Just stuff that she was doing. No mention of her ex, but no mushy stuff either. On the Fourth of July, Jimmy fixed me up with a friend of his current girl and we doubled to Coney to watch the fireworks. My date was a real dog and at an impromptu conference in the men's room he promised to make it up to me. He better. The prick had the balls to admit that he knew she wasn't a queen, but he had to find her a date to keep his girl happy. At least the fireworks were cool, so the night wasn't a total loss. When I dropped Jimmy and his chick at the Vette he told me he couldn't meet me later at Farm Acres, but that I should stop over in the morning. I caught his drift.

Sunday morning was a beautiful day and I drove up to Jimmy's thinking it sure would be a nice day to take the Crosley for a spin, if I still had it! Maybe I had made a mistake in selling it, too late now.

Jimmy was still in bed, but his Mom told me it was time he got up anyway.

"Hey, sleeping beauty, it's time to rock & roll," I said, as I entered his room.

"Jesus Christ! It's only eleven. What are you doing here so early, asshole? And why are you waking me up, I didn't get in 'til after three!"

"Three? What were you doing 'til then? As if I didn't know. Was it any good?"

"Son," Jimmy began, waking up rapidly now that his favorite subject had been mentioned. "There's only two kinds, good and better. Now, how 'bout you what did you do with that sweet young thing I so honorably fixed you up with?"

"Shit! I took her straight home, man. Then checked out Frisch's, which was dead, so I was in bed very early, thanks to you. Now what are you going to do to make it up to me?"

"Well, just because I like you, tell ya what I'm gonna do," Jimmy said, in a circus barker's voice. "I know this little honey that is a sure thing and I'm gonna let you in on it."

"Well, what do I have to do? Are you gonna call her? Do it now. Man, I'm so horny I'd fuck a snake."

"Hold on now. I can't call her now, it's Sunday and she's probably in church. Shiksas go to church, you know.

"Fuck the church, call her anyway. Maybe the Lord talked to her and told her that she's the answer to my prayers. I just gotta get laid!"

Jimmy called from the phone in his room. No answer.

"See, I told ya. Now let me tell you about this chick. She's not allowed to go out, some kind of strict religion or something. That's why she's in church now with her family."

"Well, if she's not allowed to go out, how am I going to slip it to her?"

"Keep your pants on, I'm coming to that. The only way you can go out with her is to pick her up after eleven at night, when the rest of the family is asleep. She will sneak out her window and meet you on the corner. Now this is no shit. This is the way I took her out. The only bad part is that you have to wait so long and she lives at the end of Westwood Northern Boulevard, at Harrison."

"Ah, shit. It'll take a tank of gas just to get there." I complained. "How'd you meet her, anyway?"

"This kid that works for us part time fixed me up, way back in April. She'll only go out with you if she's fixed up by somebody she knows and it's to go to a party. I'll tell her you're going to take her to a big party when I get a hold of her. Now get the fuck out of here and let me get some sleep. I'll call you when it's all worked out."

Jimmy came through but Debbi, the chick he fixed me up with didn't. We ended up at Frisch's early in the evening, where I found Ivan with two of his buddies. Leaving Debbi for a minute I casually approached the loser of the big race, "Hey, man how's it goin'?" "I've been lookin' for you. What did you do to the Spider's stage coach to make it run os good? He never could have beat me if he was stock," Ivan demanded.

"Hey, we can't give up our secrets, man. But just to make it up to you, I'll tell you what. There's this chick in my car that I'm finished with…if you catch my drift, and I don't want to take her home. So, if you want, I'll introduce you to this sure thing and I'll even let you take her tonight. Now how's that for a real buddy?"

"What makes you think she'd go home with me after shtupping you?"

"Because I'll tell her to, that's why. Now come out to my car, check her out, and if she won't go, then there's nothing lost. Is there?"

It was days later when I learned that Ivan had dumped her on some street corner, miles from her home, and was looking for me to kick ass. He didn't look very hard because I was always available and nothing ever came of it.

The weather had gotten very hot and dry which wasn't doing the grass any good, so I was put to work painting the guard rails in the factory parking lot. The hot, dirty, thankless job took the better part of two weeks with a little time off for occasional grass cutting. Some days I was so beat that I even went to bed before ten. I was rolling in the bread, but didn't have any time to spend it. It was during these lonely, tiring days that I wrote Donna. I told her how I missed her and wished she was back and in my arms. I had never really written anyone before—well, not counting thank yous to relatives—and was embarrassed by my handwriting and inability to say on paper what I thought. I wasted quite a few pieces of my Confirmation gift stationery before figuring out that it was better to write a draft on plain paper. The letters I wrote paid high dividends in her following letters, which out numbered mine by at least three to one. She too, it seems, really missed me and found that all her friends in Denver, mostly the boys, were just a bunch of squares. The bad news was that their stay was going to be extended another two weeks because one of her mothers relatives had suddenly died. It would now be the middle of August before they would be home.

I was getting pretty horny, not having even kissed a girl for what seemed like years. It was early on a hot August Saturday night that I found Louie and Howard in Hard's '57 rag top parked at Frisch's. Louie was singing the words to "Little Star" and trying to teach Hard the chorus. I climbed in the back seat and soon was inducted into the new group. When Louie was satisfied with our sound he announced that it was good enough and we should head for Norwood to pick up chicks.

Sometimes you get lucky. On the first pass down Montgomery Road, we saw two chicks on a corner talking to some guys in another convertible. We pulled around the corner and waved to them. One of the young things came over to our car as Goldstein broke out with:

> "Where are you little star,
> Where are you?"

Hard and I picked up the chorus:

> "Oh ,oh, oh, oh, ratta, ta, ta, to,
> oh, oh,...."

Louie smiled at the chick. "We're the Elegants and we just got into town. Wanna hop in and take a ride with us?"

The chick looked to her girl friend and called out, "I've got my car load, see ya later."

As soon as she was in Louie introduced us, first names only, as Howard patched out onto the pike. Her name, she said, was Jerri and she lived in one of the apartments above the stores near where we found her. Right smack through the heart of Norwood we went, top down and Louie crooning:

> "Tinkle, twinkle little star,
> how I wonder...."

CIRCA 1957

I didn't know if Jerri believed we were really the Elegants, but she didn't dis-believe it either. We drove around in an aimless manner, Louie and Jerri in the back seat making out and giggling, until it got dark. Hard then found a deserted street that had a lot of construction of new houses on it and we parked. Goldstein, always in command, ordered, "Hard. Put the top up and then you and Paul can take a walk while I talk to Jerri."

We complied and within fifteen minutes Hard and I heard the car door open, from a half block away. We started to walk back. Louie met us half way and, in a very subdued voice, said, "Well, you guys can decide who's next, she ready."

I started to walk in the direction of the '57 but, Hard grabbed my arm, "Wait a minute, hot dog, it's my car, I get seconds!"

"Well you can't blame a guy for trying, can you?" I said.

In less time than it took Louie, Hard was back. Now it was my turn, and boy was I ready! In the dark back seat I struggled to pull my pants down and grope at her large titties. It was very cramped and as I was attempting to slap it to her, she murmured for me to make it quick because she was starting to get sore. Being a true gentleman, I offered, throbbing cock poised over a moist patch of hair, to let her suck me off instead. She thought it was a great idea, saying that she had only done it once before and thought it was fun. As I was vocalizing my satisfaction during its peak, I could hear the guys laughing and kibitzing while they watched through the open window. Pricks! I'd fix them.

We allowed Jerri the courtesy of dressing alone in the car and then took her back to the corner where we'd picked her up. As soon as we were back north bound on Montgomery, I laid it on them. "I really hate to tell you guys this, but I only got a blow job because she said the sores on her pussy were starting to hurt," I said, enhancing a little.

"Oh shit. VD! You're not lying about this are you, Auer?"

"Hell no. Why would I lie about a thing like this?" I said, doing a good job of keeping a straight face.

Hard piped up, "I heard that if you wash right away with kerosene you can keep from getting it. Whatever "it" is."

"Well, get us to a gas station, asshole," Louie ordered.

At the first gas station we came to I went to get some

kerosene from the attendant while they went to the rest room. I handed in the fuel and stood outside, listening to their cries of pain as the kerosene burned their balls and dongs. It was all I could do to keep from laughing. In due time, we ended up back at Frisch's where Louie made us promise not to say a thing about the events of the night, at least until he and Hard were checked by a doctor.

Donna's return was a real high point in the long, work filled summer. I hadn't realized how much I had missed her or how much I actually liked her. Her first night back we went to the pit and never watched the show. I can't even remember what was playing other than it was some kind of war movie. We made out nonstop for the duration of the picture and again I never tried to go past first base. We both talked about how we missed each other and that maybe this was the real thing. I had stuffed my class ring in my pocket before leaving the home, in hopes that she might want to go steady. I don't know why I bought it in the first place, as I never wear jewelry, but it sure came in handy when I fished it out of my pocket to show her. She said she couldn't wait to fix it all up with tape and nail polish, so she could wear it. We talked about what we had done all summer and maybe a little about dreams of future summers. I told her of my boring and tough job of painting the guard rails and of my date with the chick I had to take out to keep Jimmy happy. I didn't tell her about Debbi or Jerri!

After the show we went to Silverton Frisch's to show off the ring, which she was now wearing on a chain around her neck. We were greeted by a lot of snickers, due to her beard rash and a big passion mark she had managed to make on my neck. I was sort of impressed that I could now give a girl a rash.

We saw each other almost every night right up until school started. Most nights I would just go over and play a little toss with Artie, which seemed to really bug Donna, and then we'd talk until the rest of the family went to bed. Then it was snoof time. Most of our talk centered around the upcoming school year and what lie ahead. I told her that if I went to college and joined a fraternity, then I would give her my pin and we'd be pinned. She said that getting pinned would be the greatest thing that could ever happen, explaining that being pinned meant being engaged to be engaged, which was news to me. It was a nice period of time, no pressure, no games, just nice.

CIRCA 1957

"WHAT'S THE WORD?
THUNDERBIRD!
WHAT'S THE REASON?
'CUZ GRAPES..."

CHAPTER 18

The senior year began much as had the last few years, with Jimmy and I walking up the front circle together to join the herds of kids in their gangs of friends.

"Hey, there's Auer and Cohen. You two cocksuckers going steady?"

"How's your muthah?"

"Where's Goldstein, the third member of your circle jerk club, fuckers?"

"He's probably giving Richards a blow job."

Laughter followed each attempted put down and the rhetorical profanity never seemed to end as Jimmy finally said to one group, "Grow up little boys."

"Man, did you hear the language those kids were using? We never talked like that, did we?" Jimmy commented to me once we were away from them.

"Naw, we were never nerds like that. What a bunch of squares," I replied.

We joined a few other seniors standing near the entrance and compared schedules for the final year. The only thing we all agreed on was that the first semester better be a good one, because the second half we'd need a lot of time for parties. I was way ahead of them, signing up to take the hardest courses first and leaving a lot study hall time for the second part of the year.

At lunch I joined Stan, the Zap, Zappin on the ramp, taking in the rays with some of the other smokers. "Well, fellahs, being this is the first day of school and due to the fact that I turned eighteen last week, I'm going to treat you all to a beer. Now if someone will offer to drive me to Schuster's, I'll pick up a few cold ones to celebrate this, our final year," The Zap offered.

"I don't care what they say about you, Zappin, you're alright," I ribbed. "Now, just to show you that I'm an equally generous man, I'll drive. Anybody not worried about being late for class, follow me," I added, starting down the ramp.

Five of us piled into the '56 and we raced to Schuster's where Stan, true to his word, brought out the Hudey. It was going to be a good year!

Tooling back to Swifton, one hand on a beer and the other on the wheel, I asked my benefactor, "Did a rich uncle die or something? Or are you working?"

"Work? Please don't ever mention that word to me. I'm

allergic to it. But, just between you and me, I had a good day at the track last week. In fact I plan to have an even better day this coming Saturday. Wanna go?" the Zap asked.

"I don't know, man, I've only bet on the ponies once before and I took a bath then."

"Well, this is a sure thing, if the Goose shows up."

"Yeah, who's the Goose?"

"Roger Fowler, you know him. He goes to Walnut Hills and drives a '58 T-Bird. He's a COS.

"Oh yeah. Didn't he used to go with that blond cheerleader, what's her name?"

"Right, that's the guy. Anyway his father is a trainer at River Downs and sometimes he can find out who's going to win some of the races."

"Has he done this before?" I asked.

"No, but he indicated that because he has been working there all summer as a stable hand, they would let him in on a few races now that he had to quit and go back to school. Saturday is supposed to be the day and he said he'd share the info with me."

"Sounds good to me. Who else is going and what time? You're not planning on any early morning trip are you?"

"No. We don't have to be there until a little before one. Alex has been going with me, but this week he has something he has to do with the family. Baker has also gone a few times and the last time I talked to him he said he's going. Tell you what, why don't you talk to me later in the week, after I have had time to talk to the Goose again."

"Okay, and if you don't have to leave before noon I can still get some grass cut, not that it needs it much in all this hot weather we've been having," I answered.

River Downs might have been a more impressive place, with its white clapboard sided, spire topped, clubhouse, if it wasn't for the fact that it was right next to Coney Island's parking lot that was always a dust bowl. It was just a little much to take the place serious when it felt like it was part of a carnival, dust and all.

We found the Goose at the prearranged location only he wouldn't talk to all of us, so George and I went to our seats while the Zap and the Goose conferred. The outcome of this meeting was that jockey Bill Hathaway, was going to win three of his four races today. The Goose didn't know which three, but he was sure of his information. We quickly checked the racing form and saw that Hathaway was riding in races two, four, seven and nine.

The three of us went to the win window and placed modest bets on the horse ridden by Hathaway in the second. The race was exciting, especially since our man won. We collected our winnings, which weren't much because the horse was the favorite.

In race number four we bet a little heavier and won again. Congratulations all around were in order as we celebrated with cold beer and fresh cigars, agreeing that this was the only way to play the ponies.

For race number seven we each bet half our winnings, still not absolutely sure of our good fortune. Hathaway lost. Now came the big question. In the last race of the day, number nine, the gilded jockey was supposed to win, this being his third win of four races. However, he was riding the favorite again and it paid low odds. If the Goose was wrong we could lose more of our winnings. In addition, it meant that we would have to stay for the last race and then have to fight the traffic. Since we all had dates that night we decided to pass on the last race and walk away winners, agreeing to meet for dinner at the Fox and the Crow.

The dinner was an outstanding four course meal complete with wine and dessert, in one of the areas finest restaurants. Stan had a date with Ginger, who had been his steady since, well, forever. George was with a new chick he had just met at school and obviously never been to such a fancy place. She was very good at waiting to see what everybody else did before attacking her food. Donna loved putting on the dog and we all toasted our success at the track and future good times together. When the check came it was a real pleasure to be able to reach into my pocket and not have to worry, as usual, that I wouldn't have enough. We all left generous tips, feeling quite grown up in a real adult world.

Stan had doubled with me as his parents were using the car. George had a football team party to go to after dinner, so Stan and I and our dates just drove around for a while finally ending up in Eden Park. The weather was still on the warm side so we sat on the park benches and watched the, ah...submarine races in the river. Donna had become one of the best kissers ever. We just sort of fit together without a lot of the awkward situations of having a nose or arm in the wrong place at the wrong time. Neither one of us felt the need to constantly profess our love for each other verbally. It was just kiss and hug and stuff like that for hours on end. It felt so natural. There was no need to rush into other things.

Sunday I checked the paper: Hathaway won in the ninth.

****

It was a rumored fact that teachers piled on the homework for seniors, it being their last shot at us. There was no question in my mind that it was true. It seemed like every day I had to study in the evening and thus didn't get to go to Carters' or Frisch's except on the weekends. But by the end of the first grading period I had earned at least a passing grade in all subjects and could afford to slack off if need be.

It was on the Friday the report cards came out that I made the rounds of the drive-ins to celebrate with friends. Around eleven I walked into Carters' and found BB and Janice in a booth sipping coffee.

"Hi, good lookin', you still hanging around with this animal? When are you going to dump him and latch onto a real man?" I said, in a teasing way, sliding in next to her.

"No jokes man, we're not in the mood," BB said, quietly.

"Why? What's wrong? You two having a spat or something."

"No man, haven't you heard?"

"No. What. What's going on?"

"Frank died. You didn't know?" Janice stated coldly.

"Frank? You mean Frank the accordion player with the Keynotes. The one married to Sharon?"

"Yeah man, the same cat."

"When? How?" I pleaded.

"I think it happened this morning. I only heard about it a couple of hours ago. He went into the hospital yesterday, complaining of stomach pains and dizziness and must have had a heart attack or something while he was there. There wasn't any warning or anything. I heard about it from Isky, who had gone to visit him. Isky's pretty tore up about it. He's their kid's godfather and all. The only other thing I know is that Frank's family, on his father's side, has a history of heart trouble. I think both of his uncles died of heart attacks before they were fifty and his father has had one heart attack that I know of," BB related.

"Hey, man, I didn't know, I'm sorry, How's Sharon taking it. Have you seen her or his parents?"

"No. Like I just told you, we only just heard about it, but from what Isky said she's taking it pretty hard. Shit, she's only eighteen and already a widow, and with a kid to boot. Man life sucks."

Janice added, "At least they got the record cut, even though it didn't sell very well. He was such a nice guy. Everybody liked him."

"When's the funeral," I asked, getting very somber.

"We don't know. I guess we'll all just have to watch the papers."

I left Carters' knowing I should try to find Laine because she had become somewhat of a friend of Sharon's. It was weird, driving down Reading Road toward Frisch's. I was sure at any moment I would pass Frank's musical instrument packed Ranchero, and we'd wave just like always. I could just see him now, with his duck tails blowing in the wind from the cozy wing that he always kept cranked wide open. I thought of all the times I had enjoyed his playing at jam sessions and the Drift Inn. I didn't really know Frank very well, but he was one of the guys— I didn't know anybody very well. I thought of his little kid, who would now be growing up without a father. Then I thought about Willie. Now the old feelings came back and my stomach began to hurt. I hadn't thought of Willie for a long time, much less gone to visit him. I promised myself I'd take care of it tomorrow.

I didn't want to think sad thoughts or tell Laine, but I knew I had to. Maybe she wasn't there, though I had seen her pull in with a guy and another couple as I was leaving a little over an hour ago. No such luck. I saw her sitting in a booth with the others and walked right over, knowing that if I hesitated I might chicken out, "Hi Laine. Can I see you for a minute?"

They were all laughing and having a good time, the table covered with straw wrappers and empty coke glasses.

"Well, Mr. Auer. Where's Miss Donna? Have a little spat?"

"Laine, I'd like to talk to you, please."

"It's over big boy, can't you see. I've got a date so leave us alone."

They got silent as I continued to stand there, not saying anything. I wanted to speak, but I couldn't. I was mad. Mad because I couldn't talk and tears were starting to well up in my eyes. I didn't know if it was because I was sad about Frank or Frank's son or just the memory of Willie...or maybe just everything.

Laine's date, looked at me with contempt and started in, "What're you going to do Auer, cry and beg her to come back to you, man? Hey everybody, look at this, big bad Paul Auer's got tears in his eyes."

I knew I should punch him out, but I just didn't feel like it. I took a deep breath, put my hands on the table top and leaned over toward Laine and said, in a voice that cracked, "Frank died. I just wanted to tell you that." As soon as I said it I felt my ears getting hot and I knew it was a rush of adrenalin, similar to the feeling I used to get just before a swim meet, back so long ago. I back off, turned and started to walk away, hearing Laine telling her friends to let her out of the booth.

She caught me at the door before I got out. Pulling my arm she begged, "Paul, what happened? Are Sharon and the baby alright? When Where? Paul?"

I turned to face her and she saw the tears.

"Oh Paul, I'm sorry. I didn't know. Tell me. Hold me."

I told her all I knew and she hugged me burying her face in my shoulder.

"We were all friends. How could this happen?" She was crying now and I just held her. When I realized that others were staring at us, I said, "Maybe you better go back to your boyfriend now. He might be getting jealous."

"Oh he's just a nerd, let him. Will you call me when you know something," Laine said, wiping her eyes."

"Sure, and you call me if you talk to Sharon, okay?"

The funeral was Monday morning and I had to get Stan Schwartz, the gentile, to write the early excuse a note. Elaine was also going as I had promised to take her. She looked terrific, all dressed up with her hair piled up on top of her head, high heels and a dark suit. Maybe I was a little premature in dumping her, I thought, as we drove to the funeral home together. If I played my cards right I might be able to have both her and Donna. One to love and one to make love to.

After the services, we drove in a procession comprised of a few family cars and a long line of hot rods. There was BB's dust covered '35 with the rear window now completely fogged that gray blue that old glass gets, Isky's Stude-lac its twin pips rumbling deeply, Harry's '56 Chev now completely customized including a flame job and a full set of chrome lake pipes, Benny's '57 convertible with rust colored primer over his recent nose and deck job, Gil's '39 Ford minus the engine side panels which exposed the fully chromed 283 Chevy and George and his brother in the '52 Olds, sans mufflers, and showing D/GAS 37 in white paint on the side. Other clubs were also in attendance with an appearance by Larry's '51 nosed and decked, and still in gray primer Merc, from the Hellcats, and Charlie's Flat head coupe, its Camlifters plaque swinging below the rear bumper. I'm sure Frank's parents weren't impressed, but I know Frank would have been proud. It had begun to drizzle and I could see BB in my mirror, left arm stretched in front of the windshield, trying to get his wipers to work while Janice held the wheel. I wished I still had the Crosley, so I, too, could pay a proper homage.

On the way back to school Laine got back to normal, "I think it was just awful, having all those noisy hot rods following a hearse. And did you see how, what's his name, the guy with the blue car was dressed? He didn't even have on a coat and tie. Honestly Paul, I don't know why you go around with people like that. And that car of BB's—"

"Cut it, Laine. They're friends of mine and they were friends of Franks. As to their cars and clothes...well, maybe that's all they can afford." I wondered what I ever saw in her.

ARE YOU FOR REAL?

CIRCA 1957

Chapter 19

On the Friday after Thanksgiving, I had planned to catch up on some Z's except Mom woke me around nine, telling me my father wanted me at Queen City Chevrolet right away. This had happened before, whenever the Company bought new cars and ended up a car or driver short in the exchange. I showered and dressed in a hurry forgoing a shave and breakfast figuring I'd be gone only about an hour. At the dealership I inquired around until I found a salesman who introduced himself as Johnny Mitchel and then produced a set of keys. "They just finished washing the car and are probably bringing it to the front lot now," he said in that knowing way adults sometimes have. Suddenly, I was quite curious about what was going on here. "If you'd be interested in joining our club, I'll be happy to get you an application."

"Huh. What club, sir?" If his aim was to confuse me, he had succeeded.

"There's the car now," Mr. Mitchel said, starting to walk to the door. I followed as my eyes focused on the only moving vehicle on the lot—a brand new 1960 Corvette!

"Ah, excuse me, sir. Is that Corvette the car I'm supposed to take?" I asked, afraid to hear the answer.

"If you're Sid Auer's son, it is. How do you like it?"

It had to be the most beautiful thing I'd ever seen! It was the same color exterior as my sister's and Jimmy's, only this year it was called Ermine White. I approached the car and held my breath while offering a little silent prayer, "Please let it be a stick." It was, only it was a three-speed and not the four-speed that all the fast ones had. I wasn't going to complain as I now knew what I'd do with all the money I had saved over the summer.

Mr. Mitchel handed me a paper. "This is the invoice," he said. "Please see that your father gets it and if you're interested in joining the Queen City Corvette Club, just fill out the application and drop it off. We meet the first Monday of each month right here at seven o'clock."

I glanced at the invoice and saw that I was getting a radio, heater and white wall tires for a total sale price of $3433.01 plus tax and title. I thanked the salesman and went over to the '56, after he told me that it stayed, to clean out my personal stuff.

I was so proud and excited that I just had to show someone, so I stopped by the Knights garage on the way home. The guys that were there weren't impressed—after all it was only a stocker, but they advise me to break it in slow like the book said, and change the oil after the first five hundred miles. As I was about to leave, the club president, pulled me aside, "Listen, Paul, Ole buddy, we don't mind if you miss a few meetings once in a while, but we haven't seen you in at least the last three, and besides that you owe us back dues."

"Well it's like this—"

"Yeah I know, you've got other expenses and just because you have a rich father doesn't mean you've got any bread. Right?"

"Hey Gil, you ought to be a detective, the way you figure things out. How'd you know my problems?"

"I've been there myself."

Isky pulled me aside next. "Now listen, I want you to be careful with that new machine of yours and I don't want you to let either the power or the prestige go to your head. Ya dig?"

"Yeah, I hear ya, but what do you mean by prestige? You mean that just because I drive a fancy, new and fast car that my shit don't stink?" I asked.

"Well, yes, but there's more to it than that. I've watched you since you first become a member here and you're a nice kid with a good head on his shoulders. I haven't forgotten the lesson you taught us all about boring out the venturi of a carburetor, and you did a good job on the Crosley too. I just want to see that you don't mess up in life. I've got a feeling that your interests will change and you won't be coming around here much anymore. What I'm trying to say is, don't let this be the high point of your life. To some kids, especially ones who are big shots in high school, either through sports, social events or cars, this is the greatest time of their life. Now don't get me wrong, it is a great time, but if you let it be the highest point, then the rest of your life will seem anti-climatic. Do you know what I'm trying to say?"

"Well, sort of. Like I should always be looking for a higher point."

"Okay. But change that to always working for a higher point. Try to keep in mind that this is just one step on the road to greater things. Some people don't really come into their own until middle age, or even older. For them life doesn't really begin until much later, while for others life is over once they start living in the past. Now this can be really hard for you because you have a rich daddy who can make life too easy for you. I guess what I'm trying to say is that anything you get that you didn't earn isn't worth having. I'm not saying that you didn't earn that car, only that if you didn't or even if you did, don't let it stop there. Make it the best car there is, or become the best driver there is and when you've mastered that, move on to something else. Am I making any sense at all?"

"Yeah, I dig what you say and I really thank you for having an interest in me. You're right that I probably won't be around the club much anymore. I might join the Queen City Corvette Club because sports car racing is where my main interest is. But man, I'll still come to the strip and still see you and the guys at Carters' and such.

For the next four weeks I logged over 3,000 miles just to get though the warranty period and gain experience in handling the car. I took trips to Dayton to visit my Aunt, trips to Oxford to visit Bobbi and once to Louisville with Jimmy for a cup of coffee. Most of the driving was by myself, but Donna went many times too. She was very excited when I first took her for a ride, but soon realized that, at least for a while, she was no better than the second most important thing in my life. The Corvette Club that Jimmy and I joined was not what I expected. They were mostly older people, squares who only wanted to stage rallies and other non- speed contests. Of the thirty or so members there were only two who were into racing; they were much older than I was not very interested in helping a kid who had over three years to go to get an SCCA license. As the miles piled up I began spending my hard earned money on speed equipment and other necessities, to be added once the warranty period was up. By the start of Christmas vacation, I had accumulated in the garage:

1	Four speed transmission	$254.56
1	Heavy duty clutch	30.21
4	Heavy duty chocks	29.40
4	Set, metallic brake linings	35.21
1	Quick steering adapter	11.33
1	Dual point distributor	40.40
3	Two barrel Carter carburetors	54.88
1	Edelbrock intake manifold	53.20

1 Fuel block and fittings	28.49
1 Used 50M volt coil	30.00
1 Duntov 098 Camshaft	22.43
1 Set solid lifters	21.17
1 Set of gaskets	12.18
2 Marchal head lamps	14.20

The six hundred and thirty odd wholesale dollars represented almost all of the money I had saved, plus the cash I had gotten from the sale of the Crosley. Except for Christmas night and New Years Eve, I spent the entire vacation tearing down and building the Vette

On Christmas night, Bobbi let me borrow her car and I went to church with Donna. It was very impressive service, with the singing of many songs, most of which I knew by heart from my years at Lotspeich Grade School. I didn't feel very Jewish, but I didn't feel like a Christian either; I just felt American. The minister's message wasn't any different from what the Rabbis said in their sermons. They all wanted peace on earth and more money for the church/temple. On the way out, I overheard one of the congregation say, "The Jews sure don't know what they're missing". I wanted to laugh, but didn't, because this Jew sure wasn't missing anything! Donna heard it too and we both had a good laugh later when we talked about the service and compared notes on each others religion.

Neither one of us had very strong spiritual ties or beliefs, which was one more thing we had in common. In fact, the only thing we really didn't have in common was children. I liked kids and planned to have a few when I married, but I got the feeling that she didn't because of the way she treated her little brother. I had never heard her say a kind thing about him, or to him, for that matter. One time when I read in the newspaper about some children being killed in a fire and mentioned how sad it was, she acted very indifferent. I put that on my mental list of things to talk to her about. I mean I didn't want to waste time on a chick who there wasn't any future with. This wasn't puppy love anymore. I was almost eighteen and if we became pinned next year, well, who knows, lots of college kids get married.

New Years Eve Donna and I doubled with Stan and Ginger. Stan drove his father's Buick sedan and we saw the movie The Mouse that Roared at the Guild. It was a great movie and afterward the Zap and I fanaticized about what it would be like to own our own island in the Caribbean. We both believed we would be millionaires by the time we were twenty-five and could pool our money and just buy an island to set up our own government. Oh sure there were a lot of details and technicalities to be worked out, like maybe the island already belonged to some government, but we figured money could buy anything. After the show we stopped by one of the younger fraternity member's homes, who was having a party since his parents were out of town. Most of the kids were well on their way to getting drunk and were carrying on like it was their first New Years Eve. They were acting like such juveniles that we only stayed a short time and left, ushering in the new year at a stop light in the Zap's Buick.

We ended the evening toasting in 1960 at Jazz Bohemia, a new beatnik espresso house in Bond Hill. Before the bottle of wine that Stan ordered was gone, we were making plans on how to establish our new government on our island. The Zap was quite a guy with figures and in no time he had budgets and allowances all figured. We agreed to share the office of President and he would be the Treasurer while I would be the Commerce Secretary in order to set up a race course for International Grand Prix races, which we hoped would be our main income. It all seemed to get simpler and easier as the bottle got emptier. While Stan and I conferred on these matters of international importance, the girls had turned their backs on us to hear some beatnik chick in a halter top recite poetry on the little makeshift stage. The chick was good looking enough with her long straight hair, except she hadn't shaved under her arms. I couldn't understand what the poems were about and I don't think the Zap did either, but men of the world, such as we, couldn't be bothered with such trivia. The girls, on the other hand, clapped politely and said how beautiful it was.

The day after New Years I finished the Vette and took it for a test run. It performed better than my best expectations and I was very glad I had opted to install the three-twos, instead of the usual two-fours that most others had done. I even went the hot rodders one better by making straight linkage for the carbs when the norm was to use progressive linkage. This set up allowed total control in the corners, where power had to be metered just so.

It was late afternoon when I stopped by the gas station

where Hard worked, only to learn that he had been laid off. I found him at home in a very depressed state. After he thoroughly checked out my work, he wanted to see what it would do. I knew just the spot. I had heard that they were building a new shopping center way north of the city on some farm land, a place called Tri-County. We found this huge center, with its newly paved blacktop, completely deserted, it being a Saturday. We drove slowly all the way around the buildings looking for hazards or holes in the pavement. It must have been at least a mile all the way around and the only dangerous conditions we found were the light poles, which were spaced a hundred yards or so apart. On the second trip around, I picked the speed up to about seventy as we weaved in and out of the light poles testing the quick steering and new shocks. The Vette stuck like glue. On the third try I got on it hard with full acceleration up to red line in third before leveling off at ninety and again weaving in and out of the poles. We hadn't completed the third trip when, from out of nowhere, two cop cars, lights flashing and sirens screaming, converged on us. With one squad car coming from the rear and one from the front, I decided now was to good time to test the new metallic brake linings! At ninety miles per, I clamped on the binders hard, just short of locking up the wheels. The cop from the rear couldn't stop that fast and he overshot me by about four or five car lengths, while the scout car in front underestimated my stop also and came up short. When everybody got stopped, I put the Vette in first and drove up to them. The uniformed nerds, obviously highly excited, approached each side of our car with guns drawn! "Okay, assholes, out of the car and keep your hands where we can see them," came the command.

We got out and I looked at Hard as he gave me one of those, I-don't-need-this-shit-after-losing-my-job-and-all looks.

"Let me see your license, hot dog," one officer demanded, as I stood facing them. I didn't say a word as I handed him my permit.

"You boys better lock that machine up and come with us. It might be a long time before you get back," the first officer said, in a still excited voice.

"Better wait a minute, Sarge, the Chiefs coming now," the second officer said.

As the third car pulled up, I started to feel a little sick myself, with the thought of another visit to the twenty-twenty club coming up. The chief pulled up right next to us, got out and said, "Paul, what the hell are you doing? I heard your daddy got you that Corvette, but I sure didn't expect to see you out here trying to kill yourself."

With a wave of relief, I said, "Sure is good to see you Doug."

"Sergeant, you and Patrolman Rudniki can go. I'll take care of this," the Chief ordered. As the other cops turned to leave, the Chief continued, "Well, what the hell are you up to? Your daddy's gonna skin you alive if I take you in."

"I'm sorry, Doug. It's just that I got it running after putting a lot of speed equipment on it and we wanted to test it out in some safe place. I didn't want to drive like that on the street- -"

"You damn sure better not drive like that on the street! Now open the hood and show me what's in it."

I popped the hood. "Woo wee," Doug exclaimed. "That's some motor. How fast will she go?"

"I haven't run top end yet, but on paper, at 6500 RPM in top gear, true speed would be 140. I don't have any doubts that it'll do it. Want to take it for a spin?"

"Not me. I'd probably kill myself. Now listen, you take that bomb out of my bailiwick real slow like and don't you ever come back unless it's the same real slow pace. Otherwise I'll lose my job and you're daddy'll have both our hides. You got that, boy?"

"You bet, and thanks, Doug," I said, as I turned to Hard who was still standing where the Sergeant had placed him, his mouth hanging open. "Come on Hard, time to go."

It was almost a mile before Howard could talk. "What happened? First I thought we were going to hit those light poles and I was going to be dead. Then I knew I was going through the windshield when you stood on the binders, and finally, I was sure I'd never see my dear sweet mother again after they threw away the keys to the slammer. Who was that masked man?" Hard said, in a slightly exaggerated way, half joking and half crying.

"Oh, You mean my ole buddy, Doug," I said, starting to feel a little more at ease.

"Yeah, man, The Chief of Police you so lightly call by his first name. Who's he and what have you got on him?"

"Well, you see, it's like this. Doug is a part time driver for the company. He's a real cool guy, in case you haven't noticed.

He even taught me how to drive the company semi. I knew he was a cop, but I didn't know he was the Chief. Lucky for us he was, eh?"

"Auer, you're the luckiest son-of-a-bitch I've ever seen."

"Luck? Your ass. It was pure skill that we didn't hit any of those light poles."

"I wasn't referring to that, that giant steel picket fence that you snaked through. I have the utmost confidence in your driving ability. It's your mastery of staying out of trouble that involves the element of luck. And I only hope I'm not there when it runs out."

"Well, anyway, I think I learned something about the car. Did you feel the slight pause whenever we went from a hard left to a hard right? There seemed to be a little miss, like the carbs were running out of gas. What do you think?" I asked Howard.

"Now that you mention it, I remember thinking the same thing on the last hard corner we took. But that's all you can expect from carburetors. The only cure for taking corners as hard as you drive is fuel injection."

"An injector is out of the question. Too much bread. I'll have to figure on something else."

Instead of cracking the books hard for the upcoming exams, I spent the next two weeks working on a way to improve the cornering aspects of the three-twos. I didn't even bother to consult some of the Knights, because they had all been so wrong about the boring of the venturi on the Crosley. After much trial and error, I finally hit on a system utilizing multiple fuel blocks, pumps, lines, and special fittings to keep fuel flowing through the carburetors at all times. This negated the tendency of the float to close during hard cornering, in addition to reducing the risk of vapor lock.

Finals proved to be a disaster. I was passing in all subjects, but just by the skin of my teeth. On the Friday after the semester finals, I was not in a very good mood and in need of whiskey, fast driving and loving. I ended up at Donna's where she was baby-sitting. She got real upset because I was talking baseball with Artie and looking at his collection of baseball cards. Around nine she came into the living room and announced, "All right creep, it's time for you to go to bed."

"How come, DD? It's not my bed time. I get to stay—"

"Because I said so, you little brat. Now get going or I'll

tear up all those silly cards and give you a spanking."

"She grabbed him by the arm and jerked him out of the chair, raising her hand as if to smack him. I jumped up and stepped between them. "Easy now," I said. "Why don't you just go to your room, Artie, so Donna and I can talk. I'd really like to see the rest of your cards, but not right now, Okay, buddy?"

"Well, okay, but if she hits me, I'm tellin' Dad this time."

Artie left and I looked at Donna, thinking how some guys say their girls looks cute when they're mad. Donna didn't look cute at all! Considering the mood I was in, I figured maybe this was the time to find out about her reasons for such behavior.

"Say, ah, Donna. How come you're so hard on that kid? He's only, what, ten or eleven and seems to be just a normal little brother to me."

Putting her arms around me, she said, " I don't want to talk about him. Can't we just sit on the couch. I'll rub your back if you want."

"No. I want to talk about it. Is it him, or do you hate all little kids? What about after you're married, do you want kids of your own?"

"I don't know. Certainly not if they're like him, and besides, it's none of your business how I treat my brother, is it?"

"Well, in a way it is. If, or when, we get married I wouldn't want you to treat our kids that way. And besides that, it hurts me to see a kid treated that way. In all the time I've known you, I've never seen or heard you be nice to him. Are you ever?"

"Sure I'm nice to him, whenever he does the dishes for me and stuff. I didn't hit him just now, did I? You see how it is. He never minds me and always wants to argue and tell Mom and Dad about me. What difference does it make to you, anyway? Tell me, I want to know, what right you have to say how I treat my own brother? What are you, a judge or something?"

She had gotten very indignant and defensive. I thought maybe I really didn't want to know this about her and that if we just kissed and made up now, things would all work out later. I sat on the couch, suddenly thinking of her soft firm boobs, "Let's not fight. Come over here and—"

"No. You started this. Now tell me what bothers you so much about Artie and me. This isn't the first time that you have tried to tell me how to treat him. Well?"

"Well, okay and since you asked...I don't know if you know this or not, but...I had a little brother once. He was just about the same age as Artie is now, only my little brother died. It was a brain tumor and it happened quite suddenly. In fact, I didn't even get to say good-by. He was a, well...a playmate in addition to being a brother and I really liked him. So when I see Artie, or for that matter, any little kid get treated badly, it makes me sad.

Without showing any sign of softening Donna said, "Yeah, so what was your brother's name and how long ago was it he died?"

"Willie. He name was actually William, named after old Uncle Will, but we called him Willie. He's been gone now, lets see, about four years or so. I really liked him. We used to play together all the time and he was great at helping me and the other kids at building tree houses and—"

You mean he's been dead for four years and you're still grieving for him? Isn't that a little morbid? I mean really, Paul."

"I'm not grieving, just remembering. I hope I never forget him and the good times we had. When I get married I plan to name my first boy after him."

"Well, I think that's dumb. And if you marry me there might not be any kids. I don't think I want any, they're too much trouble, the brats. Do you want a coke or something?"

I was having a hard time believing what I was hearing. The callous, detached tone of her voice was exposing a trait I was afraid had always been there. I didn't answer her. After a short silence she came over and sat on the couch next to me. In a softer tone, but still without compassion, she said, "What's wrong Paul? Are you just upset because of the exams? Don't be mad at me. I really love you. Now why don't you put your head on my shoulder."

I did as she suggested, but it didn't help. I knew, in the back of my mind, that the relationship wasn't going to be. She kissed me on the forehead and squeezed my hand. Maybe I was wrong. "I don't know Donna," I began, searching for the questions that would yield the answers I wanted to hear. "All I want is to get through school, go to college, get married—married to you— and raise a family."

"Well, that's all I want too, except the part about a family. Don't you want to make money?"

"Sure, but I don't have any doubts about that. I'll make

a lot of money someday, but I want a family and you don't."

"Well, if we make a lot of money, maybe we could have a nanny or something to handle the kids. Yeah, that's it. I wouldn't mind having the babies, that's cool, but if we had someone to take care of them then we, you and me, could just keep on doing things together. Wouldn't that be alright?"

The scene flashed through my mind of the hurt look in a little Willie's or Artie's eyes, while the nanny waved good-bye to Donna and me, as we left to party every night.

"Well? Wouldn't that be okay, Paul?" Donna asked again, obviously pleased with her idea.

"What? I'm sorry, I was just thinking. Yeah, sure that might be just great," I lied.

She must have sensed that things weren't the same between us because she asked me to unhook her bra and rub her back. I had the feeling that I could get past first base, but somehow my desire was lacking.

GOT THE PICTURE, DADDY-O

CHAPTER 20

The weekend was not a total loss. Sunday, my parents informed me that they were leaving for Florida the following Saturday. A good party sure could go a long way to lifting the spirits. At school that week I spread the word that I was having a blast. Jimmy promised to come up with a couple of quarts of Arnold's homemade wine for the event, and George was sure that he could swipe a bottle of booze from his old man's liquor cabinet. The only problem we had to get around would be keeping old Bessie, who was going to stay in the spare room, from telling. Friday night brought another problem: Bobbi had come home for the weekend, but with careful and discreet questions I learned that she was planning to be out with John on Saturday night.

The big night rolled around with the Stan, the gentile, Schwartz being the first to arrive, carrying a half a carton of Burger.

"Where's the rest of it?" I asked as soon as he was in the door.

"In here," he said, patting his belly. "I'm just trying to get a head start."

"Come on down the basement and for God's sake don't let Bessie see that beer."

"Who's Bessie?"

"She's the old colored lady that's staying here while Mom and Dad are gone," I replied.

"What'd they do, get you a nurse maid?" he said, ribbing me.

"Wouldn't you? If you were my parents?"

Stan laughed, "You got me there."

It wasn't long before the driveway was filled with cars and the basement was packed with guys in various stages of intoxication. Schwartz was the first victim, passing out on the stairs. Hard helped me half carry, half drag him all the way to the second floor where we dumped him, clothes and all, in the shower. As Stan sputtered to life under the cold stream of water, Bessie walked in.

"Masser Paul, wha's yew doin' in dere? An wha's all dat racket down de basemen? Why lookie 'ere...dat dere boy's done gots all his clothes on. Wha's—"

"It'ssss OOOkay Bessieeee," I slurred.

CIRCA 1957

"Now yew lis'en 'ere, Masser Paul. Yew git dis 'ere boy outta dem clotheses an put 'im in t'other bed in yourn room. I'm a goin' ta see fer maself wha's ah goin' on down dere. Ya'ere?"

Hard and I struggled to do as we were told, which had become very difficult, not only because Stan had collapsed in the tub, but we were both feeling the effects of all the booze. By the time we got to the head of the basement stairs I could hear Bessie telling those that were still sober to clean up the mess and those that weren't to get out. I started down the stairs just as Bobbi and John came home. At the bottom of the stairs I could smell vomit and before I could even turn my head for fresh air, up it came. Boy was I sick. As I heaved onto the clean floor, I kept promising myself I'd never drink again while Bobbi screamed something at me. The last thing I remembered saying was something about promising to clean it up in the morning.

The morning came too early and too loud. I had the worst taste in my mouth and someone was sleeping in the bed next to me who smelled worse than me. Then I remembered. Other than the bad taste in my mouth I really didn't fee to bad. Shit, I can handle my liquor. Time to get rolling...ohhhh. I shouldn't have moved. My head exploded and then everything hurt at once. I tried for the medicine cabinet, but as soon as I laid my hand on the bottle of aspirin I knew that anything going down was coming up. I did manage to brush my teeth while Stan took his second shower in eight hours. I traded him my tooth brush for the hot shower, after which we both put on clean clothes. He didn't fit into my jeans very well being at least fifty pounds heavier, but at least they were dry and smelled fresh. We slowly and gingerly clumped out of the house and into Stan's '55 Olds, his nice quiet Olds, his nice quiet Olds with an automatic transmission and working muffler. So that's why you never see old drunks driving hot rods.

Three cups of hot, black, Carters' coffee later we stopped at the Center Pharmacy for a box of candy. Our timing was perfect. Bessie had just finished with the clean-up as we strolled in. "Ah Bessie, you didn't have to do this. We were going to clean it up," I said, a sincere tone of voice.

"What yew meen I's don' 'ave ta do dis. It's ma job! Yourn Mama gonna beat knots on yer haid when she gits home...an fire me too!"

"Now, we don't have to tell her. Here I brought you this candy," I said, handing her the paper bag from the drug store.

"Shucks, I's still gonna hav'ta tell 'er. Now yew git up in dat kit'en an let me fix yew an yer frien' som'in ta et. Now git."

There was no arguing with Bessie when she got like this.

The next week in school was a real bummer. I saw Donna every day, but we really didn't have anything to talk about. At least that's how I felt. She was still wearing my ring and seemed to talk like nothing was wrong, but I knew it was over. I was mad at her for being the way she was, and I was mad at myself for being the way I was. Maybe I was wrong and shouldn't care about little kids so much or worry about having my own, which might never happen. With Donna on the way out, my grades on the way down and my parents on the way back I was ready for drastic action. What I needed was a change, any change. It seemed like everybody was having trouble: Donna with me, Hard with his steady in addition to having blown the engine in his '57, the Zap had lost big at an all night poker game in Newport and Jimmy had gotten taken on the two-fours he bought for his Vette.

Thursday night I tried doing my Trig homework, but I couldn't figure it out. I was hopelessly behind and it was only the first full week of classes. I got in the Vette and drove to Roselawn hoping to find a shoulder to cry on. Jimmy's Vette was in the lot at the Center Pharmacy, so I stopped in to join him at the soda fountain. The Zap was also there too and Hard and George came by a few minutes later, making it a foursome to commiserate. Without any previous conscious thought I said, "The weather sucks, Donna doesn't, my grades aren't what you'd call cherry, and my parents are going to take my Vette away as soon as they get back from vacation. I think I'll go to Florida. Anybody want to come along?"

"You mean Florida, where the sun always shines and it's not so fuckin' cold?" Hard asked.

"That's the place."

"Sounds good to me. When do we leave?"

"Shit, I don't know. Can you be ready in half an hour?"

"No sweat," Howard answered, as both our spirits began to soar.

"Now listen, man. I'm serious. I want to go there and not come back. I figure we can get our grades transferred to a high school down there and get jobs and just live there. I don't want to, wait make that, can't come back if I leave, ya dig."

219

"I'm hep. That's the only way I could go too. If I leave I'll never be able to come back either," Howard solemnly stated.

"Now don't do anything stupid and get caught, like Perkins and Keebler did last year when they took off to Florida, "Jimmy advised.

"Ah, those candies were only gone four days. And besides, they were hitch-hiking. There's no way they're gonna catch us. This isn't a vacation, we're moving to The Sunshine State, suckers! Now we expect you real gone cats to come and visit us this summer, when we get set up in our own pad and all," Hard said, starting to get in the swing of things.

"Now we're cookin' with gas. How much bread you got? I've got about a hundred at home," I said.

"I don't know man, at least that much. How 'bout you guys coming up with a little scratch, say maybe a sawbuck each. It ought to be worth that much just to be rid of us," Howard said, in a joking way, but George and Jimmy forked it over.

"Okay, everything's set. Cohen, if you'll take Hard home to pack, I'll get my stuff and meet you guys at the Cities Service station in half an hour.

It was nine-thirty when we pulled onto Reading Road for what was sure to be the last time. We hadn't even talked about a final destination because we didn't want anyone to know. But once in the privacy of the tiny cockpit of the Vette I suggested, "How's Tampa - St. Pete sound?" And without waiting for an answer, I continued. "I checked the atlas at home and it looks like we can follow U.S. 27 all the way to Atlanta and then pick up U.S. 41 which is direct to the Gulf Coast, beaches, sunshine and pussy. I don't think we should go to Miami because that's where my parents are and that's the first place they look for run-a-ways. What do you think?"

"Any place in Florida is alright with me, just wake me when we're there, ole buddy," Hard sighed, as he snuggled into his coat turned pillow.

"Ole buddy, my ass! You're going to have to do your share of the driving too. Tell ya what, we'll change off every tank of gas which ought to be about every two hundred miles or four hours, okay?"

"Yeah sure. What is it, about a thousand miles?"

"Something like that. It sure will be nice when Ike gets that expressway system in I've read about. Won't that be neat? A thousand miles without a stop light, and if you want to pass someone all you have to do is pull over in the next lane."

"Shit. We won't live that long."

Once through Newport, the traffic thinned out and I could really let the Corvette roll down the short straights and around the countless turns through the semi-mountainous hills of Kentucky. The chicken shit speed limit of sixty, which we had to adhere to when behind some old fogy, was frustrating and agonizing. Hell, the Vette could do that in first gear! But to me, every car I passed and every corner I entered was a challenge, a challenge to drive to the limit. I loved it. I loved the changing down for the bends, feeling the metallic brakes hauling the beast to a safe speed and then the surge of raw power as I opened her up coming out of the corners. I relished the exhilaration of passing a string of cars at red line in third gear. I felt the machine and I were one, and at times I was so intent on the task at hand I was totally unaware of anything, including my passenger. It wasn't until we were deep into the Bible belt that I began to slack off. The powerful Marchal lamps had no trouble finding the small, old and rusty signs peering out of the brush from between Burma-Shave jingles and Mail Pouch sided barns: "PREPARE TO MEET THY MAKER". It's not that I'm a very religious person, but those ominous signs had a sobering effect. At least for a few miles, anyway. The only cop we saw was on a straight stretch just outside Atlanta. He was parked on the side of the road and took off after us as we sailed by at the usual ninety. Hard was driving and as soon as we crested a small hill and were out of his sight, Howard panic stopped, as I braced myself with the chicken bar. During some of our brief conversations over the past ten hours or so we had planned for such a situation. As soon as we stopped we both got out and took off our shirts. Standing there in our T-shirts, we watched with subdued glee as the State Trooper overshot us. The new brakes had done it again! The cop had to back up the shoulder of the road to get to us and was obviously mad, jamming his hat on as he got out of the patrol car.

"Ya'll goin' a mite fast back there, weren't you, boys?" The Trooper snarled as he looked us over.

"No sir. If we were going as fast as you we couldn't have gotten stopped this quickly, sir," I said, in my most sincere and innocent voice.

"Don't smart mouth me boy, and which one of you was drivin'?"

"Gee, I don't remember. Whose turn was it to drive? Do you remember, Howard?"

"Why no, I'm not sure, maybe...."

"Alright boys, I'm trying to be patient, now which one was driving because he's going to jail and the other one can then go on his way. Now, come on, and fess up. Ya hear."

Howard and I looked him right in the eye, but didn't say a word. We had him. He couldn't write a ticket unless he could place one of us behind the wheel and since we both had dark hair and white shirts there was no way he could honestly say who was driving. We were lucky he was an honest cop. He checked his hot sheet to see if the Vette was reported stolen and finally sent us on our way with the admonishment, "Ya'll drive slow now. We don't cotton to no Yankees racing through our fine State, ya here."

We hit the Florida State line and stopped to put the top down. This was really living. Of course, in less than fifty miles we had to put the top back up due to the buffeting of the wind at ninety per. It wasn't until we hit he city limit sign of St. Pete at one- thirty-five in the afternoon, that we could put it down again and soak up some of that glorious sunshine. Within a few minutes of that momentous occasion, we pulled up next to two chicks walking on a sidewalk. Hard didn't waste a minute. "Hi. I wonder if you two good lookin' girls could help us out?"

They looked at each other, giggled, and then walked over to the car. Howard continued, "We just got in from the North, the cold, cold North, and we need directions to the beach. I've just gotta wiggle my toes in the surf."

"Well," the taller of the two began. "If you take this—"

"That sounds too complicated. Why don't you two just hop in and show us," Howard interrupted and then continued. "My name's Howard and this is my buddy, Paul, and we sure would appreciate a little southern hospitality in showing us the way to the ocean."

The taller one giggled again and then spoke once more. "I've never ridden in a Corvette. Can we all fit in there? Will you bring us back? We can't be gone long."

This time I spoke. "Sure there's plenty of room, and we'll bring you back whenever you say, if you can keep us from getting lost. So hop in."

"Well, okay, but we can't be gone long. Cecilia, you go and tell Mom that we'll be right back. That's Cecilia, she's my sister, and I'm Barbara," the tall one said.

Sixteen-and-a-half hours after leaving the soda fountain we each had a chick on our arm and were lying on a real beach! Barb and I were hitting it off real good, even doing a little kissy face. Howard and Cee didn't seem to be having any trouble getting to know each other either. Man, life doesn't get any better than this. The girls told us that the best place to find work was at the motels that fronted the beach, so before taking the chicks home we hit the closest one. Much to my surprise the manager told me that if I came back at six I could have a job parking cars. I was elated.

Back at the girls' house we cleaned up and I took a nap, while Hard went looking for a job at some of the gas stations. When he got back with the news that he had been hired to pump gas starting the next morning, we just had to call and tell somebody. We called the Zap collect, who related that Howard's Mom had been calling him, looking for her son. He said that he told her in all honesty that he didn't know where we were. The Zap was most impressed with our good fortune and promised to tell the guys.

At six Howard dropped me at the motel, promising to pick me up again around eleven. Of the four men shuttling cars, I was by far the youngest. Two of the guys looked to be in their fifties, but they could run just as fast as I could. It was pretty neat getting to drive all those fancy new cars and get paid for it too. By the end of the dinner hour I had earned over twelve bucks in tips!

Hard and the girls picked me up a little after eleven and we stopped for some burgers and fries. Between bites I asked my chick, "Do you think we could stay at your place for a few nights? Or at least until we get a pad of our own."

"I don't know for how long, but I did talk to my Mom before and she said that we really don't have the room. Maybe one of you can sleep on the couch tonight."

"Well Hard, it beats a blank. I'll flip you for the couch." I lost.

"How come you girls weren't in school today? And where is the school anyway?" Howard asked.

Cee said, "It was a teachers' day and the school is only two blocks from our house. Why?"

"Well, we'd like to enroll there on Monday so we can finish our schooling and graduate. Is it a cool school?" Hard probed.

"It's okay, I guess. What grade are you guys in?"

"We're both seniors and only need the last semester to get our diploma. I think if we register there, they'll let us go to class while they send for our transcripts. At least, that's the plan. Right, Paul?"

"Sounds good to me, but I've got to get some serious sleep soon."

Corvettes were not made for sleeping and as tired as I was I still woke up many times that night with aches and pains in different spots each time. Saturday, Howard worked and I washed the car in the girls' driveway. I met their mother, Mrs. Griffith, and learned that she worked the second shift as a nurse in the big hospital over in Tampa. She was divorced and had just the two girls and a cat. Mrs. Griffith was very understanding when I told her that the reason that we ran away was because our parents beat us. She said we could sleep, one on the couch and one on the floor, until Monday and then we would have to find a place of our own. She was most impressed that we wanted to finish school and hold jobs. Around five I picked Hard up and as we headed for the motel. I told him of my conversation with the girls' mom.

"Oh shit! I hope she doesn't talk to Cee," Howard exclaimed.

"Why not. What did you tell her?"

"I told Cee that we took the car and left because the cops were looking for our parents 'cuz they were involved in the Mafia.

"Well if comes up—"

Wrrrrrrrrrrrrrr, Wrrrrrrrrrrrrr

"Shit! Now what! It's the cops!" I said, looking in the rear view mirror and pulling over to the curb.

"One of you named Auer and the other Richards?" The cop demanded, walking up to the drivers side.

"What if we're not?" I said, feeling cocky. I mean who did he think he was talking like that to a man with a job, a car and a chick.

"Well, if you're not, then you're under arrest for driving a stolen car. Now lets see some identification."

"Oh well, in that case we're the guys you're looking for." I said, sheepishly.

After looking at our driver's licenses, he took Howard

with him and told me to follow.

Once inside the old City Jail building, Howard was led to another room and the desk sergeant made me put all my stuff from my pockets, except my fags and Zippo, in a brown envelope marked "PROPERTY".

"Where's my friend, Howard? And why are you taking my things?" I wailed.

The sergeant moved the cigar from one side of his mouth to the other. "Son, I'm the only friend you've got in here. Now mind your own business and you'll do alright. You're going to be our guest until your mommy comes and gets you. I don't want you to get worried, but we don't have any more room in the juvenile cell so I'll have to put you in one of the regular cells. I'll try to find one that doesn't have any killers or real hard cases in it, if you just behave. Understand?"

"Yes, sir and thank you, sir."

This was nothing like the Twenty-Twenty club. This was big time with eight double steel bunks in each cell and bars and smelly, scruffy men everywhere. There were already seven in the cell I was assigned, so I immediately climbed onto the only vacant bunk and tried to act as tough and cool as I could. Trying to act nonchalant, I pulled a cigarette from the pack rolled up in my sleeve and lit up. Hey, I had it made. I was one of the guys. All I had to do was look cool and keep blowing smoke. I finished the fag and casually tossed the butt in the toilet just below my bunk. Within a second, one of the hardened criminals I shared this "home sweet home" with, jumped up and grabbed me by the shirt front. Fish breath, his scarred unshaven face, inches from mine, then ground out. "Listen punk, around here we pass the butts on to the next guy. We don't never throw 'em in no shit can. Understand?"

"Sure, sure, man, I can dig that. I'm, I'm, I'm sorry. Here do you want my whole pack?" I said, meekly reaching for my shoulder.

"No, asshole. Just pass the butts on, okay?"

In the Twenty-Twenty Club there was nothing to do but stare at the walls, jack off, and sleep. Here I was afraid to sleep and I had seven other guys to watch—without staring—and I sure couldn't beat my meat in public. Sleeping on a flat steel plate with holes in it, and nothing but a dirty blanket for a cover, was not conducive to good rest. However, I managed to cop a few Z's and woke up feeling a little better, especially since I hadn't been robbed, raped or beaten, by my bunk mates. Breakfast was served in a large room on steel tables with steel benches for seats. Everything was steel, even the cups which the prisoners banged on the table top until coffee was served. A big fat colored man with one gold tooth in an otherwise toothless mouth, passed out the trays of good and kept the coffee cups filled. I ate the yellow stuff that was supposed to be scrambled eggs, but didn't taste like it. They sort of tasted like salted chalk dust with maybe a little pepper. The toast was great and the coffee better, but as hungry as I was I couldn't handle the grits.

By early afternoon Eddie—that's the guy who had grabbed me by the shirt—and I had become jail house buddies. I told him I was up for Grand Theft Auto and he said he was in for Armed Robbery, but he didn't think they could make the charge stick because he had tossed the gun he used in the bay. He told me he was from "somewhere up north", where he had a wife and two kids. He also said that he was almost thirty, but had spent six of those years in the "big house" for burglary. He looked at least fifty, with scars and tatoos all over his body and all his front teeth were missing. Somewhere around three, they came and got me. As I walked out, not knowing if I'd be back, I tossed the remainder of my fags to Eddie who gave me a big toothless grin and said he'd save them for me in case I was sent back.

I was taken to an office marked "SHIFT OFFICER" where I was surprised to see my Mother seated across from the uniformed cop. She didn't look very happy to see me, and after the officer explained that he was releasing me in her custody, we walked out. That's all there was to it. Once outside she stopped and hugged me, saying, "Paul, I just want you to know that we love you. Now I'm still a little nervous from the plane ride up here, it was my first, you know, so if you will take me to your car we can get started for Miami.

"Sure Mom. And I'm sorry. It just seemed like such a good idea at the time. I hope I didn't cause you any trouble?"

"No, your Father's a little upset, but he'll get over it."

"Do you know what happened to Howard?"

"Oh, he left yesterday. His Mother sent money for a plane by Western Union, right to the police station and they put him on the plane. At least that's what the Captain said. He was such a nice man. I didn't want to have you arrested, but that was the only way we could see to get your attention. I hope they treated you all right."

During the ride to Miami Mom tried to find out why I had run away, "You can tell me son. What is it that makes you so unhappy that you'd want to leave your parents? We've tried so hard to give you the things that we never had and to make life as easy as possible. What's wrong, Paul?"

"Ah, Mom it's not that I don't appreciate what you've done for me and all, but...well it's just I want to plan my life and make some decisions of my own."

"Wasn't there a movie, Rebel Without a Cause, that was playing a year ago or so?"

"Yeah, I think so. It starred James Dean, I think."

"Is that what you're doing? Rebelling without a reason?"

Maybe I was. Maybe it was time I gave some serious thought to what I was going to do with my future. I tried playing out different scenarios for next year, ten years, anytime in the distant and was surprised—and a little scared—that I really couldn't see myself.

The rest of the ride to Miami, at the legal speed limit, was boring and uneventful. Ditto for the stay at the Fontainebleu Hotel. I mean how much fun can a guy have, surrounded by bikini clad chicks, with a parent always, and I mean always, in tow. I figured that must be part of my punishment, and that's what hell must be like—lots of temptations, but unable to get away with anything. Purgatory only lasted two days and then we were on the road home, me in the Vette and the old man in his Caddy. The only high point of the entire return trip was that the old man got a ticket for following me too closely. I got a real kick out of it but knew better than to say anything to him. During the few times Mom rode with me, we talked about my future and she promised me that if I graduated from school this year, I would get to keep the Vette. The only punishment I would have to endure would be grounding on school nights for the rest of the grading period.

Back home, the school suspended me for three days so I spent the time helping around the house. During the next few weeks, when I wasn't cracking the books, I installed a switch panel in the Corvette. This little plate of aluminum contained controls for both tail lights, just one tail light, and both brake lights.

At the end of the grading period I learned that I had pulled all my grades up to a passing level except Trig. There was no way I could ever pass that and summer school was a must again. Only this time I would be able to take a snap course because I already had enough credits in math to graduate. I also learned that I would be permitted to participate in the graduation exercises, but would only receive a blank piece of paper instead of the diploma. The actual diploma would be mailed to me upon successful completion of summer school.

Two weeks later, the first day of spring, I turned eighteen. Dad took us all out to Grafton's for dinner and I ordered my first "legal" beer. It was sort of anti-climatic.

NO SHIT, SHERLOCK

CHAPTER 21

With the advent of my eighteenth birthday and the end of the school year in sight, things were starting to look a whole lot better. Even Howard fared well; his father gave him enough money to rebuild his '57 and he landed a job at another gas station. He swore that when he was finished with the re-build it would eat Corvettes, and thus, another challenge was made. Jimmy had failed English, but like me, had enough credits in that subject so he would only have to take a snap course in summer school for total credits. We got together in the counselors office one afternoon and both signed up for a course in Government that was being given at Walnut Hills. Almost everybody was going to college and had been busy making applications and campus visits.

My relationship with Donna had been...well, nonexistent since my return from Florida. It seems that she told everybody who would listen that she had broken up with me and because of that, I was so hurt that I ran away to St. Pete. I didn't see any point in a confrontation, so I never really had any contact with her. I got my ring back, sans tape and nail polish, from Louie who had gotten it from Natalie. Just before opening day I made it a point to talk to Donna, stopping her in the hall at school. "Hi, good lookin'. Got a minute for an old flame?"

"Sure handsome. I've been wanting to talk to you anyway."

"Yeah, what about?" I asked.

"No, you first. What did you want to talk to me about?"

"Okay. I've got two tickets to the Redlegs opening game and- -"

"Wait a minute. If you think I'm going to go out with you, well, I can't. I going steady with William now."

"William? I heard you were going out with him, but I didn't know you were going steady with old nerd face," I said, getting my licks in.

"He's not a nerd, and if that's all you wanted, then I have better things to do. Like go to class," she said, in a huff.

"Wait. You didn't let me finish. Before I was so rudely interrupted, I just wanted to know if you think Artie would be allowed to go to the game with me?"

"Well! I guess you'll just have to ask him or my mother," Donna coldly said, as she stormed away.

229

"Hey wait. You said you had something you wanted to talk to me about, Didn't you?" I called after her hoping for another chance to put her down. She said something I couldn't understand and just kept right on walking. I really didn't give a hoot. I knew she would be p.o.'d if I took Artie to the game, but that wasn't the reason I wanted to take him. I did like the kid and he loved the game so. Maybe it was because I could see Willie in him or maybe because of the way Donna mistreated him. I didn't know and didn't want to think about it, I just wanted to see him enjoy the game. That night I called Mrs. Diamond and got permission to take Artie, promising to call again the night before the game to confirm a time.

Friday night, while enjoying a coke at Frisch's, I noticed a good looking young chick sitting with a group of girls not far from me and just for fun I winked at her. When she smiled back, I winked again and after a few minutes she got up and walked over to me.

"Something in your eye, Paul?" she asked.

"How'd you know my name, and what's yours?"

"Oh, everybody knows you."

"Yeah? Who's everybody?" She was very cute with short blond hair and a face full of freckles, with a little button of a nose that turned up and slightly to one side. Her body wasn't all that great, but her boobs, nicely projecting from her sweater, were in proportion to the rest of her diminutive stature. They looked to be about a mouth full. I took an instant liking to her forwardness and the way she sort of half giggled, half-smiled with everything she said.

"Well, me for one and I guess those girls over there," she said, nodding toward the booth her friends were still sitting in.

"Anyway the answer to your question is, no. Now tell me what your name is and where you're from and where you go to school," I asked.

"What question?"

I shook my head in mock exasperation. "Tsk, tsk, tsk. You asked me if there was anything in my eye. There's nothing wrong, I just like to wink at pretty girls. Now tell me your name or kiss me."

She got a big smile on her face, blew me a kiss and walked away toward the ladies room. As soon as she was gone, I got up and walked over to her table and asked the girls who she was. After a few giggles, one of them said her name was Suzie

Rosen.

I sat down back at the counter and waited the few minutes for her return. "So tell me Miss Rosen, how 'bout a movie tomorrow night?"

Her face lit up again as she replied, "I thought you didn't know my name?"

"I didn't say I didn't know your name. I just wanted you to tell me what it was. Now what about Saturday night?"

"I can't. I've already got a date."

"Okay then. How 'bout Sunday?"

"Sunday! I can't go out on a school night!"

"See. There you go again," I said, really beginning to enjoy this banter. I felt like an elder statesman, because she obviously only had the poise and sophistication of a fifteen-, or at best, a sixteen-year-old. Since I hadn't seen her or any of her friends before and they all looked Jewish I played a hunch. "What grade are you in at Walnut Hills?"

"Now how would you know I go to Walnut Hills and what do you mean, `there I go again'?"

"Well, I just figured that you go to Walnut Hills because most kids that go there have a hard time understanding what everybody else is talking about."

"It must be true, because I sure don't have any idea what you're talking about," Suzie said, in utter bewilderment.

"I only asked you a simple question. I asked if you would like to go out with me, Sun-day. I didn't day anything about night. Now this time you'll either have to give me a hug or agree to go out Sun-day."

"What time, Sun-day. And I think it's you guys from Woodward who don't talk straight."

"How about noon?"

"Where are we going?"

"It's a surprise. Now tell me where you live."

"I only live about two or three blocks from you. We live in what I'd guess you'd know as the Keefe house, you know, in Brookwood."

"Sure. Doctor Keefe's old house," I said, thinking that George wouldn't mind squeezing in a good looking chick for the ride to Flenner's Gymkhana Course near Hamilton what we had agreed to visit Sunday.

The grass cutting season had once again arrived and I worked myself to near exhaustion all day Saturday. Man, I was getting too old for this kind of hard manual labor. There was no question that I was going to go to college so I could get some nice soft cushy desk job. No wonder old Bill had had a heart attack. On top of that I was only making a lousy two dollars an hour which meant that I'd only get sixteen dollars, less the damn taxes, for working all day. Shit, it cost that much for gas, dinner and a show with a chick! Here come the summertime, fuckin' blues again.

Sunday I drove down Fair Oaks, crossed Section and then half way down the back straight of the old Crosley test track, I pulled into the former Keefe estate driveway. I hoped that Mr. and Mrs. Rosen hadn't been living here long enough to realize I was the one who had raced around these streets a few years back. Best not to volunteer any information.

The day was one of those perfect midwestern spring days, with the temperature already into the low seventies and the humidity so low that you could feel the moisture being sucked out of the greenery. The air was clear and smelling of blooming trees and bushes. Ugh! I get to smell that stuff every time I cut grass. I'd rather have the odor of gas and oil filling my nostrils. At the end of the Lockland Highway, where it ran dead into One-twenty-six, we stopped and uncapped the lake plugs. The Vette was running prime and the noise from the open exhaust was awesome. We put the top down and all enjoyed the ride in the country, noise and all. Turning from Seven-forty-one to route Four, just south of Middletown, I put my foot in it to blow the carbon out. The noise from the 300 horse mufflerless exhaust, even in an open cockpit, was deafening as we topped a little over a hundred at 6500 in third. The thrill didn't last long because, unknown to us was that this brief shake down run took us right past a State Patrol Post! Our greeting committee was waiting for us at the turn-off for the gymkhana track in the form of a Trooper, complete with operating bubble gum machine. I tried every trick I knew to talk my way out of a ticket, but the young officer related that he had orders to issue a citation. It seems that the noise and vibration from the car as it passed the Post had caused the desk Sergeant to spill his coffee and he had put out a broadcast to, in the words of the young Trooper, "nail his hide". Well, it was only a ten dollar ticket and now that I was over eighteen I could just pay it out and wouldn't have to go to Juvenile: Bye, bye Twenty-twenty Club forever!

This race course, which I was seeing for the first time,

was nothing more than a dirt track carved out of an undulating pasture on some farmer's back forty. It was five-eights of a mile long with three short straights and ten right and left hand corners. Contestants were allowed to run one at a time against the clock and passengers were permitted. After removing the hub caps I took a test run alone to familiarize myself with the conditions of the track. The hard packed dirt yielded surprisingly good traction as I had to really get on it to break the tires loose. I noted that at the end of the longest straight was the widest turn where I was sure there was enough room for a full four wheel drift. After my test trips around the track I handed my old stop watch to George, asking him to check my time when my turn came again. Suzie looked a little bored, but I promised to take her for a ride on the track before the day was done. When my turn came again I eased out on the track, glanced over my gauges and let her rip. The first few turns had to be taken on rails due to their narrowness, but I learned that the number four turn, like the last bend, could be taken in a drift if I got my front wheel on the edge of the grass infield. After three trips around I pulled in to let others have a turn. George had a time on me of 102.3 which was the same time the track owner had on his watch. He told me the track record was 101.6, set last year by another Corvette. I was feeling pretty good having only been seven tenths of a second off the track record on my first try.

Once the track was clear again, I helped Suzie fasten her seat belt and we took off. I had no idea how fast we were going because I was so busy on this tight course, and my concentration so high, that I couldn't look at the speedometer or tach. I had to rely on the sound of the engine and feel to know when to shift. The top speed must have been a little over sixty because as soon as I got into second gear I would have to shut down for the next bend. On the second circuit, with Suzie in the car, I really got the feel of it as I slammed around each corner at the limit of adhesion. Coming out of turn nine I trounced on the throttle, as the three- twos sucked all the air they could. Half way down the main straight, I grabbed second and poured the coal to her for only a brief instant before having to heal-toe back into first as I went deeper than I had gone before into the final turn, the tires chirping as they came close to locking up. Just before the apex, with the left front tire chewing turf on the edge of the infield, I cranked the wheel hard inducing the now familiar understeer. The front end began to slide toward the outside of the turn and as I reached the point of no return I fed gas to her, breaking the rear tires loose and completing the all wheel drift. The car came around at the appropriate and exaggerated angle—the front end pointed in toward the center of the corner while the front wheels were hard turned the other way and the rear end sliding out trying to catch the front end. It must have looked like a car skidding on snow, but this was a very controlled slide because as I came out of the bend I was all lined up for the next turn, just as it should be.

I took another lap to get slowed down and let the engine cool. About half way around I remembered my passenger, and was surprised to see that she was as white as a sheet and holding onto the chicken bar with both hands. We were down to around thirty or so, but the noise level was still very high. "Hey, are you all right?" I shouted. I think she nodded okay, but she never took her hands from the chicken bar or her eyes from the road until we stopped.

George ran over all excited, "Crazy man, you just broke the record. I got you at 101.1! Man, I don't know how you kept that thing on the track. It looked like you were skating on ice, always sliding first this way and then that way."

The track owner walked over and showed me his watch which had the same time as George's, "Congratulations son. You've just set the track record. That was some driving you did. Best I've seen."

I looked at Suzie. She was still a little on the pale side and she was shaking a bit, as she rummaged through her purse for a comb. "You okay baby? You were as white as a sheet," I said, with concern.

She ran her tongue over her lips, blinked a few times and said, in a voice that sounded strained and broken, "I thought we were going to be killed for sure. I kept seeing that telephone pole coming right at us and then WHAM! At the last second we're suddenly going the other way. Then I was sure we were going to turn over. But it was fun. Wow was it." Recovering very quickly, she continued. "This was even better than the Shooting Star at Coney! Can we do it again?"

We got back to the Rosen's around five and then, sat for a while, in the open, dust covered, hub capless Vette.

"So anyway, you never told me what grade you're in or anything," I said.

"I'm only a Freshman now."

"You mean you're only fifteen?"

"Well, I'll be fifteen next month!"

"Mornin' Judge," I moaned.

"Morning Judge? What's that supposed to mean?"

"I don't know. It's a little joke or scenario or something about what the conversation would be like when they take you before the Judge."

"I'm from Walnut Hills, remember? I don't understand what you're talking about," Suzie mimicked.

"Okay. It goes something like this: `Mornin' Judge. What could the matter be? You know what the matter is boy. But Judge, she said she was eighteen. Ain't you ever heard of girls lyin' before, boy? But Judge—No buts about it, boy that'll be thirty days'."

"You mean you could go to jail for dating me?" Suzie asked.

"Well, not exactly for just dating you; if you catch my drift."

"Oh."

"Anyway, how 'bout next Saturday night?"

"I can't. I have a date."

"Ah baby, I hope you're not going to be too busy for me. I'd like to get to know ya better. Where're ya goin'?"

"We're going to a place in Hamilton to see the Skyliners."

"Hamilton? Oh, you must be going to Spatz's Show Bar."

"That's it. Is it a nice place?"

"Oh yeah. It's a cool place. Maybe I'll see ya up there. I was thinking of taking in the show too."

I got home in time to wash the Vette before dinner. Bobbi's car and a late model VW were also in the driveway. While I was soaping down the recorder holder, John came out to watch and talk.

"What'd-say, hot rod. How'd you get that thing so dirty on such a nice day?"

"Now don't tell the old man, but I've been to a dirt track today and the dust is everywhere. Is that your VW over there," I said, holding my thumb over the end of the hose to produce a spray of water.

"Sure is. What do you thing of it. It's a '58 model and it gets over thirty miles to the gallon!" John said, obviously proud.

"Well, if you're looking for economy, then from what I've

read and heard, you've got one of the best cars on the road."

"I'm glad to hear that. I value your opinion, Paul. So tell me, how did you do at this race track and where is it. Is it a drag strip track?"

"No, it's a sports car track and it's up near Hamilton. I set the record there for fastest time." It was my turn to be proud.

"That's very impressive, but what happens if your Dad finds out? Are you allowed to race?"

"Well, he never said I couldn't and I don't want to ask, so please don't say anything, okay?"

"My lips are sealed."

John was an alright kind of guy for a square. He had gotten his degree and graduated in January and was now working as an accountant for some big office downtown. He even looked like an accountant, with his ever present bow tie and premature receding hair line.

"So what's new with you and how's life in that bachelor pad of yours," I asked trying to keep a conversation going, because I was enjoying the company.

"Well, now I can tell you a little secret. Life in the 'bachelor pad,' as you call it, is going to end. That's why I'm here and that's why Bobbi's in town. We are going to announce to your parents at dinner this evening that we are going to be married!"

"Oh Wow! Like, crazy man! Congratulations! When?"

"I think it's to be the sixteenth of June and I'd like you to be one of the ushers."

"Why, thank you, John. I'd be honored. How much does it pay?" I said, kidding him.

"Pay? You've got it all wrong. Tradition says that you have to pay me!" John could kid right back. Bobbi could do a lot worse.

"I guess you guys are going to live in your Mt. Adams pad, eh?"

"Well, no. Your sister doesn't want to live in that neighborhood, so we're looking at apartments in the Hyde Park area."

An inspiration struck me. "Say, ah brother, ole buddy, how much rent has been paid on your apartment? I mean if it's going to be vacant for any length of time, I might be available to ah, keep and eye on for you."

"You say you might be interested in sub-letting it? The lease isn't up until September and I can let you have it for—"

"Wait a minute. Brothers don't charge brothers, especially if one brother is holding a hose in his hand, Brother," I joked.

"Okay, you win! Sure we'll give you a key when we move out which probably won't be until the first part of June. And, of course, a brother wouldn't charge a brother to help him move. Would he, brother?"

Mom called us for dinner and John helped me wipe the Vette down and put the stuff away. Man, this apartment thing was going to be the coolest ever. I couldn't wait to tell Jimmy.

After this significant dinner, for which the old man uncorked a bottle of his finest wine, Mom pulled me aside to remind me that next week was my Father's birthday. She thought that since he was also my employer, I should get him a tie or something like that. Her advice was to try Henry the Hatter because they knew him and could help me select an appropriate gift.

CHERRY

CIRCA 1957

CHAPTER 22

Tuesday after school, I went downtown to the suggested haberdashery only to be waited on by a stunning young lady. I was glad I was wearing my good school clothes because she was a real looker, with long, strawberry blond hair, bright green eyes, a smile to match, and a perfect figure to go with her tall frame.

"Hi. Do you work here," I said with a stammer.

"Only when they pay me," she said, looking me up and down.

"Well, I'm looking for a gift for my Father and I was hoping you could help me."

"Sure, no problem. You pick it out and I'll take your money."

She wasn't being flip or intimidating, just fresh, but in a friendly sort of way. She was no ordinary salesperson/chick. I guess if I had to describe he in a word, that word would be: refreshing.

"That's not exactly what I had in mind. You see, I was hoping you knew my Father and could sort of pick out something he'd like," I said in a shaky voice, much to my horror.

"Well, how could I know him if I don't know who you are? Men are so dumb."

"I'm sorry. I'm Paul Auer and it's just that your beauty overwhelmed me and—"

"Your father's Sid Auer? Must be! You sound just like him, always with the sweet talk. I know just what Sid likes. How much do you want to spend?"

"Ah, as little as possible. I'm—"

"No question about it. You're Sid's son. He never wants to spend any money either. Now, how about a nice tie?"

I took a deep breath to regain my cool, "A tie? That would be fine if you pick it out and tell me your name, so I'll know who to blame if he doesn't like it."

"Oh, I pick out all his clothes. He loves to come here. You just tell him Jill, Jumpin' Jill, picked it out."

"Jumpin' Jill? Is that a first and last name or—"

"That's just what I go by. Now if you want, I'll gift wrap it for you."

With a master stroke of quick thinking, and my most business like voice, I said, "I have some other pending transactions, but if you would meet me for a drink after you get off work, I could pick it up then."

She got a big smile on her face and her eyes lit up. "Say, if you're anything like you old man, then I can't go wrong! We close at eight and I always go to the Cricket. If you want to stop by it's fine with me."

"In the bar or one of the other rooms?" I asked.

"Oh honey, just come in and ask for me. They all know me there."

I had no trouble finding her. She was holding court in the back room, surrounded by waitresses, kitchen help and patrons of the bar. As I approached her booth, she immediately presented me to all present as though I was her long lost and best friend. She knew everybody and everybody certainly knew her. I sipped a beer while she had two or three somethings with a twist of lime in it that the bartender kept bringing. In between conversations with everybody else, she told me that she was nineteen, came from a small town in Indiana and lived in an apartment with another woman who also worked downtown. She didn't own a car, saying that she can walk every place she needed to go downtown, and that the bus took her to and from work. It didn't seem to bother her that I was only eighteen and still in high school. She was very easy to talk to and in the short time that we were in the bar, I must have told her my life story without really learning much about her. I even told her things about me I didn't know about me. Jill insisted that I drive her home when she learned that I had a Corvette, and then made me wait in the parking lot of her apartment complex while she got her roomie to come and look at the car. I decide to play it cool and not ask for a date just yet, but I did hint that I might call her sometime. She seemed to know that.

Before going home I stopped at Jimmy's. "Man, this is going to be one great summer. I've got two chicks lined up and my future brother-in-law has promised me a key to his soon to be vacant, Hill Street apartment."

"That's just great. You've got all the honeys in the world and I haven't even had a date in over two weeks," Jimmy said, dejectedly.

"When it rains, it pours, man. Besides, I remember not too long ago when you had a date almost every night and I was like, tap city."

"Well that's different. I'm better lookin'."

"Yer ass. But, I'll tell you what. Why don't we go to Spatz's on Saturday night and maybe you can show me how to pick up chicks? I heard there's a lot of single slits that go there," I said.

"Yeah, maybe. So anyway, tell me about this new chick? Do you think you'll score with her?"

"Please! Too crude. But if things don't work out...well, you can have her. How's that for a true buddy?"

"A true BF, you mean. And what about the one from Walnut Hills? Isn't she a little young? What's her name, Suzie? Her old man could put you in jail if you shtup her."

"Hey, man, I only had one date with her and I don't plan to do anything they could put me in jail for...unless she forced me, that is. Hey, how about my old flame, Laine? I could try and see if she wanted to go out with you."

"Shit, I wouldn't take her to a dog fight...even if she was the main attraction," Jimmy said, continuing to joke.

"Nice talk. I think you're jealous. She's the best lookin' thing around and probably wouldn't go out with you anyway."

"Oh, she's good lookin' enough, but when she opens her mouth- -"

"Well, that's why I'm not going with her anymore, but I thought that since you're such an asshole it'd be a perfect match," I kidded Jimmy, as he threw a pillow at me.

Saturday evening we took Jimmy's Vette, paid our way into the now semi-famous Hamilton night spot, and secured a table near the dance floor. The Skyliners whose only hit, "Pennies From Heaven", had just made the charts, were performing that night. Their lead singer was a pretty good lookin' chick and that alone was worth the price of admission. During the first intermission, when they played the jukebox, Jimmy went back stage and enticed this lead singer to come out on the dance floor. We took turns dancing with her for a couple of numbers. It was defiantly a cool thing to do as many of the other dancers then thought we were members of the troupe. In addition, Jimmy had picked up on a chick seated nearby, but the chick's girlfriend was a real dog so we didn't try to move to their table. He was some smooth talker. Just before the second show was to begin, I spotted Suzie and her date, seated way back in the corner where you could hardly see. As I approached their table, I was surprised to learn that her date was a fellow fraternity brother from the Walnut Hills chapter.

CIRCA 1957

"Hey, Allen, How's it goin'? Hi Suzie," I said, while shaking hands with Allen and winking at Suzie as Allen looked at his shoes. Suzie sort of giggled at me as Allen fumbled, "What's say, Paul? We thought that was you dancing with the singer. How'd you meet her?"

"Hey, I get around, man. Would it be alright if I danced with your date?"

With a nod from my frat brother I turned to Suzie, came to attention, and extended my hand, "Miss Rosen?" Walking to the dance floor I continued, "Isn't he a little drippy for such a class chick like you? I heard he drives a '58 many-door with reflector-covered mud flaps and a neckers' knob."

"Now, Paul, don't put my date down. He can't help it. He's really very nice."

The jukebox was playing "In the Still of the Night" and I pulled her in close, getting a whiff of her perfume and feeling her little boobs press against my chest. I knew we didn't have much time before show time so I pushed. "I'd like to do some more of this. How 'bout if I come by after Allen drops you off?"

"What? You mean a late date?" Suzie asked incredulously.

"Yeah, sure. Tell me which window to knock on and I'll be there."

"What if I get caught? Where would we go? Oh Paul, I don't know."

The music stopped and the dance floor thinned as we stood their, arm in arm, smirking at each other.

"Nobody's going to catch you. It's hardly against the law. Now tell me quick. Which window?" I said, as we started back to her table.

As we reached the table, she whispered under her breath, "On the right, all the way back in the corner."

Back at our table, Jimmy proudly displayed the phone number of the chick who he had been hustling from the nearby table.

At the end of the final show, we went back stage and again got to talk to Becky, the lead singer.

"Hey, Baby, good show. Want to dance some more?" I asked.

"No, I can't. The manager doesn't want me to dance with the customers, but thanks anyway," she said, with a sincere smile.

242

"Well, ah, how about a ride? We've got a Corvette outside and we could take you to your hotel or for a quick trip to see Cincinnati and the river." Jimmy jumped in with promise and a smile.

"Yeah, that would be neat. Will it take long?"

"Naw. The river's only a few minutes from here."

"Okay. Meet me at the stage door in the back in about five. I've never seen Cincinnati and I've never ridden in a Corvette," she said, her eyes flashing.

It was not a very productive trip. She really couldn't stay out, wasn't going to be in the Cincinnati area again, and couldn't even give us a phone number because the group would be in a different place every week. She was still a lot of fun to be with as we showed her the city from Mount Adams and the river from Eden Park, while she told us what it was like to be in a singing group.

On the way back, approaching Hamilton city limits, we were stopped at a road block. The police were checking the interior of every car with a flashlight. Only when we pulled into the motel parking lot, where Becky was staying, and saw more cops did we learn that it was us they were looking for. It seems that Becky had failed to tell anyone that she was going for a ride and the leader of the band thought she had been kidnapped. We all had a good laugh, except for the leader, and the cops who took our names and addresses.

Jimmy dropped me at my Vette in Carters' lot and wished me luck. He was in a little better mood, having gotten a phone number for the future.

I fired the big two-eighty-three and listened with pleasure to the rumbling of the twin pipes while scanning the gauges. Satisfied that all was well, I headed up Section to Brookwood where I parked on the back straight, two houses down from the old Keefe place. I couldn't see any lights on in the back of the house and I felt a little funny walking through their dark side yard at one something in the morning.

Peering in the window at the far right corner of the house, I could only make out a bed and dresser from the light of the clock radio. I held my breath and knocked lightly. The figure in the bed stirred, sat up and stared at me for a moment before coming to the window. I guess there was second or two there that we both weren't sure what—or who—we were looking at. Suzie opened the window and whispered, "Paul! I really didn't think you'd come."

"Yeah, well, I don't like standing here, where I can be seen from the street. Where can we go."

"Walk around to the garage and I'll meet you there. And be quiet."

She didn't have to tell _me_ to be quiet. Shit, every shadow I approached looked just like Mr. Rosen holding a shotgun! We met in the open garage and immediately fell into an embrace. She was scared stiff and wouldn't go out to the car so, we just stood there and made out. She was wearing a long thin night gown with nothing underneath and I could feel every curve, protrusion and indentation on her small firm body. That, coupled with the excitement of the clandestine embrace, produced a throbber in nothing flat—any thought of the Mister and his shotgun vanished from my mind. I was confident that, given time, I could score with her, but she was such a cute little thing I wasn't sure I wanted to spoil her. Plenty of time to think about that, especially if things with Jumpin' Jill turned out.

Tuesday, April the twelfth, was opening day and true to my word, I took Artie. He had now become a real Redleg fan having learned all the players names, numbers and batting averages. We sat in the company box with my mother and father and a few customers. Mom took an instant liking to Artie and before the game was over many of the people around us were checking with Artie for explanations of the game. It was a great game, with the home team creaming the Phils, nine to four.

Later at the Diamonds, Mrs. Diamond insisted that I stay for dinner, which was a big mistake. Donna wouldn't eat with us, until Mr. Diamond ordered her to come to the table. She glared at me the whole time and I felt compelled to leave right after the meal was over. Artie walked with me to the Vette and I told him that I wasn't going to take him to any more games because it was obvious that it upset the family too much. I also told him that if he wanted some tickets I would try to get them for him and if he ever needed someone to talk to he could always call me on the phone. He didn't really understand what I was trying to say, but I had the feeling that by the time he became a teenager, he was going to need someone to talk to.

Friday afternoon, as I was finishing cutting the lawn at the house, two squad cars and a fire truck, sirens wailing, raced up the street. I quickly shut the mower down and ran to the end of the street to see what was going on. I couldn't see any smoke, but there were people running from the fire truck to the last house on the street. For a better view, I walked back the old overgrown path that led through "no man's land". It seemed strange in those woods, as though I were in "The Twilight Zone" or something. It was the same area, but maybe because I was bigger, the hills and valleys didn't seem so large and the path looked so much shorter and not a bit scary. I left the path and started down one of the hills, into the valley to get closer to the end house. It took only a minute and a few steps, but I smiled as I remembered how, as little kids, we had struggled to climb out of this valley lugging toy rifles while dressed in remnants our uncles or fathers had brought home from the war. On the valley floor I easily stepped over the small stream that was the beginning of the creek that flowed past the front of our house on old lady Palmer's place.

Something caught my eye as I started up the other side of the valley and I stopped to look. It was an old rusty tricycle and for just an instant I could clearly see Willie, racing down a homemade ramp that the Fritschi boys and I had made in order to jump the creek. Willie hadn't made it, crashing into the bank on the opposite side and breaking the front wheel. We just left the bike there and I now looked for evidence of the ramp, but I couldn't remember what we did with it, for there was no sign of any boards or timbers. It seemed like it happened to somebody else; it happened so long ago I couldn't visualize myself as a little kid anymore. A fireman yelled something and it jarred me back to the realization that this was 1960 and I was trying to find out if there was fire in the old Hastie house. The fire turned out to be just a pot on the stove that overheated so I headed home. The memories recalled in "no man's land" stirred more recollections as I scanned the trees, on the walk back, for signs of old tree houses and vines that we used to swing on. I saw the big clump of bushes where Willie and I had hidden to rest, the day we dragged home the wood that was to become the work bench. I made a promise to take some flowers or something to Willie's grave, but not right now. I still had to put the mower away and then Suzie and I were going to a movie tonight. Maybe tomorrow. Yeah, tomorrow sure.

At the drive-in, with Suzie, I taught her how to kiss with her mouth open and never saw the show. This could work out okay, but I still felt a little guilty putting the make on such a young chick. I wasn't going to push it, just sort of let nature take its course. The only problem with her was that she sure had a lot of guys wanting to take her out and I didn't like competition. I liked my women the way I liked to run the old Crosley: I never had to race anyone else, but I always got the trophy!

Saturday, on my lunch break, I called Jill at Henry the Hatter's.

"Hi baby, It's Paul Auer...'member me?"

"Why sure I remember you. Did Sid like the tie?"

"He loved it and even asked if I had gotten it from you. What do you two have going?" I said in a kidding way.

"I'll never tell. Now listen, I have customers and I can't stand around and gab all day. Is there anything else you needed?"

"Sure is. I wanted to know if we can go out tonight?"

"Oh no. I can't possibly go out on such short notice."

"Well then, how about next Saturday night?" I continued to press.

"I can't possibly plan that far in advance. Why don't you call me next week sometime? Where are we going?"

"If we go. I promise it'll it be someplace you've never been."

"Where's that?" she said, getting interested.

"You'll just have to wait and see, bye now."

Chicks/women—dating—it was all a game, and the older I got the more I loved it!

Thursday night I stopped by the Cricket and found Jill holding court in one of the back rooms. In between the stream of friends and acquaintances that kept stopping by the table to kibitz, she agreed to a date, telling me that she didn't care where we went just so long as it was fun and she was back in time for work on Monday. She was sounding more and more like my kind of girl:

I called for her at her apartment around seven and had to clear a place for myself to sit amid piles of clothes and stuff strewn all over the living room. The pad looked like a cyclone had hit last month and the insurance adjustor had failed to appear. Neither of the girls offered any apologies and it sure wasn't my place to say anything.

Once in the Vette I headed south, as Jill said, "Okay handsome, tell me where we're going and I'll bet I've been there. I've been everywhere!"

"Well, since the Vette needs a little blowing out I

thought we'd just drop in at Cumberland Falls."

"Cumberland Falls? You mean you want to take me across a state line for immoral purposes? Why that's hours away, at least."

"Hey, you ought to be a detective the way you figure—

" "Well listen here. I'm not going to play house without a ring, so you'll just have to get me one before we go any further."

"Ah...a ring? Does it have to be expensive?" I inquired, not knowing whether she was joking or for real.

"I don't care if it's free just as long as it's big!"

I turned the white bomb around and headed for Swifton where I was sure I could find something at the Five & Dime. This chick was just plain zany. We had a great time putting on the air that the ring we were selecting was going to be a real wedding ring. The sales lady was very nice and wished us the best of luck, as I slipped the ninety-eight cent imitation diamond on Jill's finger, while she exclaimed, over and over, how happy we were going to be. The ring was an oversized piece of Emerald cut glass in a Tiffany setting, and from any distance looked very real.

Back in the car Jill grabbed my arm and looked at me real serious like. "This is just for fun, no strings. I'm not the marrying kind, big boy."

What could be better, I thought, as I swung the Corvette into a gas station for a fill up. I stood next to the attendant as he pumped the gas and watched Jill, flashing her left hand, as she strutted past two old ladies standing on the island. After she passed them, en route to the ladies room, I heard one old biddy say to the other, "Did you see the size of the rock on that girl's hand?" The other old maid replied something about flaunting one's wealth. I related the conversation to Jill when we were back in the car and she got the biggest kick out of it.

We got as far as Newport before we had to stop again. This time to let a long train pass. I shut the engine down and turned on the radio, which couldn't be heard when the engine was running due to the combination of stranded copper spark plug wires and a fiberglass body. Little Richard was doing one of his gotta-shake- and-dance numbers and Jill cranked the volume up. We danced in the street until the track cleared much to the astonishment of the entire line of waiting traffic. We drove most of the rest of the way in silence as I had fun on the now fairly familiar U.S. 27, passing everything I could.

At the big old Inn, deep in the Kentucky hills, we

registered as Mr. and Mrs. Paul Wilson and then enjoyed each other's bodies until falling asleep in the early hours of the morning. We had breakfast in the huge, open rustic dining room of the Inn and then just walked along the trails and savored the view of the falls. It was too cool for swimming or sun bathing so after another fling in the sack we were on our way home by two in the afternoon.

TAKE A LONG WALK OFF A SHORT PIER

CHAPTER 23

In the Auer household the official start of summer was Memorial Day weekend, because that's when the pool was filled. Rain or shine, hot or cold, it got filled sometime that weekend. I slaved all day Sunday cleaning the pool, the lawn furniture, and bath house. By Monday, the holiday, I was ready to party. Since it was very hot, I didn't have to do much enticing to get Jimmy, George, Louie and Howard to bring dates and join the rest of the family for a swim and cook out. Suzie was my date for most of the day. It seems she had a date with Allen at eight o'clock and it really pissed me off that she wouldn't break it. She did agree to see me for a late date and to be my date to the up coming Senior Prom on the following Saturday night.

The party broke up a little after eleven and we all ended up at Frisch's for coffee to sober up. Around one in the morning I parked in the usual spot, two doors from Suzie's, only as I was about to get out of the car a set of headlights appeared and I ducked down in the seat, thinking it might be a cop. The car pulled up behind me, turning its lights off. Strange, I thought, cops don't turn their lights off and very few residents park on the street. I lay still until I heard the car door open and close and then I peered out to see some guy walking across the grass toward Suzie's room! Now what? She's got so many boy friends she doesn't know who or when they're coming. I got out and was trying to figure out what to do next, when another car came around number three bend and headed down the straight. It was too late to hide so I just stood casually by the side of the car. This time it was the fuzz. Sergeant Trueblood, an alright guy, stopped next to me, "That you Paul?" the officer said, playing his spotlight on me and the car.

"Yes sir, How ya doing', Sarge?

"I thought that was your car. What are you doing over here on this side of Section and at this hour of the night?"

"Well, it's like this. I have this late date with the Rosen girl and I think somebody beat me to her."

"What do you mean?"

"Not two minutes ago a guy got out of that car, the one right behind mine, and walked over toward her bedroom, which is where I was supposed to meet her."

"Oh yeah," the officer said, getting interested. "Do you know who it is?"

"I'm not sure, but I think the car looks like the one a guy by the name of Tom Miller drives. Do you think you...ah might be able to have a little talk with him. I mean, it's not right having strangers running around the Village at all hours of the night. Is it?"

Which house is it?" the Sergeant asked getting out of his cruiser, flashlight in hand.

"Rosen. You know the one the Keefe's used to live in."

I got in the Vette and as quietly as I could drove around the old Crosley race course, stopping at the head of the main straight, lights out, to see what happened. Within a few minutes I watched the kid get in his car and follow the squad car out of the area. Now it was my turn. Suzie was very excited when she finally met me at the garage. I told her now that she lived in the Village, she would have to get used to the fact that residents have privileges that others don't. I assured her that they wouldn't do anything to the cat this time, but she better tell him, and any one else with the same ideas, not to try it in this neighborhood. We made out in the back of her dad's sedan that was parked in the garage but I was worried that the law might be back and come looking for me so it wasn't all that great.

It was after two when I dropped by the police station. Patrolman Bloomfield was on duty as the dispatcher and he greeted me with a sly smile, "What's this I hear about you using the Department to cut down on your competition, Mr. Auer?"

"All's fair in love and war. Isn't it?"

"I'm tellin' you, I hear about more shit that you're always getting into. How old is that little Rosen girl, anyway?"

"I don't have to answer that. I know my rights. I'm taking the fifth," I joked.

"You'll get a fifth alright. About a fifth of Mr. Rosen's boot when he shoves it up your ass for messing around with his little girl."

"Hey, I never laid a hand on her...yet. Besides, she's not the only chick I'm dating. You sound like you're jealous, old man."

"Old man, eh? If I didn't have to watch this radio I'd jump out of this chair and give you the good sound whipping you need." Tony said, keeping the banter going.

"If? If my aunt had balls, she'd be my uncle. If!"

"Alright, alright. So what else you been up to?"

"Nothing much. What about the guy the Sarge picked

up? Was his name Tom and what happened to him?" I asked.

"Yeah, I think that was his name. The Sergeant hasn't written up his report yet. We just gave him a scare and let him go. Now why don't you be a good boy and run down to Carters', before they close, and get me a large cream and sugar. I've got a stack of paper work to do. The damn Sergeant always sticks me on the desk when the monthly report is due.

"You got it. I'll be right back. Should I bring one for the Sergeant?"

"Fuck him. He's got a car. Let him get his own."

Graduation was Thursday night and they had to use Music Hall, downtown, because our class was so large. Both my parents came which surprised me. It was uncomfortably hot in the rented cap and gown they made us wear, and very boring as "Pomp and Circumstance" was played over and over while we walked single file to receive our diplomas. Only in my case, as well as a few others, including Jimmy, it was just plain paper. I didn't know whether to thumb my nose, give thanks, or cry. I had sure had some good times in that school and now I was facing the real world where termination was in lieu of three-day suspensions and prison took the place of detention for doing wrong. In the short time after the ceremony, everybody was shaking hands and saying good-by, knowing that, except for the Prom on Saturday night, it would be the last time some of us would ever see each other again. It was a very sobering thought, standing there watching all the glad-handing and promises to "keep in touch". I knew, as I'm sure other's did too, that somewhere down the road when we were old, like thirty or so, we'd have a reunion and learn that some of the ones we were shaking hands with tonight would be dead, lost, famous, infamous, or God forbid, just average.

For the Prom, Mom let me borrow her Caddy convertible so the six of us could go in style. The Zap, Hard, and I had agreed along time ago that we would all be together for the Prom. Stan had a date with Ginger, who else? And Howard was with Carol, his steady of two weeks. The girls were all dressed in strapless formals, which looked dumb, but I sure didn't say so. I mean what's so beautiful about a chick whose boobs looked like they're where her belly button should be. I liked my tits up high, not all sagging down. The Zap and Hard had on rented tuxedos and looked real sharp. The only part of my costume that was rented were the trousers. My Mom bought me a shirt and a jacket because of Bobbi's upcoming wedding. The weather was perfect, but the girls wouldn't let us put the top down for fear of ruining their hair-dos. The Prom was held in the Hall of Mirrors of the Netherlands Hotel, downtown, with the local band of Sammy Leeds providing their not so good renditions of current rock & roll hits. Howard had a flask of some of his parent's finest bourbon, which we mixed with the punch. It only made the drink worse, but nobody really wanted to get smashed and miss anything on this, our last night together. It was sort of anti-climatic. I mean, how could one night, this night, top all the stuff we had done over the past few years? As the Band played memories for the three-hour dance, my thoughts ran the full spectrum of emotions, from melancholy to sobering knowledge that some of my class mates and friends, and maybe even me, might not make it in the real world to the euphoric belief that others, and again maybe even me, would become the movers and shakers. It was over all too quickly. Now all that was officially left of our high school life was the traditional boat ride on the Ohio.

Once on board Suzie and I went to the top deck and in the cool night air, nuzzled, all curled up in one of the giant lounge chairs. She was a nice girl, in spite of the fact that she had too many boy friends. I somehow envied guys like the Zap who at least had a steady to help him start into the future. They had this night and years of memories they could share together while to Suzie, this was just another date and she still had her prom to look forward to. I tried to find words to say how I felt, watching the city lights grow dimmer as the big stern wheeler pushed us further up stream. She sensed my distress by whispering that it was okay if I just held her and thought my own thoughts. Very perceptive for a fifteen year old.

By the time the ship had made its turn for the down river leg, I had begun getting feelings of frustration and anger. Frustration from the realization that it would be years, maybe decades, if ever, before the impact of the class of 1960 would be felt on the world. Anger, from knowing that there was nothing I could do about it. I wanted to make things happen, the way we had done in high school. But trying to change the world was much harder than just becoming known as a builder of one race car in one circle. For the first time in my short life, I felt very small and insignificant, just a bolt on an engine in a world of full race mills. To put these thoughts from my mind, I led Suzie to the main deck and danced a little to try and get back in the swing of things.

I saw Mr. Herne, one of the chaperons, and shook his hand thanking him for educating me not only in the operation of machine tools, but for teaching me a little about life itself. He made me promise to come back and visit sometime. I talked to Stan Schwartz, the gentile, and we had a good laugh over the drunken party. I told him I'd kick his ass if he tried to charge anything at Shillito's using my "Mother's" signature. I had to pry Louie off his steady to say good-by just to hear him mumble something about don't get all mushy. Well what else could I expect from "Louie the Tough". Jimmy and I commiserated on the impending summer school and George told us that he'd be seeing us there too since old Lady Cantrel had flunked him in English. I saw Donna and Laine, but didn't think I should say anything in front of their dates.

The next week I helped John move, after which he gave me a key to the almost vacant pad. Almost, because he left an old couch and over-stuffed chair, which was all Jimmy and I would need to entertain our dates. The apartment was one of the renovated old row houses that had a super view of the river and city through new floor to ceiling picture windows. It was Thursday night before we got to officially dedicate the new pad. Jimmy brought his new, as in umpteenth, girl friend and her sister over to help in the clean up. Some help! Jimmy and Barbie spent most of the time making out on the couch while Joanie and I did all the cleaning. Not that I didn't try to put the make on Joanie.

Summer school was good and bad. Bad that I had to go at all, and good that not only was it educational, but finally, in the last class of the last year of school I got a really cool teacher. On the first day of school he announced that he understood why we were there and therefore was going to give us all "A's" if we just showed up and kept quiet. His only instruction was in the form of studying the daily newspaper. Each day he would bring a copy to be read out loud and then a discussion would take place among those who wanted to. Others could sleep, read books or what ever, as long as they were quiet. It was very enlightening as I got a good understanding of the now progressing space race and learned about the candidates in the coming presidential election. If nothing else, the class gave me the realization that I really didn't know much.

Sometime in July Suzie told me she was going steady and we wouldn't be able to date anymore, not even late dates.

She also told me she thought she was pregnant and I felt like a schmuck for not even trying to slap it to her. Nice girl indeed! Of course, then again, it might have been me facing marriage. I mean she was alright, but I sure didn't want to have to marry her. Not now, anyway. Later, I learned that she hadn't been knocked-up and then I really felt like a schmuck!

I had been neglecting the Vette and so toward the end of July, I spent a few afternoons cleaning and tuning her up. The Saturday I finished, Jill and I went to dinner, afterwards I dropped the Vette's top and she dropped her top for a quick spin through Frisch's to give the gang a thrill. She was always game for anything and was not the least bit inhibited. We ended up in French Park, which was closed during the night hours, but still young lovers parked there until run out by Amberley's finest. We hadn't been there, parked amid three other cars, more than half an hour when a cruiser pulled up next to us. Shinning a spotlight in the cockpit, Patrolman Bloomfield said, "Oh, it's you Paul. That's not the Rosen girl is it?"

"No man. Smooth move ex-lax," I replied.

"Uh, sorry. How 'bout if I run these other cars out of here, so you can a little privacy?"

"Hey, thanks, Tony. That'd be great."

As he pulled up to move the other cars on, Jill asked, "Who's the Rosen girl, and how do you know him so well?"

"Ah, she's just some chick I used to date. She lives here in the Village and they know her too," I said, trying to worm my way out of a tight spot.

"Is he really going to let us be here all alone? This is really cool. How'd you do it? You never cease to amaze me, Paul."

"Well, living here does have its rewards, and besides Tony's a friend of mine. We go way back, to the first time he stopped me for hitch hiking.

When the park cleared of cars and people, we got a blanket from the trunk and spread it next to the car on the grass. Jill found some good music on the radio and within a short time we were both bare ass naked and locked in the missionary position. I hadn't gotten more than a few strokes in when Jill pushed up on her elbows exclaiming, "Paul! There's a car!"

"So who cares. Lay down."

No sooner had I said that when a blinding light covered us and the sound of laughter could be heard above the radio. Jill rolled me off and pulled the blanket over us as I got a glimpse of the intruder—Tony! The spot light went out and the squad car backed away as silently as it came. The mood was broken. We got dressed and relaxed on the soft blanket covered grass. Jill said she loved the smell of fresh cut grass because it reminded her of her hometown back in Indiana. It didn't smell so good to me; I had to smell it every day.

It was after one when I finally took her to her pad. On my way home, I noticed Howard's '57 in the lot at the White Castle in Bond Hill. Pulling up next to him, I said, "Hey man, I see you finally got that Junker runnin'."

"This "junker" will dust you off any time you're ready," came the reply from Hard.

Before I could think of a good come-back, Goldstein walked over saying, "It's about time you two smoked one off."

Howard and I looked at each other and grinned.

"I'm ready, if you are," he said.

"Wait a minute. What have you got in this thing? You're too eager. Pop the hood and let me see," I demanded.

"Okay with me. It's just a stock two-seventy."

"Bull shit! You never drove a stocker in your life."

He opened the hood, but all I could see was that he had two- four's. Anything else had to be hidden in the engine. "Fire it up one time, Howard," I insisted.

When the engine caught I could tell by the sound that it had a hot cam but I wasn't sure if it was any hotter than mine. "How big did you bore it and what's the cam?" I said, probing for information.

"Now look, do you want to talk or do you want to race?" Howard took a hard line and I knew it was now or never.

"Okay. But no standing start. We go from a roll. I'll take Louie and you get a passenger to count."

"Okay. But since I only have a three-speed, we have to start at less than say, thirty."

The rules were made and we pulled onto north bound Reading Road. Just past Elizabeth Place we leveled off, side by side between twenty-five and thirty. I rolled my window down to hear the count, as Howard's passenger shouted above the din, "One, two, three!" The recent tune up had not been in vain. At the sound of the magic word, I stabbed the throttle and hit the high beam switch, the big Marchal's lighting up all of the four lane road. The sudden acceleration slammed me back in the seat and I fixed one eye on the tach and put my full attention into hearing the engine. I got the jump on him, the three-two's having and advantage over his quads on the low end. I increased the lead in second, but as we neared the top of the hill just, before Langdon Farm Road, he began to close the distance, his two-four's now having the edge. Cresting the hill, almost side by side, at a little over a hundred, the powerful French headlights picked up the reflective decals on the side of a city police car waiting for the light at Langdon Farm. It was too late now. I could see by the condition of the "walk-wait" signal that the light was about to change to red for our north bound cars. We went through the red light, side by side at fifty, hand on horns, high beams on and engines revved tight. The cop didn't waste anytime in turning on his bubble gum machine, pulling out around the line of cars waiting with him. Howard stopped in front of Woodward, but I kept right on going, reaching over in front of Louie to hit the switches, turning my tail and brake lights out. At Seymore Avenue, I turned right and got on it all the way to where it curved around and backed into Langdon Farm. Approaching this intersection I set up for a four-wheel drift, after seeing that there was no other traffic. The big Vette slid around the bend in perfect control, smoke billowing from the wheel wells as I poured the coal to her. From Langdon Farm we wound our way through the back streets of Golf Manor and Amberley. The last time I saw the cop, he was about a half-mile behind me and losing ground. I wasn't worried about a road block because the City and the Villages were on different radio frequencies.

At home I put the Vette in the garage and found a key to Bobbi's car which we took back to White Castle. Howard was waiting for us, grinning from ear to ear. He explained how John-law pulled next to him, told him to wait, and took off after me. As soon as the cop was out of sight, Howard merely turned around and drove back to the drive-in. The cop, obviously a rookie, had failed to copy license plate numbers or even get a good look at Hard and we were now both scot free.

SO THE BEATNIK SAYS, "OKAY MAN, YOU'RE AN AMBULANCE"

CHAPTER 24

August, high school was over...FINALLY! The only thing that remained was to present my transcript to Ohio State, which Mom and I did on a one-day excursion to Columbus. Within two weeks I had my acceptance to college. Jimmy has also been accepted, and we spent hours talking about what it would be like, being away from home and all.

On the day before I was to leave for OSU, Mom and I were packing when, quite unlike her, she sat down on the edge of my bed and began to cry. I stopped what I was doing and sat next to her   "What's wrong, Mom?"

She wiped her eyes on one of my clean T-shirts and softly said, "Oh, nothing. I'm just happy, I guess."

"Well then, let's have a laugh," I said in a joking way, trying to cheer her up. It didn't work.

"Oh Paul, I'm so happy for you and for Bobbi. But, I'm going to be so alone now. Somehow I knew this day would come, but then I would still have your brother here, for a few more years at least. He was such a loving little boy. Not that you and your sister aren't, but I still miss him. I don't—"

"I know Mom, I'm sorry. I miss him too."

"I know you do, son. It's been such a happy time. It's, it's just too bad that Willie wasn't there to enjoy it with us. Every year, on his birthday, your father and I have put flowers on his grave. On his next birthday he'd be, let's see...oh, I can't think straight now. I want to go and lie down for awhile. We can finish the packing later, okay, son?"

"Sure, Mom, no hurry. Look, I have someplace to go for a few minutes. I'll be back in time for dinner. Is there anything I can get you before I go?"

"No, thank you, son. But, where do you have to go on such short notice?"

"Just something I have to take care of. I won't be long," I promised, heading down the stairs.

I fired the Vette and slowly pulled out of the drive. Damn, it was loud. I hoped the noise didn't disturb her. I never realized how loud the thing was and that maybe I had annoyed others in the neighborhood with my constant comings and goings. I slipped the gleaming white sports car in and out of traffic and arrived at the cemetery gate in less than fifteen minutes. This time I had no trouble finding the little marker that represented all that was left of Willie. I stood there awhile, finally sitting on the grass next to the small memorial. Realizing that I hadn't even brought any flowers I looked around, but I didn't even see any dandelions. I searched the grass at my feet, finally picking a clover which I placed on Willie's memorial. It took me a little while longer to find any words, guilt almost overwhelmed me.

"Say, listen Willie, I'm awful sorry that I haven't been to see ya in such a long time, but I've thought about you a lot. I got a Vette, Willie, and it's one of the fastest there is. You should have been there when I dusted ole Howard off...maybe you were there Willie. Maybe you've been watching over me all the time. Somebody must have been to have kept me alive during some of the crazy stunts I've done. Yeah, maybe you were there. Thanks, Willie. I'll try to make your job easier in the future. I guess you know that I'm going to Ohio State and it's going to be a whole new ball game. They don't mess around up there. You screw up and out you go. I'm going to try real hard, Willie, I promise. And speaking of ball games, I got to know this little kid, Artie's his name, and he really loves baseball. Except I feel so sorry for him. His sister is always treating him bad. She has no idea what it would be like to loose a little brother. I don't know what to do about it. Maybe I should just mind my own business. I need some help. I guess I need a lot of help, Willie. Here I am, eighteen years old, ready to leave for college and I still don't know what I want to do. I don't know what I want to major in, I don't know what kind of girl I want to marry or even if I ever want to marry. Damn, Willie, it doesn't change. I've always got these doubts and worries. That's probably why I do all those crazy things I do, so I'll be so busy that I don't have to think about stuff I don't want to worry about. Maybe I should just stop and spend a whole lot of time trying to plan my life, instead of running around like a punk kid. Yeah...maybe I am just a punk kid. I mean, making all that noise with my cars and driving so fast. I never realized that until just this minute that I probably cause more grief than I give...ah, what's the word...pleasure? consolation? Well, you know what I mean. I take more than I give. I guess I've been a little selfish and now it's time I grow up." I kicked at a twig lying next to his little plot and tried to think of good things, as the realization of what I had just said sank in.

"I was going to tell you all about the Vette, but it seems kinda dumb now. It's just a piece of machinery that anybody can have. I'd thought of being a race car driver, but I know that's not a real future. I guess I'm good enough, but man, it would just be fun and games. I want to make an impression on the world and do something to help people. This guy, Jack Kennedy, he's going to be the next President and he's going to make things happen. I don't just want to read about it in the paper, I want to be part of what's coming. And maybe, since I like cars so much, I could study engineering. Then I'd really be able to make changes on automobiles, changes that would be used and needed everywhere. Yeah, that might be the thing to do. Since I proved them all wrong on the boring of the venturi, there's no telling what I might invent or improve upon with the proper training. What do you say, Willie? Think I could cut it, man?"

Suddenly feeling better and full of fresh ideas, I turned to leave, then realized I had forgotten to say good-by. I knelt by the stone, brushed at the grass clippings and twigs and tried to impress in my mind every little mark and notation.

"You know a couple of months ago there was a small fire at the old Hastie place and I went up there to see what was going on. Well, I walked back the trail into "no man's land" and it seemed really different, but maybe it was just because I was taller. It was still the same woods and all, but the hills didn't seem so big and I found that tricycle that you tried to jump the creek on, you remember that don't you, Willie? It's still there, buried in the mud, the same mud that covered you from head to toe. I remember how you kept Mom from getting mad because you were so dirty, by telling her that you were lucky the mud was wet and soft to break your fall and keep you from breaking any bones. She just stopped bawling you out and hugged you, telling you that it was she who was sorry! You were the greatest con man ever, Willie! We sure had a lot of good times and since then I've had a lot of good times; I wish you'd been there, Willie. I don't know, man. Thanks for letting me talk to ya. I gotta cut out now Willie, take it easy, man."

There were some other people coming in and I stopped to dry my eyes on my sleeve again before getting in the Vette. I fired the engine, embarrassed by the noise it made. I had planned to rap the pipes, sort of as a last salute to Willie, but somehow didn't think it would be proper, much less needed. Willie knew how I felt about him. Suddenly, for the first time in my life I realized that I didn't have to prove anything to anybody. Pulling out into traffic, I taxi-cab-shifted into fourth gear and

CIRCA 1957

kept to the posted limit.

SEE YA LATER ALLIGATOR

EPILOGUE

Jimmy Cohen: After trying two wives finally found his soul mate and is currently living and working in Cincinnati.

Howard Richards: Hard is married with two point three kids and living in suburbia with a stock stage coach for transportation.

Big Bart: BB married Janice and had two kids. Struggling with a job, night school and cancer, he finally received his BS degree, only to die from the disease in 1964.

George Baker: Is lost

Louie Goldstein: Came all the way from his home in Texas to attend the 25th high school reunion. He looked as fit and tough as the day he graduated.

Donna Diamond: Married and divorced and currently running her own company in California.

Artie Diamond: Became a psychiatrist.

Bobbi and John: Are still married.

Isky: Still building cars in his spare time.

Knights of the Twentieth Century: Disbanded in 1962. Of the fifty-three members that belonged at one time or another, twelve have never been found and six are known to have died.

Paul Auer: Paul's first born, Willie, is now 22.